This book is to be returned on
or before the date stamped below

UNIVERSITY OF PLYMOUTH

PLYMOUTH LIBRARY

Tel: (01752) 232323
This book is subject to recall if required by another reader
Books may be renewed by phone
CHARGES WILL BE MADE FOR OVERDUE BOOKS

Stock Exchange Listing
The New Requirements

Stock Exchange Listing
The New Requirements

Robert R Pennington LLD

Solicitor, Professor of Commercial Law at the
University of Birmingham

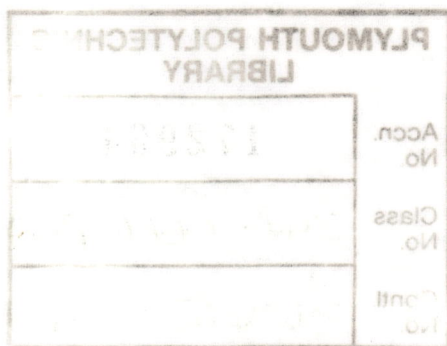

London
Butterworths
1985

England	Butterworth & Co (Publishers) Ltd, LONDON WC2B 6AB
Australia	Butterworths Pty Ltd, SYDNEY, MELBOURNE, BRISBANE, ADELAIDE, PERTH, CANBERRA and HOBART
Canada	Butterworth & Co (Canada) Ltd, TORONTO and VANCOUVER
New Zealand	Butterworths of New Zealand Ltd, WELLINGTON and AUCKLAND
Singapore	Butterworth & Co (Asia) Pte Ltd, SINGAPORE
South Africa	Butterworth Publishers (Pty) Ltd, DURBAN and PRETORIA
USA	Butterworth Legal Publishers, ST PAUL, Minnesota, SEATTLE, Washington, BOSTON, Massachusetts, AUSTIN, Texas and D & S Publishers, CLEARWATER, Florida

© Butterworth & Co (Publishers) Ltd 1985

ISBN 0 406 33700 4

Typeset by Latimer Trend & Company Ltd, Plymouth
Printed and bound in Great Britain
by Billing & Sons Ltd, Worcester

Preface

In January 1985 a fundamental change took place in the status of a listing of a company's shares and debentures on the Stock Exchange. Previously for over two hundred years the fact that securities were admitted to dealings on the Stock Exchange merely signified that they were recognised by the rules or practices of the Exchange as eligible for sales or purchases between members of the Exchange. Since January 1, 1985 a listing of securities on the Stock Exchange signifies that they have a legal status which makes them a distinct legal category from unlisted securities, and subjects them to different rules of law from unlisted securities.

This has come about as a result of the issue of the Stock Exchange (Listing) Regulations 1984 (S.I. 1984 No. 716), which were made under the powers conferred by the European Communities Act 1972, to give effect to three harmonisation directives issued by the Council of Ministers of the European Communities under art. 54(3)(g) and art. 100 of the Treaty establishing the European Economic Community. The three directives prescribe respectively the conditions which must be fulfilled by a company to obtain a listing for any of its securities on a stock exchange in the member states of the Community, the requirements which must be satisfied in respect of listing particulars (or prospectuses) published in connection with an application for a listing of securities and, finally, the requirement that a listed company should publish a half-yearly report in respect of its activities and financial results as well as the yearly report already required by law.

The Stock Exchange of the United Kingdom and Ireland is the designated competent authority to administer the new law governing listings of securities, and in November 1984 it published a new edition of its Yellow Book on the Admission of Securities to Listing so as to incorporate a statement of the new rules together with the Stock Exchange's own supplementary rules which companies must comply with to obtain and maintain a listing for their securities.

This book seeks to set out and explain the practical implications of the new Regulations and the Stock Exchange's supplemental rules so as to provide a guide for directors, lawyers, accountants, company secretaries, stockbrokers and others concerned with the administration of companies which have or qualify for a listing. The book does not pretend or attempt to be encyclopaedic. Many points of law and practice are bound to arise in the future which a book published at the inception of the new régime cannot anticipate, and undoubtedly it will take several years of accumulated rulings by the Stock Exchange before all the problems arising in practice are dealt with. Nevertheless, an initial account of the new Rules and the suggestion of possible answers to some of the questions which they will raise will, it is hoped, prove helpful.

The detailed provisions of Section 4 of the Yellow Book deal with the rules for the preparation of accountants' reports which must be included in certain listing particulars and certain circulars issued to shareholders, and Section 10 deals with the variation in the normal rules of the Yellow Book in their application to property and mining companies and to investment trust companies and unit trusts. These are highly specialised and detailed matters, and space does not permit their inclusion in this book.

The law and Stock Exchange practice is set out in this book as at May 1, 1985.

The text of the Stock Exchange (Listing) Regulations 1984 is set out in an appendix to this book, but not the text of the Yellow Book. This is because the Yellow Book is likely to undergo fairly frequent amendment to deal with practical problems as they arise and also with new developments, and the inclusion of its text in its present form would soon be misleading.

Robert R Pennington
University of Birmingham
May 1985

Contents

CHAPTER 1

The Regulations and the Yellow Book

The three directives issued by the Council of Ministers of the European Community to harmonise the laws and practices of member states in respect of stock exchange listings for companies' securities[1] are given effect as part of the law of the United Kingdom by the Stock Exchange (Listing) Regulations 1984,[2] which came into force on 1 January 1985 as regards companies and most other issuers of securities, two of the directives having already come into force on 1 June 1984 as regards securities offered by or on behalf of a Minister of the Crown or by or on behalf of a corporation controlled by such a Minister.[3] The Stock Exchange (Listing) Regulations 1984, are subordinate legislation made under the authority of the European Communities Act 1972,[4] which empowers a Minister of the Crown (here the Secretary of State for Trade and Industry) to make provision by regulations 'for the purpose of implementing any Community obligation of the United Kingdom' (ie any obligation created or arising by or under the EEC, ECSC or Euratom Treaties[5]) and 'for the purpose of dealing with matters arising out of or related to any such obligation'. Regulations made under the European Communities Act 1972, may include any 'provision (of any such extent) as might be made by Act of Parliament',[6] and may therefore repeal, modify or exclude the application of any statute or subordinate legislation currently in force. The Stock Exchange (Listing) Regulations 1984, do exclude the application of certain provisions of the Companies Act 1948, and the Prevention of Fraud (Investments) Act 1958, when an application for a stock exchange listing of securities is made, but it contains only one repeal[7] and leaves the statutory provisions which are simply excluded in full force in other contexts.

Concurrently with the Stock Exchange (Listing) Regulations coming

1 The directives are the Directive 79/279/EEC of 5 March 1979 co-ordinating the conditions for the admission of securities to official stock exchange listing (the Admission Directive); the Directive 80/390/EEC of 17 March 1980 co-ordinating the requirements for drawing up, scrutiny and distribution of the listing particulars to be published for the admission of securities to official stock exchange listing (the Listing Particulars Directive); and the Directive 82/121/EEC of 15 February 1972 on information to be published on a regular basis by companies the shares of which have been admitted to official stock exchange listing (the Interim Reports Directive).
2 S I 1984/716.
3 The Stock Exchange (Listing) Regulations 1984, reg 1(2). The Interim Reports Directive does not apply to corporations and persons other than companies.
4 European Communities Act 1972, s 2(2) (42 Halsbury's Statutes (3rd edn) 81).
5 Ibid, s 1(2) and Sch 1, Part II.
6 Ibid, s 2(4).
7 The Companies Act 1948, s 39 (which empowered the Stock Exchange to exempt a company from including in a prospectus all the information required by the Act if the company had applied for a Stock Exchange listing) is repealed by the Stock Exchange (Listing) Regulations 1984, reg 7(4).

1

into force as regards companies on 1 January 1985, a new edition of the Stock Exchange manual *Admission of Securities to Listing*, (usually known as the Yellow Book) became effective. The new edition was made necessary by the fact that the Stock Exchange (Listing) Regulations 1984, designated the Council of the Stock Exchange as the competent authority under the three directives to grant listings for securities and to apply and enforce the requirements of the directives.[8] Consequently, the Stock Exchange's own manual had to be made conformable to them. In fact, the new edition of the Yellow Book repeats the provisions of the directives with minor verbal changes and in a re-arranged form, but it also contains additional requirements and material derived from the Stock Exchange's own rules and earlier editions of the Yellow Book. Some of these additional requirements do not relate directly to the grant or maintenance of a listing for securities, and so take effect as non-legal rules which are sanctioned only by the Stock Exchange's own disciplinary powers (primarily suspension or cancellation of a listing). Other additional requirements are imposed in exercise of the power conferred on the Stock Exchange by the Stock Exchange (Listing) Regulations 1984, to impose 'more stringent or additional conditions or obligations' so long as they are not inconsistent with the directives;[8] this power reflects the powers conferred by the directives themselves to impose more stringent conditions or obligations than the Admission Directive on the admission of securities to listing,[9] and to require listing particulars to contain information additional to that called for by the Listing Particulars Directive.[10] Insofar as the Stock Exchange imposes additional disclosure requirements in respect of the contents of listing particulars so as to ensure that they comply with the rule in the Listing Particulars Directive that listing particulars shall give all necessary information 'to enable investors and their investments advisers to make an informed assessment' of the issuing company's financial position and prospects and of the rights attaching to the securities to which the particulars relate,[11] the Stock Exchange exercises the power conferred on it by law, but insofar as it imposes additional requirements under its own rules or in exercise of its general discretion, it does not act as a public authority exercising powers conferred by law. This, as will be shown below, makes a difference if review by the court is sought of a decision of the Stock Exchange on a listing application.

The Stock Exchange (Listing) Regulations 1984, give effect to the three directives by incorporating them in the Regulations *verbatim* and by expressly making the conditions and obligations imposed by them legally binding as part of United Kingdom law.[12] This is an unusual way for a member state of the European Community to give effect to directives in fulfilment of its obligation under the EEC Treaty.[13] Unlike a regulation issued by the Council of Ministers under the Treaty, which is effective and applicable in the law of each member state as soon as it is issued, a directive is binding only on each member state as to the result to be achieved by

8 The Stock Exchange (Listing) Regulations 1984, reg 3(3).
9 Admission Directive, 5(1) and (2).
10 Listing Particulars Directive, art 4(1) and art 18(2) and (3).
11 See Chapter 3, below.
12 The Stock Exchange (Listing) Regulations 1984, reg 3(1) and Sch 1.
13 EEC Treaty, arts 5 and 189.

implementing it, and the government of each member state is left with a discretion as to the form and methods by which that result is achieved.[14] Consequently, legislation giving effect to directives is usually expressed in the form and manner in which purely national legislation is enacted, and national legal terminology is employed in place of the unavoidably vaguer and more general terms of the directives.[15] Fortunately, because of the nature of the subject matter, the three directives on stock exchange listings on the whole employ terminology which is either internationally uniform or which can be related immediately to the equivalent terms of national law, and with very few exceptions the incorporation of the three directives *verbatim* into United Kingdom law does not give rise to problems of interpretation. What problems there are relate mostly to the substance of the three directives, and not to their expression in the official Community languages.

IMPLEMENTATION OF THE DIRECTIVES

The Stock Exchange (Listing) Regulations 1984, give effect in United Kingdom law to the conditions and obligations imposed by the Admission Directive and the Listing Particulars Directive in respect of applications for the admission of companies' and others issuers' securities to listing on the Stock Exchange and the grant and maintenance of such listings, and to the obligations imposed by the Interim Reports Directive on companies whose shares are listed on the Stock Exchange.[16]

The conditions which must be fulfilled for securities to be admitted to listing are objective in character and are identical, whether the application for listing is made by the company which issued or proposes to issue the securities in question or by other persons.[17] Similarly, the conditions which must be fulfilled in respect of the contents and publication of listing particulars in connection with an application for a listing of securities are the same, whether the listing is applied for by the issuer of the securities or by other persons (such as existing holders of shares or debentures who wish to create a market in them).[18] Under the present practice an application for a listing on the Stock Exchange of shares or debentures of a company or the securities of any other issuer can only be made by or with the concurrence of the company or other issuer itself. This is because, in the case of a company issuer, the Stock Exchange requires the broker who sponsors the application[19] to lodge certain documents with the Quotations Department

14 Ibid, art 189.
15 See, for example, the Second and Fourth Directives on the harmonisation of the companies legislation of the member states (Directive 77/91/EEC, published in the Official Journal dated 31 January 1977, No L26/1, and Directive 78/660/EEC, published in the Official Journal dated 14 August 1978, No L222/11) which were respectively given effect in British law by the Companies Act 1980, Parts I to III and the Companies Act 1981, Part I.
16 The Stock Exchange (Listing) Regulations 1984, reg 3(1).
17 Ibid, reg 3(1)(*a*); Admission Directive, art 4(1).
18 Listing Particulars Directive, arts 3 and 4, art 18(2) and (3) and arts 20 and 21.
19 All applications for listing must be made through a broker who is a member of the Stock Exchange; he is responsible for lodging all necessary documents in support of the application and is the channel of communication for the discussion of all matters arising in

at least two business days before the application is considered, including a formal application for listing signed by an authorised officer of the company, a certified copy of a resolution of the board of the company authorising the making of the application for listing and the publication of the listing particulars, four copies of which must be submitted (one copy being signed by all the directors and proposed directors of the company),[20] and because after the application has been considered a declaration by a director or the secretary of the company must be lodged deposing that all conditions for the grant of a listing for the securities have been fulfilled and all necessary documents have been lodged.[1] A listing cannot therefore be forced on an unwilling company. Nevertheless, although it is unlikely to happen in practice, the listing particulars which are published in connection with an application for a listing may be prepared by persons other than the company or other body which issued or proposes to issue the securities for which a listing is sought (eg the holders of a block of shares or debentures who wish to make a market in them). The obligation to ensure that the listing particulars conform to the Listing Particulars Directive is then imposed on the persons who prepare them,[2] and it is they, and not the company, who will be named in the listing particulars as the persons responsible for them and who will make therein the declaration of responsibility for the accuracy and completeness of the listing particulars.[3] In the case of a public body whose securities are to be listed (other than the UK Government), an application for a listing by the issuer itself must be lodged with the Quotations Department at least 48 hours before the application is considered,[4] and in practice no one other than the issuer would seek a listing since a public body's securities must be marketable from the moment they are issued.

The obligations imposed by the Admission Directive in connection with securities for which a listing has been obtained are imposed on the issuer of the securities, whether a company or other body,[5] and it is immaterial who obtained the listing in the first place. Disregard of the obligations imposed by either directive may result in the listing for the securities being suspended or cancelled.[6]

All three directives require member states to designate a national authority or authorities competent to give effect to the directive, and also require the competent authority to be vested with all necessary powers for that purpose.[7] The Stock Exchange (Listing) Regulations 1984, appoint the Council of the Stock Exchange to be the competent authority for all purposes under the directives, and vest in it all the powers required or permitted to be conferred on a national competent authority by the

connection with the application (The Stock Exchange *Admission of Securities to Listing*, Section 1, Chapter 1, para 4).
20 The Stock Exchange: *Admission of Securities to Listing*, Section 2, Chapter 1 para 5.1, 4 and 9.
1 Ibid, Section 2, Chapter 1, para 8 and Sch 3, paras 1 and 2.
2 Listing Particulars Directive, art 4(2).
3 Ibid, Schedules A and B, Chapter 1, para 1.1 and 2.
4 The Stock Exchange: *Admission of Securities to Listing*, Section 2, Chapter 2, para 6.1.
5 The Stock Exchange (Listing) Regulations 1984, reg 3(1)(*b*).
6 Admission Directive, art 14.
7 Ibid, art 9(1) and (2); Listing Particulars Directive, art 18(1) and (3); Interim Reports Directive, art 9(1) and (2).

directives.[8] This form of defining the powers of the Council is unsatisfactory in that the scope of the Council's ancillary powers is left uncertain, although its main powers to grant, refuse, suspend and terminate a listing are clearly conferred by the terms of the directives themselves, and certain ancillary powers (such as the power to call for further information than is specifically required by the directives[9]) are also conferred expressly in the same way. However, no investigatory powers are conferred on the Council of the Stock Exchange by the directives or by the Stock Exchange (Listing) Regulations 1984, and it has no power to compel persons who are not parties to an application for a listing, or to compel a company or other body which already has a listing for its securities, to supply it with evidence or information which may assist it in exercising its functions. For this reliance must be placed on the investigatory powers of the Secretary of State for Trade and Industry and the court.[10] The Stock Exchange (Listing) Regulations 1984, empower the Council of the Stock Exchange to discharge any of its functions as the competent national authority through any committee, sub-committee, officer or employee of the Council, and therefore to delegate any of its powers to such a body or person.[11] The Council has under this provision arranged for all its functions under the Regulations and the directives to be discharged by its Committee on Quotations, advised by the Quotations Department.[12] In practice decisions and rulings on matters arising in connection with applications for listing and waivers or derogations from the rules normally applicable to listing applications are given by the Quotations Department, and questions are referred to the chairman's panel (comprising the two chairmen and the two vice-chairmen of the Quotations Committee) or to the Quotations Committee itself only if the company or other person concerned is dissatisfied with the Quotation Department's decision.

CRIMINAL SANCTIONS

The three directives to which the Stock Exchange (Listing) Regulations 1984, give effect require member states to ensure that securities are not admitted to a listing on a stock exchange in their respective territories unless the conditions prescribed by the Admission Directive are fulfilled and the issuers of such securities are subjected to the obligations set out in the same directive,[13] that the admission of securities to listing is conditional on the publication of proper listing particulars,[14] and that companies whose securities are listed fulfil their obligation to publish reports on their activities and profits or losses for the first half of each financial year.[15] None of the directives specifies the sanctions which the law of each member state must impose to ensure that the conditions and obligations are fulfilled, and,

8 The Stock Exchange (Listing) Regulations 1984, reg 4(1).
9 Admission Directive, art 13(1); Listing Particulars Directive, art 4(1) and art 18(3).
10 Companies Act 1948, ss 164–167, 268 and 270; Companies Act 1967, s 109 (now Companies Act 1985, ss 431–434 and 447).
11 The Stock Exchange (Listing) Regulations 1984, reg 4(2).
12 The Stock Exchange: *Admission of Securities to Listing*, Section 1, Chapter 1, para 2.
13 Admission Directive, art 3.
14 Listing Particulars Directive, art 3.
15 Interim Reports Directive, art 2.

in particular, no directive requires contraventions of it to be made a criminal offence. The mode of enforcement of the directives is left to the discretion of each member state, provided that the enforcement measures applied are effective to ensure compliance. It is therefore open to each member state to decide which contraventions of the directives shall be made criminal offences and, if any such offences are created, what the penalties for committing them shall be.

The Stock Exchange (Listing) Regulations 1984, create only one criminal offence,[16] and that offence and the obligation for which it provides a sanction,[17] do not result from any provision in the directives. The Regulations require a copy of listing particulars in connection with an application for a Stock Exhange listing to be delivered to the Registrar of Companies on or before the date when they are published under the requirements of the Listing Particulars Directive;[18] if they are published without such a copy first being delivered to the Registrar, the issuer of the securities in question[19] and every person who is knowingly a party to the publication is liable on summary conviction to a fine not exceeding £200 and, on conviction after a continued contravention, to a daily default fine not exceeding £20 for each day that the contravention continues after the first conviction.[20]

Curiously, the Stock Exchange (Listing) Regulations 1984, do not make it an offence to publish listing particulars which do not contain all the information required by the Listing Particulars Directive, or which contain false or misleading information. It therefore appears that if a copy of incomplete or false listing particulars is delivered to the Registrar of Companies before the particulars are published, no offence is committed, but if complete and accurate listing particulars are published without a copy of them being delivered to the Registrar, there is an offence. However, listing particulars which offer the shares or debentures of a company for subscription by the public, or for purchase by the public if they were allotted for the purpose of being so offered, are within the definition of a prospectus under the Companies Acts,[1] and subject to what is said below with regard to the application of the provisions of the Companies Acts, to listing particulars,[2] it would seem that a person who authorises the issue of such listing particulars which contain any untrue or misleading statement commits an offence which is punishable on indictment by imprisonment for not more than two years or an unlimited fine or both, or on summary conviction by imprisonment for not more than three months or a fine not exceeding £1000 or both.[3]

16 Stock Exchange (Listing) Regulations 1984, reg 7(7),
17 Ibid, reg 5(5).
18 Ibid, reg 7(5) and Listing Particulars Directive, art 20(1) and 21(1).
19 The references to the issuer is presumably to the issuer of the securities and not to the persons who publish the listing particulars (see Stock Exchange (Listing) Regulations 1984, reg 2(2)).
20 The Stock Exchange (Listing) Regulations 1984, reg 7(7) and (8).
 1 Companies Act 1948, s 45(1), s 55(1) and (2) and s 455(1) (now Companies Act 1985, ss 59(1), s 60(1)–(3) and s 744). Not all listing particulars are prospectuses; they will not be if no new issue of securities is involved (as on a Stock Exchange introduction), nor if securities are offered to a limited number of persons who do not constitute the public or a section of the public.
 2 See p 18, below.
 3 Companies Act 1948, s 44(1) and s 46; Companies Act 1980, s 80(1) and Sch 2; (now Companies Act 1985, s 70(1) and s 71).

In any event, a person who publishes listing particulars in respect of a company's or public body's securities which contains a statement, promise or forecast which he knows to be misleading, false or deceptive, or which he makes recklessly (whether dishonestly or not), or who dishonestly conceals a material fact, is guilty of an offence if he thereby induces or attempts to induce another person to subscribe for or purchase or acquire securities to which the listing particulars relate,[4] and on conviction on indictment he may be punished by imprisonment for not more than seven years or an unlimited fine or both,[5] or on summary conviction he may be punished by imprisonment for not more than six months or a fine not exceeding £1000 or both.[6] It is uncertain whether the omission of material information from listing particulars[7] amounts to a concealment for the purpose of this offence; it has been said obiter that an offence is committed by concealment only if the omission of information makes the positive statements in the investment invitation misleading,[8] but it is doubtful whether this is correct, particularly when the omitted information is expressly required to be disclosed by law.

Finally, a person who publishes listing particulars in respect of a company's or public body's securities which are deceptive with the dishonest intention of inducing another person or other persons to subscribe for or purchase those securities for a consideration which is delivered to the accused or another person (eg the issuer of the securities or an issuing house acting for it), commits an offence under the Theft Act 1968,[9] and may be punished on conviction on indictment by imprisonment for not more than ten years or an unlimited fine or both,[10] or on summary conviction by imprisonment for not more than 6 months or a fine not exceeding £1000 or both.[6]

CIVIL SANCTIONS

The Stock Exchange (Listing) Regulations 1984, and the three directives contain no provisions imposing liability to pay damages or compensation on any person who participates in an application for a listing of securities on the Stock Exchange, or in the publication of listing particulars or half-yearly reports required by the Interim Reports Directive, if a third person suffers loss as a result of a condition for a listing not being fulfilled, or as a result of listing particulars or a half-yearly report containing false or misleading information or omitting information which they should contain. Likewise, the Regulations contain no provision imposing liability on the

4 Prevention of Fraud (Investments) Act 1958, s 13(1) and s 26(1); Protection of Depositors Act 1963, s 21(1) (22 Halsbury's Statutes (3rd edn) 980).
5 Ibid; Powers of Criminal Courts Act 1973, s 30(1) (43 Halsbury's Statutes (3rd edn) 327); Criminal Law Act 1977 s 32(1) (47 Halsbury's Statutes (3rd edn) 164).
6 Criminal Law Act 1977, s 28(1) and (7) (47 Halsbury's Statutes (3rd edn) 709).
7 The information may be material either because it is specifically required to be included by the Listing Particulars Directive, or because it 'is necessary to enable investors and their investment advisers to make an informed assessment of the assets and liabilities, financial position, profits and losses and prospects of the issuer and of the rights attaching to the securities' (Listing Particulars Directive, art 4(1) and art 5(1) (see p 53, below)).
8 *R v MacKinnon* [1959] 1QB 154, [1958] 3 All ER 657 at 659, per Salmon J.
9 Theft Act 1968, s 15(1) and (2) (8 Halsbury's Statutes (3rd edn) 792).
10 Ibid, s 15(1); Powers of Criminal Courts Act 1973, s 30(1); Criminal Law Act 1977, s 32(1).

Council of the Stock Exchange if it fails to fulfil its functions properly under the Regulations or the directives and thereby causes loss to the applicants for a listing of securities, the persons responsible for listing particulars or third persons. The Listing Particulars Directive and the Interim Reports Directive (but not the Admission Directive) do, however, provide that those directives shall not affect the national competent authority's liability, which shall continue to be governed solely by the national law of each member state.[11]

The only provision in the Regulations in respect of liability in damages contains an exoneration from liability. The Regulations provide that neither the Council of the Stock Exchange nor any other person (such as the applicants for the listing of securities or the persons responsible for listing particulars) shall be liable in damages by reason only of any non-compliance with or contravention of any obligations imposed by the Regulations (including obligations imposed by the directives).[12] Nevertheless, the exoneration does not extend to the obligation to ensure that listing particulars contain all the information which is necessary to enable investors and their advisers to make an informed assessment of the issuer's financial position, record and prospects,[13] and it would seem that this exception to the general exoneration from liability extends to the Council of the Stock Exchange as well as to the persons responsible for the listing particulars.[14] However, the Council is not liable in damages in respect of any act or omission by it in connection with its functions under the Regulations and the directives unless it acts or omits to act in bad faith,[12] which presumably means deliberately, knowing that the act or omission is wrongful, or knowing that its purpose in acting as it does is improper.

Liability for breach of statutory duty

From the exoneration provision it is possible to spell out an underlying liability in damages for breach of statutory duty on the part of the applicant for a listing and the persons responsible for the relevant listing particulars, and also on the part of the Council of the Stock Exchange for approving them, if listing particulars are published which do not contain all the information necessary to enable investors and their investment advisers to make an informed assessment of the issuing company and the securities offered. The exoneration of the Council and such other persons from liability in damages for all other breaches of the directives pre-supposes that there would otherwise be a general liability in damages for such breaches, and in the one exceptional case where the exoneration does not apply (failure to ensure that listing particulars contain all necessary information), the general liability must still exist. The Council is, of course, protected by its immunity from liability unless it acts in bad faith,[12] and for practical purposes this amounts to a complete immunity, since the Quotations Committee will never knowingly approve draft listing particulars

---

11 Listing Particulars Directive, art 18(4); Interim Reports Directive, art 9(7).
12 The Stock Exchange (Listing) Regulations 1984, reg 8(1).
13 Ibid; Listing Particulars Directive, art 4(1) (see p 147, below).
14 The Council of the Stock Exchange (through the Quotations Committee) is obliged to scrutinise listing particulars before publication, and it may approve them only if they satisfy the requirements of the Listing Particulars Directive (ibid, art 18(3)).

for publication if it or officials of the Quotations Department are aware that the particulars omit necessary information or contain false or misleading information.

Another more direct reason for concluding that breaches of the requirement of the Regulations that the conditions and obligations imposed by the directives shall be complied with[15] will make the persons responsible liable in damages to others who are injured thereby in situations where the exoneration[12] does not apply, is that if this were not so the requirements of the Regulations would be backed by no sanctions at all. There are no criminal sanctions imposed by the Regulations for breaches of the directives, and the Regulations provide expressly that no transaction is made void or voidable because the Regulations or the directives are not complied with,[16] and so the only possible remaining sanction for breaches of them is an action for damages for breach of statutory duty. Because of the exoneration,[12] this liability in damages can only exist where the breach or non-compliance complained of relates to the inadequacy, falsity or deceptiveness of the contents of the listing particulars. The absence of any express statutory sanctions in an enactment is a strong factor in inducing the court to accept that the legislation intended breaches of the statutory obligations to give rise to a cause of action for damages against the person on whom the obligations are imposed in favour of those whom the imposition was intended to protect,[17] and conversely, the presence of a criminal sanction in the enactment is a factor of somewhat less weight against the court holding that an action for damages lies.[18] Where there are no express sanctions the statutory duties would be imperfect obligations if an action for damages were not available, and the fulfilment of those duties would, in the words of Lord Simonds be merely 'a pious aspiration'.[19]

Breach of a statutory obligation can give rise to an action for damages for its non-fulfilment only if the obligation was imposed for the benefit of the class of persons to whom the plaintiff belongs, if the obligation was imposed to prevent the kind of loss which he has suffered, and if the breach of the obligation was the effective cause of his loss.[20] In seeking to impose liability in damages on persons responsible for inadequate, false or misleading listing particulars, the satisfaction of these three requirements presents little difficulty. As the Listing Particulars Directive states, the requirements contained in it are designed to ensure that investors have adequate and accurate information on which to base their decisions to invest in the securities to which the listing particulars relate,[1] and the persons intended to be protected are therefore all investors who do in fact rely upon the listing particulars in question and who suffer loss by reason of the particulars being defective. Undoubtedly, the statutory obligations of the persons responsible for the listing particulars extend not only to those

---

15 The Stock Exchange (Listing) Regulations 1984, reg 3(1).
16 Ibid, reg 8(2).
17 *Cutter v Wandsworth Stadium Ltd* [1949] AC 398 at 407, per Lord Simonds; *Ministry of Housing and Local Government v Sharp* [1970] 2 QB 222,
18 *Phillips v British Hygienic Laundry Co Ltd* [1970] 2 KB 832 at 838 and 841, per Bankes and Atkin LJJ, *Monk v Warbey* [1938] 1 KB 75 at 84, per Maugham LJ; *Cutter v Wandsworth Stadium Ltd*, supra, per Lord Normand at p 413.
19 *Cutter v Wandsworth Stadium Ltd*, supra, at p 407.
20 *Clerk and Lindsell on Torts* (15th edn), p 643, et seq.
1 Listing Particulars Directive, Recitals and art 4(1).

investors who subscribe for newly created securities, but also to investors who purchase them on the Stock Exchange, whether from the issuing house or sponsoring brokers who marketed them or from other investors ·who have subscribed for or purchased them. The common law rule that only persons who subscribe for shares, debentures or other securities offered by a company or other issuer under a prospectus may sue the persons who published the prospectus for damages for deceit,[2] cannot apply to listing particulars, because the purpose of publishing such particulars is to encourage dealings in the securities on the Stock Exchange and not merely to invite subscriptions, and so even at common law in this context the liability of the persons responsible for the particulars would not be confined to subscribers or first purchasers of the securities.[3] Clearly, however, listing particulars can only be relied on by investors as stating the company's or other issuer's financial and economic situation and prospects and the rights attached to its securities and the relationship between different classes of its securities as of the date when the particulars are published or when Stock Exchange dealings begin. If the contents of the listing particulars become no longer adequate or accurate because of changes in circumstances or events occurring after their publication and the commencement of dealings, there is no obligation on the persons responsible for them to publish supplementary particulars so as to keep them up to date, and investors must rely on the issuing company's annual accounts and reports and its half-yearly reports dealt with by the Interim Reports Directive or any similar publications by a public body for information about later changes and events.[4] It may well be that when a substantial period of time has elapsed after the publication of listing particulars an investor may not rely on them at all for information, other than the historical background of the issuing company's development up to the time the particulars were first published.

Absolute or qualified liability

The duty to fulfil a statutory obligation may be an absolute one, or merely a qualified duty to ensure that all reasonable and practicable steps are taken to fulfil the obligation, so that no action for damages may be brought if the loss in question would have been suffered even if all such steps had been taken. Whether the statutory obligation is absolute or qualified depends on judicial interpretation of the content of the statutory obligation from the language in which it is expressed. If the means of fulfilling the duty is wholly or almost wholly in the hands of the defendant (such as the duty of a public officer to keep an accurate register of information given to him and to certify to third persons the content of notifications of information which he has received), the court will incline to treat the statutory duty as absolute,[5] subject possibly to the defence that the effective cause of the particular breach of duty was the act of a third person. On the other hand, where other factors than the precautions taken by the defendant, however complete, may cause a concurrence of circumstances resulting in loss, the

2 *Peek v Gurney* (1873) LR 6 HL 377.
3 *Andrews v Mockford* [1896] 1 QB 372,
4 Listing Particulars Directive, art 23 (see p 171, below).
5 *Ministry of Housing and Local Government v Sharp*, supra, per Denning LJ at p 267.

court may impose only a qualified duty, but the burden of proof on the defendant to show that all reasonable and practicable steps were taken to prevent loss occurring will be a heavy one, and the presumption will be that a breach of the statutory duty did take place.[6] An action for damages for breach of statutory duty is sometimes called an action for statutory negligence, but this is misleading, because proof of negligence on the part of the defendant is not an essential part of the plaintiff's case, and proof by the defendant that he was not personally negligent will not necessarily save him from liability.[7] The duty of the persons responsible for preparing listing particulars in connection with an application to the Stock Exchange for a listing of securities would appear to be of a qualified character. Although they have access to information about the company's capital structure, transactions which it has entered into and particulars of its directors by reason of them being its directors or governing body, or the listing application being made with the concurrence of its directors or governing body, there are items of information required to be included in listing particulars by the Listing Particulars Directive of which they may be ignorant or incompletely informed,[8] and it seems unlikely that the court would treat their duty of accurate disclosure as amounting to an absolute guarantee that all information which an intending investor ought to have has in fact been fully and accurately set out.

The statutory defences

The problem of interpreting the extent of the statutory duty is in fact made somewhat easier for the court by the Regulations providing three alternative defences to persons responsible for listing particulars,[9] and litigation is likely to be concentrated more on the availability of one or more of these defences, rather than the definition of the statutory duty. These defences in two respects reduce the responsibile person's duty to less than one to take all possible care to see that the listing particulars are complete and accurate, and they therefore raise the question whether there may be a collateral cause of action for negligence at common law against the responsible persons, to which, of course, the statutory defences would not apply.[10] The statutory defences to the liability of the persons responsible for defective listing particulars arising under their statutory duty of disclosure are as follows:

(a) that the defendant was not cognisant (ie actually aware) of a matter which should have been but was not disclosed; or

(b) that the non-compliance or contravention by the defendant arose from an honest mistake of fact on his part;

(c) that the non-compliance or contravention related to matters which

6 *Caswell v Powell Duffryn Associated Collieries Ltd* [1940] AC 152; *LPTB v Lupson* [1949] AC 155.

7 *Caswell v Powell Duffryn Associated Collieries Ltd*, supra, per Lord Wright at pp 177–179; *LPTB v Lupson*, supra, per Lord Wright at pp 168–169.

8 For example, the items set out in the Listing Particulars Directive, Schedule A, paras. 2.3.0, 2.3.8, 2.4.5, 3.2.5, 3.2.6, 3.2.7, 4.1.1, 4.1.3, 4.2, 4.3, 4.4, 4.5, 4.7.0, 5.1.5, 5.1.6, 5.2, 5.3, 6.2.1, 6.2.2, 6.2.3, 7.1 and 7.2. These items are dealt with in detail in Chapter 4.

9 The Stock Exchange (Listing) Regulations, reg 5(1).

10 See p 15, below.

the court considers immaterial or otherwise reasonably excusable in the circumstances.

The wording of the statutory defences does not reflect anything in the Admission or Listing Particulars Directive, but is taken by the Regulations directly from the prospectus provisions of the Companies Acts, under which the statutory defences may be pleaded to a prosecution or, if it lies at all,[11] a civil action for failure to include in a prospectus (other than a rights offer made to existing shareholders or debenture holders) all the statutory information called for by the Acts.[12] Under the Companies Acts it would appear that the statutory defences may only be pleaded in proceedings where failure to give the statutory information is complained of, and not in proceedings where the complaint is that false information was given and consequently accurate statutory information was not; there are separate provisions in the Act governing civil and criminal proceedings for false statements in prospectuses, and the statutory defences permitted in such proceedings impose a much more burdensome standard of exculpatory proof than in proceedings complaining of the omission of statutory information.[13] The application of the statutory defences in civil proceedings for breach of the statutory duty imposed by the Stock Exchange (Listing) Regulations to disclose in listing particulars all information required by investors to make an informed assessment of the company and the securities to be listed is much wider. The defences are available when any breach of the duty of disclosure occurs, whether it is simply by the omission of relevant information or by the giving of false or misleading information in respect of matters which are required to be disclosed. This weakens the impact of the statutory duty of disclosure (which implicitly means accurate and complete disclosure), and so makes more important the question whether a collateral action for negligence at common law may be brought when listing particulars are defective because of omission or inaccuracy.

Measure of damages

The damages recoverable for the failure of persons responsible for listing particulars to ensure that they include all necessary information for an informed assessment of the company and the securities to which they relate would appear to be the damages normally recoverable in a tort action, namely, the foreseeable pecuniary loss suffered directly by the plaintiff who has subscribed for or purchased such securities in reliance on the listing particulars. This in turn would appear to be the same measure as that for the statutory compensation recoverable by subscribers of shares or debentures under a prospectus which contains false or misleading information.[14]

---

11 There are no effective decisions that a civil action for damages does lie. There are affirmative dicta in one case (*Re South of England Natural Gas and Petroleum Co Ltd* [1911] Ch 573) and a decision of the Court of Appeal in another (*Lynde v Nash* [1928] 2 KB 93) which was overruled by the House of Lords on other grounds (*Nash v Lynde* [1929] AC 158).

12 Companies Act 1948, s 38(1), (4) and (5) (now Companies Act 1985, s 56(1) and (5) and s 66(1)).

13 Companies Act 1948, s 43(1) and (2) and s 44(1); (now Companies Act 1985, s 67(1) and (2), s 68(1) and (2) and s 70(1)).

14 Companies Act 1948, s 43(1); (now Companies Act 1985, s 67(1) and (2)).

This is normally the difference between the price which the plaintiff paid for the shares or debentures (either as a subscriber or as a purchaser) and their real value at the date he acquired them, having regard to the effect on that value of the later revelation of the omissions or inaccuracies of which the plaintiff complains.[15] But if the market value of the securities at the time the plaintiff acquired them was greater than the price he paid for them, he may recover the difference between those amounts as additional damages.[15] On the other hand, any fall in the value of the securities since the date on which he acquired them will not increase the amount of damages recoverable,[15] but if the subsequent fall in value is attributable to the discovery of the deficiencies or inaccuracies in the listing particulars and no other cause, it would seem that the market value of the securities upon the discovery being made may be given as evidence of their real value at the date when the plaintiff acquired them.

The persons liable for defective listing particulars

Finally, it would appear that the class of persons who may be made liable in damages to investors who subscribe for or purchase securities in reliance on defective listing particulars is limited to the persons who are responsible for the preparation of the listing particulars. This is because those persons are expressly obliged by the Regulations and the Listing Particulars Directive to ensure that the particulars they publish contain the necessary information,[16] and although this obligation is not expressly confined to them, the fact that the Regulations limit the availability of the statutory defences mentioned above to such persons[17] reinforces the conclusion that only such persons can be made primarily liable in damages, as distinct from vicariously liable. The persons responsible for listing particulars are the persons who are named therein as being responsible for their contents generally or for identified parts of their contents.[8] Consequently, since the directors of a company whose securities are to be listed must concur in preparing and authorising the listing particulars as published, and evidence their concurrence by signing the copy of the particulars which is submitted to the Stock Exchange,[19] the directors must all be responsible for the contents of the particulars generally. The same applies to the members of the governing body of an issuer other than a company; the listing particulars submitted to the Stock Exchange must be signed by a duly authorised officer or agent of the issuer, but a certified copy of his authorisation to do so given by the issuers governing authority must also be submitted.[20]

An issuing house or firm of sponsoring brokers will be responsible for the contents of listing particulars generally if it joins in accepting responsibility for particulars which serve as a prospectus or an offer of the securities to the public for subscription or purchase, and shareholders who market a block of existing shares on an introduction of those shares may also accept responsibility generally for the contents of the related listing particulars by

15 *McConnell v Wright* [1903] 1 Ch 546; *Clark v Urquhart* [1930] AC 28.
16 The Stock Exchange (Listing) Regulations, reg 5(1); Listing Particulars Directive, art 4(2).
17 The Stock Exchange (Listing) Regulations 1984, reg 5(2).
18 Listing Particulars Directive, Schedules A and B, para 1.1.
19 The Stock Exchange: *Admission of Securities to Listing*, Section 2, Chapter 1, para 5.4.
20 Ibid, Section 2, Chapter 2, para 6.4 and 5.

expressing their acceptance of responsibility therein. Persons who accept responsibility for part only of the particulars will be experts whose reports or opinions are included in them, for example, the company's auditors or accountants who report on the financial information given about the company.

It would seem that an issuing company itself will not normally be liable in respect of defects in listing particulars relating to its shares. It need not be expressed to be one of the persons responsible for the particulars, and it will not apparently be vicariously liable for its directors who are expressed to be responsible. This is because an action for damages cannot be brought against the issuing company, unless the plaintiff has ceased to be a shareholder of the company and the shares have been restored to the company by the plaintiff rescinding any allotment of the shares, or by a chain of successive holders rescinding their purchases from their immediate predecessor and the allottee rescinding against the company.[1] However, such rescission or ultimate rescission against the company is not possible, because the Regulations provide that no transaction is void or voidable because of a contravention of the Regulations or the directives,[2] and this deprives a subscriber or purchaser of shares of any right he might otherwise have had to recover damages from the company. This consideration does not apply when debentures or debt securities are issued by a company or other issuer, and there is no reason why the issuer should not be made vicariously liable in damages for loss suffered by an investor if its directors or members of its governing body are primarily liable.

ALTERNATIVE CIVIL REMEDIES

The principal limitation on the usefulness of an action for breach of statutory duty brought against persons responsible for defective listing particulars is that they may escape liability by relying on the statutory defences, one of which is the immateriality of the defect and the other two of which turn on the ignorance of the responsible person or an honest mistake of fact on his part.[3] It is therefore important to discover whether there are alternative remedies available under the general law which may prove more effective. The possibility of such remedies is clearly envisaged by the Regulations providing that nothing in them shall limit or diminish any liability which anyone may incur under the general law,[4] so that liability in damages for breach of statutory duty does not supersede other available remedies.

Rescission

The primary remedy for an inducement by misrepresentation to subscribe for or purchase securities is rescission of the subscription or purchase, either at common law if the misrepresentation is made knowingly,[5] or in

---

1 *Houldsworth v City of Glasgow Bank* (1880) 5 App Cas 317.
2 The Stock Exchange (Listing) Regulations 1984, reg 8(2).
3 Ibid, reg 5(2).
4 Ibid, reg 5(3).
5 *Kennedy v Panama Mail Co* (1867) LR 2 QB 580.

equity if it is made innocently.[6] However, the remedy of rescission does not lie merely for failure to disclose matters which statute requires to be disclosed to an intending subscriber or purchaser of investment,[7] unless the failure to disclose makes what is positively stated either false or misleading.[8] If a subscriber or purchaser of securities complains of omissions in listing particulars, the remedy of rescission so as to compel the issuing company or other body, or in the case of a company, the responsible selling shareholders or debenture holders, to take back the securities issued or sold and to restore the amount paid by the shareholder or purchaser will not be available,[9] but it would seem that there is nothing to prevent the subscriber or purchaser from rescinding if the listing particulars contain positive false or misleading statements of fact, and these induce the plaintiff to subscribe for or purchase the securities.[10] In this latter case the rescission is not for contravention of the Regulations or the Listing Particulars Directive, but for misrepresentation under the general law. However, if the listing particulars relate to shares offered for subscription, an investor may rescind an allotment of such shares to him for misrepresentation only if he commences an action for rescission or, at least, notifies the company of his decision to rescind before the company goes into liquidation, whether compulsory or voluntary, or before it ceases to carry on business because insolvent.[11] This does not apply, of course, if the investor purchases shares from existing holders who procure an introduction of them on the Stock Exchange and are themselves named in the listing particulars as persons responsible for their contents, which include positive false or misleading statements.

Actions of deceit and negligence

The second and third remedies available under the general law to an investor who is induced to subscribe for or purchase securities under listing particulars which contain false statements of fact, are to sue the persons responsible for damages at common law in an action of deceit if the investor can prove that they made the false statements knowingly or without belief in their truth, or in an action for negligence if the investor can show that the persons responsible failed to exercise proper care to ensure that the listing particulars were accurate.[12] The latter common law action is the more important of the two, because the burden of proof on the plaintiff is lighter, and in most situations in which false listing particulars are involved, the false information given will be about matters on which the responsible persons are far more informed than the plaintiff, and the burden of proof

6 *Redgrave v Hurd* (1881) Ch D 1; *Adam v Newbigging* (1888) 13 App Cas 308.
7 *Re Wimbledon Olympia Ltd* [1910] 1 Ch 310; *Re South of England Natural Gas Co Ltd* [1911] 1 Ch 573.
8 *New Brunswick and Canada Railway and Land Co v Muggeridge* (1860) 1 Dr & Sm 363; *Aaron's Reefs Ltd v Twiss* [1896] AC 273.
9 The Stock Exchange (Listing) Regulations 1984, reg 8(2).
10 Ibid, reg 5(3).
11 *Houldsworth v City of Glasgow Bank* (1880) 5 App Cas 317; *Re Hull and County Bank Ltd, Burgess' Case* (1880) 15 Ch D 507; *Tennent v City of Glasgow Bank* (1879) 4 App Cas 615.
12 *Derry v Peek* (1889) 14 App Cas 337; *Hedley Byrne & Co Ltd v Heller and Partners Ltd* [1964] AC 465.

will be put on those persons under the res ipsa loquitur rule to show that they exercised due care.

It has been said obiter that a common law action for negligent misstatements does not lie if statute has expressly created a right of action for damages or compensation, for example, the right to recover compensation given to subscribers under a false prospectus by the Companies Acts.[13] This would not appear to apply in the case of false listing particulars, however, because the Regulations and the Listing Particulars Directive confer no express cause of action on subscribers and investors to recover loss suffered because of their reliance on false listing particulars, and there is no general rule that an action for breach of statutory duty cannot be combined with a common law action for negligence, although damages for the loss suffered can be recovered only once.[14]

The one important outstanding question is whether the statutory defences to an action for breach of statutory duty in publishing false listing particulars can also be pleaded as defences to a common law action for negligence. If this were possible, the common law action would offer no practical advantage to an investor, because the statutory defences in effect reduce the duty of the persons responsible for the listing particulars to a mere obligation to act in good faith. The Regulations make the statutory defences available only when the investor's action is brought for non-compliance with, or contravention of, the obligation imposed by the Listing Particulars Directive to ensure that listing particulars contain all necessary information;[15] the defences are not expressed to be available when any other kind of action is brought in respect of false statements in listing particulars. Consequently, it would seem that the defences in the Regulations cannot be pleaded in a common law action for negligence, and persons responsible for false listing particulars may therefore be made liable not only when they act in bad faith, but also when they act negligently.

Statutory claim to compensation

It has been shown that listing particulars will come within the definition of a prospectus in the Companies Acts if they are used to offer shares or debentures to the public for subscription or purchase,[16] and if listing particulars qualify as a prospectus, the question arises whether a statutory claim for compensation in respect of false information in them may be brought under the Companies Acts.[17] This question is bound up with the general question as to the exclusion of the prospectus provisions of the Companies Acts in their application to listing particulars by the express terms of the Regulations, and will be dealt with below in that context.

It need merely be pointed out here that if such a statutory claim for

---

13 *Hedley Byrne & Co Ltd v Heller and Partners Ltd*, supra at pp 500–501 and 518–519 per Lords Morris and Devlin. The statutory right to recover compensation is conferred by the Companies Act 1948, s 43(1) (now the Companies Act 1985, s 67(1)).
14 *Anns v Merton London Borough Council* [1978] AC 728; *Ministry of Housing and Local Government v Sharp* [1970] 2 QB 222 at 267–268, per Denning LJ.
15 The Stock Exchange (Listing) Regulations 1984, reg 5(2); Listing Particulars Directive, art 4.
16 See p 6, above.
17 Companies Act 1948, s 43(1) (now Companies Act 1985, s 67(1)).

compensation does lie in respect of listing particulars, the burden of proof on the plaintiff investor is merely to show that the particulars contained false statements of fact and that he relied on the prospectus in subscribing for the securities offered by it.[17] There are various defences which the persons responsible for the prospectus may plead, some formal and some substantive, but the general effect of the defences is to reduce the defendant's liability to one for negligence.[18] It is not a defence to show that the defendant was ignorant of the falsity of the statement complained of or that he made an honest mistake of fact, as it is when the statutory defences are relied on in an action for damages for breach of statutory duty in publishing listing particulars which do not comply with the Listing Particulars Directive.[15] Consequently, the availability of a statutory claim for compensation under the Companies Acts could be of distinct advantage to an investor, but even if the statutory claim is not available to him, he can put himself in much the same position as though it were by combining a claim for damages for breach of statutory duty under the Regulations with a claim for damages for negligence.

Misrepresentation Act 1967

The final alternative civil remedy which an investor who has relied on false listing particulars may seek to pursue is an action for damages under the Misrepresentation Act 1967.[19] Such an action can only be brought against the other party to a contract which has been induced by a misrepresentation of fact, and it is a defence to such an action that the defendant had reasonable ground to believe and did believe up to the time when the contract was made that the misrepresentation was true.[19]

It should be noted that the defendant in such an action is the party who allots or sells securities under a contract induced by false listing particulars, that is, the issuing company or other issuing body in the case of an offer of shares, debentures or debt securities for subscription, an issuing house or sponsoring broker in the case of an offer for sale or placing of securities which the company has allotted or agreed to allot with a view to them being sold to other persons, and the vendors in the case of an offer for sale or placing of existing securities. Moreover, the defendant must be responsible for the listing particulars which contain the false information either by having itself named therein as a responsible person,[20] or by adopting or relying on the listing particulars to induce the subscription or sale of the securities.[1] A company or other issuer is not a person responsible for the listing particulars under the Regulations,[2] but it does use them as the basis for accepting applications for the allotment of securities. On the other hand, an issuing house or a firm of sponsoring brokers may be both a person responsible for listing particulars and a party to the contract with an investor for which the listing particulars have formed a basis, and vendors of existing securities are in the same position. However, although an issuing house, sponsoring brokers or vendors of securities may be sued for

---

18 Companies Act 1948, s 43(2) and (3) (now Companies Act 1985, s 68(1)–(5)).
19 Misrepresentation Act 1967, s 2(1).
20 Listing Particulars Directive, Schedules A and B, para 1.1.
 1 *Lynde v Anglo Italian Hemp Spinning Co* [1896] 1 Ch 178.
 2 See p 14, above.

damages under the Misrepresentation Act 1967, whether the plaintiff has rescinded the contract with the defendant or not, an action under the Act may be brought against a company which allots shares on the basis of false listing particulars only if the contract of allotment has first been rescinded by the plaintiff, and he cannot rescind it for misrepresentation if the company has gone into liquidation, whether compulsory or voluntary, or if the company has ceased to carry on business because insolvent.[3]

ADAPTATION OF THE COMPANIES ACTS AND OTHER LEGISLATION

The Stock Exchange (Listing) Regulations 1984, make a number of modifications to the provisions of the Companies Act 1948, relating to prospectuses in their application to listing particulars approved by the Quotations Committee of the Stock Exchange for publication in connection with a listing application.[4] The prospectus provisions of the Companies Act 1948, can apply to listing particulars only if they are published in connection with an offer of shares or debentures for subscription by the public, or alternatively, for purchase by the public if the shares or debentures have been allotted or agreed to be allotted with a view to such an offer being made.[5] Those prospectus provisions can apply and the modifications of them by the Regulations can take effect, therefore, only if the listing particulars relate to an offer of shares or debentures for subscription which is made by the company to the public at large (prospectus offer) or to a section of the public, such as its own existing shareholders (rights offer), or if the listing particulars relate to an offer of shares or debentures by an issuing house or firm of sponsoring brokers to the public at large (offer for sale) or by means of a placing with dealers on the Stock Exchange (placing) when the issuing company has allotted or agreed to allot them to the issuing house or sponsoring brokers for that purpose. If listing particulars relate to shares or debentures which are introduced on the Stock Exchange and all or some of them are to be made available on the market by their existing holders, the prospectus provisions of the Companies Acts, do not apply, and nor therefore do the modifications of those provisions made by the Regulations.

The exclusionary provisions

The main modifications made by the Regulations to the application of the prospectus provisions of the Companies Act 1948, to approved listing particulars are by way of exclusion. The prohibition in the 1948 Act that if

---

3 *Houldsworth v City of Glasgow Bank* (1880) 5 App Cas 317; *Re Hull and County Bank Ltd, Burgess's Case* (1880) 15 Ch D 507; *Tennent v City of Glasgow Bank* (1879) 4 App Cas 615.

4 The Stock Exchange (Listing) Regulations 1984, reg 7(1), (2) and (4). The modifications affect only the provisions of the Companies Act 1948, and so the prohibition in the Companies Act 1980, s 16 on the allotment of shares by a public company offered for subscription by a prospectus unless all the shares so offered or a smaller number of shares specified in the offer are subscribed, applies to an offer of shares for subscription made by listing particulars.

5 Companies Act 1948, s 45(1), s 55(1) and s 455(1) (now Companies Act 1985, s 58(1), s 60(1) and s 744).

a prospectus is issued to the public generally,[6] application forms for the shares or debentures to which it relates cannot be delivered by the company or its issuing house or sponsoring brokers to prospective applicants (other than underwriters) unless accompanied by a full copy of the prospectus containing all the information required by the 1948 Act,[7] does not apply when the prospectus takes the form of approved listing particulars.[8] Consequently, application forms can be issued or published with abridged particulars or mini-prospectuses containing summaries of approved listing particulars or with formal newspaper announcements of offers of shares or debentures, but if this is done there must be included in the abridged particulars etc a statement where full copies of the listing particulars may be obtained.[8] Again, if full approved listing particulars have been published in accordance with the Listing Particular Directive and particular sub-scriptions or purchases of the shares or debentures offered are made on the basis of abridged particulars which state where full copies of the listing particulars may be obtained, those subscriptions or purchases cannot be invalidated on the ground that no notice or inadequate notice of the contents of the listing particulars was given to the subscriber or purchaser before the transaction was entered into.[9]

The most important exclusion of the prospectus provisions of the Companies Act 1948, made by the Regulations and the one which will give rise to difficulties of interpretation, provides that 'in relation to an offer (of shares or debentures) for subscription or purchase made by means of (approved listing particulars), provisions of the [Companies Act 1948] otherwise applicable with respect to prospectuses and their contents, or with respect to the consequences attending the issue of a prospectus, or the inclusion of any statement in, or the omission of anything from, a prospectus, shall not apply'.[10] This exclusion of the prospectus provisions of the Companies Act 1948, can be read in either a broad or a narrower way. The introductory words 'in relation to an offer (of shares or debentures) for subscription or purchase . . .' could be read as a mere recognition that listing particulars may be used as a prospectus to make such an offer, but that they do not necessarily do so, and the exclusion therefore applies only when the listing particulars are also a prospectus. On that supposition the effective part of the exclusion must disapply all the provisions of the Companies Act 1948, in respect of prospectuses; this will include the provisions relating to the contents of the prospectus;[11] the prohibition on the issue of a prospectus containing a report or statement by an expert unless he has consented in writing to its inclusion and the prospectus states that he has done so;[12] the filing at the Companies Registry of a copy of the prospectus signed by every director and proposed director of the company

---

6 That is, to persons other than, or in addition to, existing share and debenture holders of the issuing company.

7 Companies Act 1948, s 38(1) and (5) (now Companies Act 1985, s 56(1), (2) and (5) and s 57(1)).

8 The Stock Exchange (Listing) Regulations 1984, reg 7(1)(*a*).

9 Ibid, reg 7(1)(*c*).

10 Ibid, reg 7(1)(*b*).

11 Companies Act 1948, s 38(1) and s 45(3) and Fourth Schedule (now Companies Act 1985, s 56(1) and s 58(1) and Sch 3).

12 Companies Act 1948, s 40(1) (now Companies Act 1985, s 61(1)).

accompanied by a written consent of every expert to the inclusion in the prospectus of a report or statement by him and a copy of each material contract which the company has entered into during the preceding two years (other than contracts made in the ordinary course of business);[13] the liability of directors, proposed directors, promoters and persons who have authorised the issue of the prospectus to compensate subscribers for loss caused by untrue statements therein;[14] the criminal liability of persons who have authorised the issue of a prospectus for false statements therein;[15] the consequences of a prospectus offering shares or debentures for sale being published by an issuing house or sponsoring brokers;[16] the minimum subscription of shares which must be obtained under a prospectus before shares may be allotted under it and the right of subscribers to rescind allotments improperly made and to recover amounts paid on the shares and damages if the minimum subscription is not attained;[17] the earliest dates on which shares or debentures may be allotted under a prospectus or applications for shares or debentures may be revoked;[18] and the consequences of a prospectus stating that an application has been or will be made for the shares or debentures to which it relates to be listed on a stock exchange and of the application being refused by the stock exchange.[19]

On the other hand, the introductory words in the Regulations to the exclusion of the prospectus provisions of the Companies Act 1948, can be read in a narrower sense as relating only to those provisions which are concerned with the offer of shares or debentures made by the prospectus, with the consequence that provisions which do not relate to the form, content or procedure for making the offer are not excluded and continue to apply to listing particulars which serve as prospectuses. The argument for this narrower interpretation, apart from the grammatical one, is strengthened by the fact that if the exclusion of all the prospectus provisions were intended, the introductory words would be unnecessary and their presence would be surplusage. The unqualified exclusion by the Regulations of all the prospectus provisions would effectively exclude them if the listing particulars served also as a prospectus; no mention of the situations where the listing particulars are also a prospectus is necessary for that purpose, because the prospectus provisions do not apply anyway if the listing particulars are not a prospectus.

If the narrower interpretation of the exclusion is correct, the result would be that the requirements of the Companies Act 1948, as the contents of prospectus would still not apply to listing particulars which are also prospectuses (including the statement of the minimum subscription of shares which must be obtained before shares may be allotted and the prohibition of allotments before it has been obtained),[20] but the remaining provisions of the Companies Act 1948, mentioned in the preceding

13 Companies Act 1948, s 41(1) (now Companies Act 1985, s 64(1) and s 65(2)).
14 Companies Act 1948, s 43(1) (now Companies Act 1985, s 67(1) and (2)).
15 Companies Act 1948, s 44(1) (now Companies Act 1985, s 70(1)).
16 Companies Act 1948, s 45(1) (now Companies Act 1985, s 58(1)).
17 Companies Act 1948, s 47(1) and (4) and s 49(1) and (2) (now Companies Act 1985, s 83(1) and (4) and s 85(1) and (2)).
18 Companies Act 1948, s 50(1), (4) and (5) (now Companies Act 1985, s 82(1) (6) and (7)).
19 Companies Act 1948, s 51(1) and (2) (now Companies Act 1985, s 86(1)–(4)).
20 Companies Act 1948, s 38(1) and s 47(1) (now Companies Act 1985, s 56(1) and s 83(1)).

paragraph would apply, including most importantly, the requirements that experts must give their written consents to the inclusion of statements by them in a prospectus and that such consents and copies of material contracts must be filed at the Companies Registry before the prospectus is issued;[1] the civil and criminal liability of persons who authorise the issue of a prospectus which contains false statements;[2] and the treatment of prospectuses by which issuing houses or sponsoring brokers offer shares or debentures which have been allotted or agreed to be allotted to them for sale to the public.[16] It is uncertain whether the narrower interpretation of the exclusion would leave intact the provisions of the Companies Act 1948, as to the earliest dates on which shares or debentures may be allotted under a prospectus or applications for shares and debentures under the prospectus may be revoked.[18] These provisions seemingly relate both to the offer made by listing particulars which serve as a prospectus and to the consequences of issuing those particulars, but they also relate to the procedure for allotting shares and liability to pay the issue price. There is no difficulty in applying the provisions consistently with the rules in the Listing Particulars Directive as to the date when a listing takes effect,[3] and there would seem to be a strong case for arguing that the provisions should apply to applications and allotment under listing particulars. The provision in the Companies Act 1948, as to a statement in a prospectus that an application has been or will be made for a listing of the securities offered on a stock exchange[4] will not apply when listing particulars are published, because the exclusion of the prospectus provisions applies only when listing particulars have been approved by the Quotations Committee of the Stock Exchange and this can be done only after the Committee has already received an application for a listing. If the application for a listing is refused within three weeks after it is made, however, there is nothing in the exclusion of the prospectus provision to prevent any allotment of shares or debentures which has already taken place being retrospectively invalidated, and the provision in the Companies Act 1948, to that effect would not appear to be excluded as one 'with respect to the consequences attending the issue of a prospectus'.

The other modifications

The remaining modifications of the provisions of the Companies Act 1948, and related legislation which the Stock Exchange (Listing) Regulations 1984, make in applying them to listing particulars and certain other documents, deal with three unrelated matters.

In the first place listing particulars by means of which shares or debentures are offered for subscription or purchase are not treated as a prospectus under the Companies Act 1948, if the offer is confined to persons whose ordinary business is to buy or sell shares or debentures,

---

1 Companies Act 1948, s 40(1) and s 41(1) (now Companies Act 1985, s 61(1), s 64(1) and s 65(2)).
2 Companies Act 1948, s 43(1) and s 44(1) (now Companies Act 1985, s 67(1) and (2) and s 70(1)).
3 Listing Particulars Directive, art 21 (see p 51, below).
4 Companies Act 1948, s 51(1) (now Companies Act 1985, s 86(1)–(4)).
5 Listing Particulars Directive, art 18(2) and art 20 and 21(1) (see pp 150 and 151, below).

whether as principals or agents (professional investors or dealers).[6] This exemption is derived from the rule in the Companies Act 1948, relating to offers in Great Britain of the shares of debentures of overseas companies;[7] it does not apply to offers of the shares of debentures of companies registered in Great Britain unless an application has been made for them to be listed on the Stock Exchange.[6]

Secondly, the provision in the Companies Act 1948, is repealed by which the Stock Exchange could in appropriate circumstances give a certificate of exemption enabling a company to comply with its rules as to the contents of prospectuses instead of complying with the requirements of the Companies Act.[8] The principal reason why such certificates were formerly given was to enable companies which already had a Stock Exchange listing for their shares or debentures to publish shorter prospectuses than the Companies Act would otherwise require when they made further issues of shares or debentures, and the contents of the shortened prospectuses were mainly confined to up-dating material.[9] The Listing Particulars Directive now deals specifically with the omission of material normally required in listing particulars when securities are issued in special circumstances, and a margin of discretion is given to the Stock Exchange to authorise omissions.[10] Consequently, the former facility of a certificate of exemption is either unnecessary or in some situations would conflict with the new rules, and has therefore been terminated.

The final modification in the existing law made by the Stock Exchange (Listing) Regulations 1984, is to extend to listing particulars and secondary advertisements in respect of securities for which a listing on the Stock Exchange has been sought and to other documents relating to securities which are listed on the Stock Exchange an exemption from the restrictions on the distribution of investment circulars which is imposed by the Prevention of Fraud (Investments) Act 1958. To qualify for exemption, however, the listing particulars, secondary advertisements or other documents must contain the whole or part of the information which the Listing Particulars Directive requires and nothing more than that information, and they must have been approved by the Quotations Committee of the Stock Exchange if any of the directives requires its approval before publication.[11] The restrictions imposed by the Prevention of Fraud (Investments) Act 1958, effectively prevent investment circulars (other than prospectuses issued generally which contain the information required by the Companies Act 1948) from being distributed by persons other than members of the Stock Exchange or an association of dealers in securities recognised by the Secretary of State for Trade and Industry, or by exempted dealers,[12] or by

6 The Stock Exchange (Listing) Regulations 1984, reg 7(2).

7 Companies Act 1948, s 423(2) (now Companies Act 1985, s 79(2)).

8 Companies Act 1948 s 39(1) and (2); The Stock Exchange (Listing) Regulations 1984, reg 7(4).

9 See the Stock Exchange: *Admission of Securities to Listing* (1979 edition) Appendix, Schedule II, Part B.

10 See p 56, below.

11 The Stock Exchange (Listing) Regulations 1984, reg 7(3). Such approval is always required for listing particulars and may be required for secondary advertisements (Listing Particulars Directive, art 18(2) and art 22).

12 Exempted dealers are banks and investment institutions whose main business is either a business other than dealing in securities, or the business of dealing in securities by marketing and underwriting them when they are issued; exemption is given by the Secretary of State for Trade and Industry at his discretion (Prevention of Fraud (Investments) Act 1958, s 16(1)).

persons licensed to deal in securities by the Secretary of State,[13] or by persons specially authorised by the Secretary of State.[14] The result of the exemption given by the Stock Exchange (Listing) Regulations 1984, is that listing particulars, abridged particulars, mini-prospectuses summarising the contents of listing particulars and announcements of intended issues of shares or debentures may, when approved by the Quotations Committee, be distributed and circulated without restriction and without the need to obtain permission from the Secretary of State. Other circulars and notifications approved by the Quotations Department of the Stock Exchange under the Stock Exchange's own requirements and not under the directives[15] are not within the exemption from the restrictions imposed by the Prevention of Fraud (Investments) Act 1958.[14] However, such circulars or notifications are subject to those restrictions only if they are investment circulars, that is, documents which contain invitations to persons to subscribe for or acquire or dispose of securities or information calculated to lead to the recipients doing any of those things,[16] and most of the circulars and notifications published by listed companies under the Stock Exchange's own rules do not contain such invitations or information.

JUDICIAL REVIEW OF STOCK EXCHANGE DECISIONS

In exercising the powers vested in it by the Stock Exchange (Listing) Regulations 1984, and by delegation by the Council of the Stock Exchange,[17] the Quotations Committee of the Council acts in the name of the Council as a public authority exercising legal powers. Consequently, any challenge to the legality or validity of decisions of the Quotations Committee must be made by an application for judicial review in the Queen's Bench Division of the High Court,[18] and an ordinary action for an injunction, a declaratory judgment or for any other relief will be dismissed as an abuse of the process of the court.[19] Nevertheless, in appropriate circumstances (which will be rare) a defendant in an ordinary civil action may rely on the invalidity of a decision of the Quotations Committee on the same grounds as he could challenge the decision directly by an application for judicial review;[20] in this situation the plaintiff's cause of action will be a normal civil claim (eg for damages because the plaintiff was induced to

---

13 Prevention of Fraud (Investments) Act 1958, s 1(1).
14 Ibid, s 14(1)–(3).
15 All circulars sent by listed companies to holders of their shares or debentures must be submitted in draft for approval by the Quotations Department before they are published (The Stock Exchange: *Admission of Securities to Listing*, Section 5, Chapter 2, para 31).
16 Prevention of Fraud (Investments) Act 1958, s 13(1) and s 14(1).
17 The Stock Exchange (Listing) Regulations 1984, reg 4(1) and (2); The Stock Exchange: *Admission of Securities to Listing*, Section 1, Chapter 1, para 2.
18 Supreme Court Act 1981, s 31(1) (51 Halsbury's Statutes (3rd edn) 625). The application is made under RSC, Ord 53, r 1. Leave of the court must first be obtained for the application to proceed, and this is done by an ex parte application to a judge, who may grant leave informally without a hearing, or may decide the matter upon a hearing in court in any other case (r 3(1), (3) and (4)). When leave to proceed has been obtained, the application is heard on originating motion to a single judge sitting in open court, unless the court orders that it shall be heard on motion to a Divisional Court of the Queen's Bench Division or on a summons before a judge in chambers (r 5(2)).
19 *O'Reilly v Mackman* [1983] 2 AC 237; *Cocks v Thanet District Council* [1983] 2 AC 286.
20 *Wandsworth London Borough Council v Winder* [1984] 3 All ER 976.

subscribe for shares or debentures which did not contain all the information required by the Listing Particulars Directive as interpreted by the Quotations Committee), and it will be the defence which raises the question of the validity of the Quotation Committee's ruling.

The decisions of the Quotations Committee which will be subject to challenge by an application for judicial review will be primarily the grant or refusal of a listing for securities, the approval or disapproval of draft listing particulars and omissions from half-yearly reports by listed companies under the Interim Reports Directive and the suspension or termination of a listing of securities under the Admission Directive. Additionally, decisions by the Quotations Committee on the proper interpretation of any of the provisions of the directives in connection with the enforcement of the directives generally by the Council of the Stock Exchange will be subject to challenge by judicial review. However, the enforcement of the Stock Exchange's own rules, as distinct from the implementation or enforcement of the directives, will not involve the Council or the Quotations Committee in the exercise of legal powers conferred on a public authority, and so any challenge to the validity of the Quotations Committee's rulings on such matters will be by ordinary action, motion for an injunction or other appropriate civil proceedings. It would appear that this is so even if the Stock Exchange rule or the Quotations Committee's ruling relates to the conditions imposed by the Stock Exchange's rules on the admission of securities to listing or on the contents of half-yearly reports by listed companies under the power reserved by the directive to member states to impose 'more stringent conditions' than those imposed by the Admission and Interim Reports Directives; this is because the Stock Exchange (Listing) Regulations 1984, and the directives do not incorporate those conditions as matters of law, but merely permit them to be imposed.[1] On the other hand, it may be contended that the Quotations Committee acts as a public authority in granting or refusing an application for a listing of securities and in approving or disapproving draft listing particulars because its powers to do these things are now conferred by law, and this is so even though its reasons for exercising its powers in a particular case are derived from the Stock Exchange's own rules and not from rules of law. If this argument prevails, the issue or refusal of listings for securities and the approval or disapproval of listing particulars by the Quotations Committee will be subject to challenge by applications for judicial review, whatever the Committee's reasons for its decision may have been.

The grounds on which an application may be made for judicial review of a decision of the Quotations Committee are:—(a) that the Committee has acted without or in excess of its legal powers or jurisdiction; (b) that the Committee has made an error of law in reaching its decision; (c) that there has been a failure to comply with the rules of natural justice; and (d) that no properly acting public authority directing itself correctly as to matters of law and acting reasonably could have reached the decision which the Quotations Committee gave.[2] The detailed application of these criteria involves questions of administrative law, for which the reader is referred to

1 Admission Directive, art 5(1); Interim Reports Directive, art 3.
2 See the Supreme Court Practice (1985 edn), Vol 1, pp 756 and 760–761.

the standard works on the subject.[3] In practice there are likely to be few applications for judicial review of decisions of the Quotations Committee in implementing the directives governing the listing of securities. This is because the questions which the Quotations Committee has to decide in exercising its functions relate principally to the exercise of discretions in giving exemptions or allowing departures from the requirements of the directives, or to matters of a technical nature where the professional knowledge and experience of the Committee (its expertise) will in practice make its rulings and interpretation of the directives almost unimpeachable. Because of the uncomplicated drafting of the directives, there are, in any case, likely to be few disputed questions of a legal character for the Quotations Committee to resolve, and the material for basing applications for judicial review will be correspondingly limited. Moreover, the remedies which the court may give on judicial review of a decision of the Quotations Committee are limited to annulling the decision and ordering the Committee to make a decision or to do any act which it is obliged to do under the directives (eg to approve or disapprove draft listing particulars submitted to it). The court cannot direct the Quotations Committee to exercise a discretion vested in it in any particular way, and so it cannot review any decision to grant, suspend or terminate a listing for securities on the merits of the case; if the discretion has been improperly exercised, the most which the court can do is to order the Committee to decide the matter again, taking account of the proper relevant factors and the court's ruling on questions of law.

3 S A de Smith, *Judicial Review of Administrative Action* (5th edn), Chapters 3 to 6; D C M Yardley, *Principles of Administrative Law*, Chapters 3 and 4; J A G Griffith and H Street, *The Principles of Administrative Law* (5th edn), pp 212–24; D Foulkes *Administrative Law* (5th edn), pp 287–304.

CHAPTER 2

Admission to Listing

The admission of the shares and debentures of companies to listing on the Stock Exchange is regulated by the Stock Exchange (Listing) Regulations 1984,[1] and the Admission Directive[2] to which it gives effect as part of United Kingdom law. The admission is also governed as a matter of Stock Exchange practice by the requirements of the Stock Exchange set out in its manual, *Admission of Securities to Listing*, published in November 1984, as amended from time to time. Insofar as the Stock Exchange's own requirements exceed those of the Admission Directive or impose heavier obligations on listed companies than the Admission Directive, they are valid in law provided that they apply generally (as they do) to all issuers or individual classes of issuer.[3] However, these additional or supplemental requirements, unlike the requirements of the Admission Directive, do not themselves form part of the law, and so the only sanctions for their enforcement are the refusal of a listing, or if a listing is given, the measures provided by the Stock Exchange's own rules. On the other hand, the Stock Exchange may waive any such additional and supplemental requirements of its own in any particular case, provided that it does so for issuers generally in situations where the conditions or circumstances are the same.[4] Waivers of the requirements of the Admission Directive are possible, however, only when the directive so provides, but any waiver of such a requirement is possible only if all issuers are treated in the same way when the conditions or circumstances are the same.[5]

The Admission Directive governs the grant of a listing for all kinds of securities, a term which is nowhere defined in the directive, but it permits member states of the Community to exclude two classes of security from the operation of the Directive and the Stock Exchange (Listing) Regulations 1984, do in fact exclude both classes.[6] These excluded securities are (i) all securities issued by a member state of the Community or by any regional or local authority of a member state, and (ii) units issued by a collective investment undertaking of the open-ended kind.[7] The exclusion does not apply to securities issued by states which are not members of the European Community or by their regional or local authorities, nor to securities issued by public international authorities, such as the European Investment Bank or agencies of the United Nations, such as the World Bank. Such issuers can issue only debt securities (bonds, loan stock or

---

1 The Stock Exchange (Listing) Regulations 1984, reg 3(1).
2 Admission Directive, arts 1, 3 and 4.
3 Ibid, art 5(1) and (2).
4 Ibid, art 5(3) and (7).
5 Ibid, art 7.
6 The Stock Exchange (Listing) Regulations 1984, art 6 and Sch 2, para 1.
7 Admission Directive, art 1(2).

notes) and they are subject to less stringent conditions and obligations by the Admission Directive than companies and other undertakings of a commercial character.[8]

Collective investment undertakings of the open-ended kind (or, in the words of the directive, collective investment undertakings other than the closed-end type) are defined by the directive as unit trusts and investment companies the object of which is the collective investment of capital provided by the public[9] on the principle of risk spreading, and the units of which are at the request of their holders repurchased or redeemed directly or indirectly out of the assets of the undertaking and while outstanding represent the rights of their holders in the assets of the undertaking.[10] The exclusion from the Admission Directive therefore applies to all unit trusts which issue circulars or advertisements offering their units for acquisition by the public, and also their foreign equivalents, American mutual funds, French *sociétés d'investissement à capital variable* and *fonds d'investissements* and German *Kapitalanlagegesellschaften* which issue *Investmentfonds-anteile*. The fact that the rights of investors in collective investment undertakings take the form of shares in the managing or trustee company would not appear to affect the exclusion from the directive, because the shareholders still have contractual, if not proprietary, rights in the assets of the undertakings, and this is expressly recognised by the Stock Exchange (Listing) Regulations 1984.[11] It is essential, however, that the shareholders should have the right to insist on their shares being re-purchased by the company under an arrangement which is legally effective,[12] and the absence of such an arrangement in the case of British investment trust companies (as distinct from unit trusts) means that the listing of their shares will not be excluded from the directive.

The securities whose listing will be governed by the Stock Exchange (Listing) Regulations 1984, and the Admission Directive will therefore be primarily the shares and debentures of companies incorporated under the Companies Acts or corresponding foreign or Commonwealth legislation. The Admission Directive relates also to certificates representing shares and permits them to be admitted to listing on a stock exchange in a member state if certain conditions are fulfilled.[13] Such certificates either represent a derivative title to shares the legal title to which is vested in a financial institution (for example, the *certificaten* issued by an *administratiekantoor* or administrative office of a bank which holds the shares of a Dutch company), or take the form of a depository certificate or receipt issued by a bank, financial institution or stockbroker as the bailee or depositary of original share certificates in registered or bearer form (such as the depositary receipts issued by American banks and stockbrokers and the

---

8 Ibid, Schedules B and C, Part B.
9 Capital is considered as provided by the public if it is raised by means of offers which would be prospectuses if the issuer were a company (The Stock Exchange (Listing) Regulations 1984, Sch 2, para 1).
10 Admission Directive, art 2(*a*) and (*b*).
11 The Stock Exchange (Listing) Regulations 1984, Sch 2, para 1.
12 Such arrangements may be established under the Companies Act 1981, ss 46, 49 and 51 (now Companies Act 1985, ss 162, 166 and 168), but they would require renewal at 18 month intervals and re-purchases could be made only out of the company's profits.
13 Admission Directive, art 4(3).

Verwahrungsscheine issued by German banks). The Stock Exchange does not give listings for such certificates, but only for the underlying shares, and consequently they give rise to no special problems in a United Kingdom context.

CONDITIONS FOR ADMISSION TO LISTING

The Admission Directive subjects the admission of securities to listing to specific conditions whose fulfilment must be verified by the competent authority appointed by the member state, which in the case of the United Kingdom is the Council of the Stock Exchange acting by delegation through the Quotations Committee.[14] When securities have been admitted to listing the issuer must fulfil certain specific obligations in order to maintain the listing, and the competent authority must ensure that this is done.[15] Member states may additionally subject the admission of securities to listing to more stringent conditions than the Admission Directive imposes, and may impose more stringent obligations on their issuers when a listing has been granted.[16]

In elaborating the conditions which must be fulfilled to obtain a listing and the obligations which must be fulfilled to maintain it, the Admission Directive distinguishes between the listing of shares and debt securities, neither of which it defines but which together must constitute the whole range of securities to which the directive applies. Shares are usually either defined expressly by the legislation of the state whose law governs the company in question, or are recognisable implicitly as such because they embody certain rights which can only be conferred on shareholders (such as voting rights, rights to the residual profits of a company or to its residual assets in a liquidation). In the British context disputes as to whether a security is a share or not are unlikely to arise, but under other systems of law there may be a grey area in which certain categories of securities may or may not qualify as shares (eg founders' shares (*parts de fondateur*) under French law and profit participation certificates (*Gewinnschuldverschreibungen*) under German law). Fortunately, in practice such problems will not be troublesome, and it may safely be assumed that if a listed security is a preference, preferred ordinary, ordinary or deferred share or carries the rights normally attached to such shares, it may be treated as a share for the purpose of the Admission Directive and also the Listing Particulars Directive; if it does not, it must be treated as a debt security. Debt securities therefore comprise all securities which qualify under English law as debentures (including debenture stock, loan stock, loan notes and loan participation certificates, whether carrying additional conversion or subscription rights or not) and also other securities which do not qualify as shares.

The Admission Directive requires the conditions set out in its Schedule

14 The Stock Exchange (Listing) Regulations 1984, reg 3(1) and reg 4(1) and (2); Admission Directive, art 4(1) and art 9(1). The functions of the Quotations Committee are in practice mostly fulfilled by the Quotations Department.
15 The Stock Exchange (Listing) Regulations 1984, reg 3(1) and (2); Admission Directive, art 4(2) and art 9(1).
16 Admission Directive, art 5(1) and (2).

A to be fulfilled if shares are to be admitted to listing, and the conditions in its Schedule B if debt securities are to be admitted. The obligations to which an issuer is subject if shares issued by it are listed are set out in Schedule C, and the corresponding obligations if its debt securities are listed are set out in Schedule D.

Conditions for the listing of shares

The Admission Directive requires the following conditions to be fulfilled in respect of a company for its shares to be admitted to listing.

(1) The company must have been formed, incorporated or registered in conformity with the law which governs it, and must operate in conformity with that law.[17] The Stock Exchange rules repeat this requirement and the Quotations Committee verifies that it is fulfilled by requiring the company to submit copies of its memorandum and articles of association with its application for a listing, unless previously supplied; and in the case of a company which does not already have a listing for any of its securities, a copy of its certificate of incorporation or equivalent document (if any) must be delivered to the Quotations Department two business days before the application is considered by the Quotations Committee.[18] The system of law which governs a company is under English Law the law of the country where it was in fact formed, incorporated or registered without regard to the locality from which its affairs are directed, or its principal business activities take place, or its principal shareholders reside. Certain other legal systems (particularly French law) regard a company as governed by the law of the country where its centre of management resides, although such systems raise a rebuttable presumption that that country is the one where the company was formed. It would seem necessary under the Admission Directive for the Stock Exchange to apply the English rule exclusively, and that the company must conform only to the law of its country of formation.

(2) The likely market capitalisation of the shares for which a listing is sought, or if this cannot be calculated, the company's share capital and revenue reserves must together amount to not less than one million European units of account (approximately £550,000), but this condition does not apply if a listing is sought for a further issue of shares of the same class as shares which are already listed, and in any case the Quotations Committee may admit shares to listing despite non-fulfilment of the condition if it is satisfied that there will be an adequate market for the shares concerned.[19] On the other hand, the Stock Exchange may require a higher market capitalisation or a higher amount of capital and reserves for an admission of shares to listing if there is another regulated, recognised and

17 Ibid, Sch A, Part I, para 1.
18 The Stock Exchange: *Admission of Securities to Listing*, Section 1, Chapter 2, para 1, and Section 2, Chapter 1, paras 2.5 and 5.7(*a*).
19 Admission Directive, Sch A, Part I, para 2 and the Stock Exchange (Listing) Regulations 1984, reg 6 and Sch 2, para 3.

regularly operating open market on which the shares could be dealt in and to which they are eligible for admission, and the requirements for admission to that market are no stricter than the conditions for a listing.[19] Such an alternative market is provided in the United Kingdom by the United Securities Market, and in reliance on this the Stock Exchange has fixed the minimum expected market value of shares which shares must have to be listed at £700,000, but the Quotations Committee may in its discretion admit shares with a lower market value if satisfied that there will be an adequate market in them.[20]

(3) The company must have published or filed annual accounts under its national law[1] for its three complete financial years preceding its application for the listing of its shares, but the Stock Exchange may waive this condition if it is satisfied that investors have or will have (eg by means of the listing particulars published in connection with the application) sufficient information to arrive at an informed judgment about the company and the shares.[2] The Stock Exchange will not normally give a listing for shares unless the company has published or filed annual accounts for its preceding 5 complete financial years or such less number of years as it has been in existence, but it may in exceptional circumstances accept a shorter period or waive the condition altogether.[3]

Additionally, on an application for a listing for shares, the Admission Directive requires further conditions to be fulfilled in respect of the shares themselves.

(1) The shares must be or have been created and issued in accordance with the law governing them (ie the law of the country where the company was formed, incorporated or registered).[4] The Stock Exchange requirements expressly provide that the shares must have been issued in conformity with the law of the country where the company is incorporated or established, and also in conformity with the company's memorandum and articles of association or equivalent instrument, and all necessary authorisations for the creation or issue of the shares must have been given.[5] Moreover, if the company already has a listing for any of its securities, the Stock Exchange rules require copies of resolutions increasing the company's capital or authorising the issue of the shares for which a listing is sought to be delivered to the Quotations Department with the application for a listing, and whether the company already has a listing or not, at least two business days before the application is considered by the Quotations Committee copies of all relevant resolutions by the

20 The Stock Exchange: *Admission of Securities to Listing*, Section 1, Chapter 1, para 3.
 1 In the case of a United Kingdom company, this means that the company must have delivered copies of the annual accounts to the Registrar of Companies.
 2 Admission Directive, Sch A, Part I, para 3.
 3 The Stock Exchange: *Admission of Securities to Listing*, Section 1, Chapter 2, para 5.
 4 Admission Directive, Sch A, Part II, para 1.
 5 The Stock Exchange: *Admission of Securities to Listing*, Section 1, Chapter 2, para 2.

board or shareholders' meetings authorising the issue of shares for which a listing is sought must be delivered to the Quotations Department.[6]

(2) The shares must be freely transferable, but shares whose transfer is subject to the approval of the board of directors or a general meeting may be admitted to listing if the use made of this provision does not disturb the market, and partly paid shares may be treated as freely transferable for the present purpose if arrangements have been made to ensure that transfers are not restricted and open dealings at a fair price and on fair terms are facilitated by the public being provided with appropriate information.[7] The Stock Exchange rules repeat this condition, but qualify it by allowing approval requirements to be imposed on the transfer of fully paid shares only in exceptional circumstances, and requiring that the need for approval of transfers of partly paid shares shall not unreasonably restrict dealings in them.[8]

(3) If a public issue of the shares precedes the admission to listing, the listing may take effect only after the period for submitting applications to subscribe for the shares has expired.[9] The Stock Exchange rules omit any reference to this condition because the contingency does not arise in British practice; if a public offering of shares is made, an application for listing is made contemporaneously, or if the public offering is made on the Unlisted Securities Market or the over-the-counter market, a listing is sought for them only after they have been held for a substantial period of time.

(4) A sufficient number of shares must be distributed to the public in one or more member states, but the Stock Exchange may accept instead the distribution of a sufficient number of the shares in a non-member state in which they are listed, and in any case it suffices that a sufficient number of the shares are to be distributed to the public through the Stock Exchange within a short period after the listing is given.[10] A sufficient number of shares is considered as being distributed, or being prospectively distributed, to the public if at least 25 per cent of the issued shares of the class in question are or will be so distributed, or if the total number of shares of the class is large and the public hold or will prospectively hold a smaller percentage of the shares which is sufficient to enable the market to operate properly.[10] The requirement that the public must hold a sufficient number of the shares is applied on an application for a listing of a further issue of shares of a class which are already listed by having regard to the actual or prospective distribution of all the shares of that class after the further issue has been made, and not only to the distribution of shares comprised in the further issue.[10]

The Stock Exchange's own rules require a sufficient number of

6 Ibid, Section 2, Chapter 1, paras 2.6 and 5.9.
7 Admission Directive, Sch A, Part II, para 2.
8 The Stock Exchange: *Admission of Securities to Listing*, Section 1, Chapter 2, para 4.
9 Admission Directive, Sch A, Part II, para 3.
10 Ibid, Sch A, Part II, para 4.

the issued shares of a class to be held by the public not later than the time when the listing takes effect.[11] However, this merely reflects the fact that where shares are the subject of a public offering a listing will not become effective until the result of applications and allotments of the shares has been reported to the Quotations Department,[12] or the fact that alternatively where shares are placed that the availability of the shares to the issuing house or sponsoring brokers and their clients and to jobbers and the public will be known in advance from the marketing arrangements notified to the Quotations Department at least 2 business days before the application for a listing is considered by the Quotations Committee.[13] Again, the Stock Exchange rules treat a minimum distribution of 25 per cent of shares of the class to the public as the normal criterion, and qualify a smaller percentage as being acceptable only exceptionally, even though the total number of shares issued is large.[11] Finally, the Stock Exchange rules define the public as being persons who are not directors or major shareholders of the company and who are not associated with them;[11] this is probably an acceptable working definition, although inexact, and it would not appear to conflict with the Admission Directive, which contains no definition of the public for this purpose.

(5) The application for a listing must extend to all the issued shares of the same class, but the Admission Directive permits member states to except shares which belong to blocks which serve to maintain control of the company, or which are subject to agreements prohibiting their transfer.[14] The United Kingdom has not exercised this option, and so the condition appears in the Stock Exchange rules as an unqualified one, with the addition of the requirement that applications must be made for all further issues of shares of a class already listed within 1 month after the allotment of the further shares.[15]

(6) If the issuer is a company which is governed by the law of another member state of the European Community, it is both necessary and sufficient that the physical form of certificates for its shares should comply with the law and practice of that member state, but if the form of the certificates does not conform to the requirements of the Stock Exchange and United Kingdom law,[16] the Stock Exchange must make the fact known to the public, and if the issuer is governed by the law of a non-member state the physical form of certificates for its shares must afford a sufficient safeguard for the protection of

11 The Stock Exchange: *Admission of Securities to Listing*, Section 1, Chapter 2, para 8.
12 Ibid, Section 2, Chapter 1, para 8.
13 Ibid, Section 2, Chapter 1, para 5.10.
14 Admission Directive, Sch A, Part II, para 5.
15 The Stock Exchange: *Admission of Securities to Listing*, Section 1, Chapter 2, para 9.
16 There are at present no requirements of United Kingdom law as to the physical form (as distinct from the contents) of share certificates. The requirements of the Stock Exchange in this respect are contained in *Admission of Securities to Listing*, Section 9, Chapter 3, para 2 (temporary documents, such as letters of allotment), Chapter 4, para 1.1 (registered share certificates) and Chapter 4, paras 2.2–2.7 (bearer share certificates).

investors.[17] The Stock Exchange rules do not deal with this con-dition, beyond accepting bearer certificates which comply with the standards of a member state and are issued by a company incorpor-ated or established there.[18]

(7) If the shares are issued or to be issued by a company which is governed by the law of a non-member state of the Community and they are not listed or to be listed in that country or in a country in which the majority of the shares are held, they may not be admitted to listing on the Stock Exchange unless the Quotations Committee is satisfied that the absence of a listing in either of those countries is not due to the need to protect investors.[19] This condition is simply repeated in the Stock Exchange rules,[20] and is intended to prevent companies from obtaining a listing for their shares on the Stock Exchange when they have failed, or would most likely fail, to convince the authorities in the country where they would naturally first seek a stock exchange listing that investors may safely invest in their shares.

Conditions for the listing of debt securities issued by companies

The Admission Directive imposes conditions for the listing of debt securities issued by companies under the three headings of conditions relating to the issuer, conditions relating to the securities to be listed and miscellaneous conditions. Certain of these conditions also apply in a modified form to the listing of the debt securities of other issuers than companies, that is, states and their regional and local authorities and public international bodies (but not to member states of the European Com-munity or their regional or local authorities).[1]

The conditions which must be fulfilled if debt securities issued by companies are to be listed are as follows.

(1) The company must have been formed, incorporated or registered in conformity with the law which governs it, and must operate in conformity with that law.[2] The observations made above in connec-tion with the identical condition imposed on the listing of shares[3] are equally applicable to the listing of debt securities.

(2) The debt securities must be or have been created and issued in accordance with the law governing them.[4] This requirement again is identical in form with that applicable on the listing of shares, but the governing law will not necessarily be the law of the country in which the company was formed or incorporated. English law treats debts

17 Admission Directive, Sch A, Part II, para 6.
18 The Stock Exchange: *Admission of Securities to Listing*, Section 9, Chapter 4, Introductory paragraph.
19 Admission Directive, Sch A, Part II, para 7.
20 The Stock Exchange: *Admission of Securities to Listing*, Section 1, Chapter 2, para 10.
 1 Admission Directive, art 1(1) and Stock Exchange (Listing) Regulations 1984, reg 6 and Sch 2, para 1.
 2 Admission Directive, Sch B, Division A, Part I.
 3 See p 29, above.
 4 Admission Directive, Sch B, Division A, Part II, para 1.

and debt securities as governed by the system of law which the parties intend. If no such system of law is designated by the terms of issue of the securities, and they are issued to many investors residing in different countries, the governing law will be that of the place where payment of principal and interest is to be made, or of the country in whose currency the loan is denominated, or, as a last resort, the country in which the borrowing company was formed or incorporated.[5] Curiously, the Stock Exchange rules in this respect are the same as those governing a listing of shares,[6] and consequently the securities to satisfy the Stock Exchange rules must be created and issued in conformity with the system of law governing the company, and also in conformity with the company's memorandum and articles of association (or equivalent documents), and all authorisations necessary for the creation and issue of the securities must have been given.[7] There appears to be a conflict here between the Stock Exchange rules and the Admission Directive, and the latter must prevail as embodying the relevant legal rule.

(3)   The debt securities must be freely transferable, but partly paid securities may be treated as freely transferable for the present purpose if arrangements have been made to ensure that transfers are not restricted, and open dealings at a fair price and on fair terms are facilitated by the public being provided with appropriate information.[8] This condition is the same as the corresponding one applicable on a listing of shares,[9] except that the approval of the board of directors or a general meeting cannot be required for the transfer of debt securities. The Stock Exchange rules permit restrictions to be imposed only on transfers of partly paid debt securities, and they may not be imposed on the transfer of such securities if they would unreasonably restrict dealings.[10] In practice restrictions on the transfer of partly paid debt securities are imposed only if they carry rights to convert the securities into shares or to subscribe for shares.

(4)   If a public issue of debt securities precedes the admission to listing, the listing may take effect only after the period for submitting applications to subscribe for the securities has expired, but this condition does not apply if debt securities are issued 'on tap', that is, if they are issued as and when applied for without a closing date for subscription applications being fixed.[11] The Stock Exchange rules make no reference to this condition because it is inapplicable in practice,[12] and companies which issue listed debt securities, unlike governments, do not issue them on tap.

5 *R v International Trustee for the Protection of Bondholders AG* [1937] AC 500; *Auckland Corpn v Alliance Assurance Co Ltd* [1937] AC 587; *National Bank of Australasia v Scottish Union and National Insurance Co* [1952] AC 493; *Campos v Kentucky and Indiana Terminal Railroad Co* [1962] 2 Lloyds Rep 459.
6 See p 30, above.
7 The Stock Exchange: *Admission of Securities to Listing*, Section 1, Chapter 2, para 2.
8 Admission Directive, Sch B, Division A, Part II, para 2.
9 See p 31 above.
10 The Stock Exchange: *Admission of Securities to Listing*, Section 1, Chapter 2, para 4.
11 Admission Directive, Sch B, Division A, Part II, para 3.
12 See p 101, below.

(5) The application for a listing must extend to all debt securities which rank pari passu,[13] that is, where no securities of the series carry a contractual right to priority in the payment of principal or interest or the benefit of a security or charge which is not equally available to all the other holders of securities of the series, and no securities of the series are subordinated to the others for payment of principal or interest or in respect of any security or charge. The Stock Exchange rules repeat this condition and extend it to all debt securities of the same series, whether ranking pari passu or not;[14] this is a distinction without a difference, however, because in practice debt securities designated as belonging to the same series will not be admitted to listing unless the rights attached to the securities are uniform in all respects. The Stock Exchange rules also require an application to be made for the listing of further debt securities of the same series as securities already listed, and the application must be made within 1 month after the further securities are issued;[14] this will occur when a company exercises the right reserved to it by the terms of issue of the original securities to issue further securities of the same series up to a specified amount or in proportion to the amount of the net assets or profits of the company or the group to which it belongs.

(6) The physical form of certificates for debt securities issued by a company which is governed by the law of another member state of the European Community, or alternatively, by the law of a non-member state, is governed by an identical condition to that applicable on a listing of shares,[15] but if debt securities of such a company are to be issued only in the United Kingdom they must comply with the law and practice of the United Kingdom, and not the law of the member state which governs the company.[16]

(7) The amount of the loan for which the debt securities are issued must not be less than 200,000 European units of account (approximately £110,000) except where a tap issue is made without a maximum amount of the loan being specified, but the Quotations Committee may admit debt securities to listing even though this condition is not satisfied if it considers that there will be an adequate market for the securities.[17] The Stock Exchange rules fix the minimum amount of the loan for which debt securities are issued at £200,000 in exercise of its power to prescribe more stringent pronolition than the Admission Directive, but permits the Quotation Committee to give a listing for smaller issues if adequate marketability is expected.[18]

(8) If the debt securities are convertible into or exchangeable for shares of the issuer or of another company, or if the securities are issued with subscription warrants entitling the holders of the securities to subscribe for or purchase such shares, the debt securities may be

13 Admission Directive, Sch B Division A, Part II, para 4.
14 The Stock Exchange: *Admission of Securities to Listing*, Section 1, Chapter 2, para 9.
15 See p 32, above.
16 Admission Directive, Sch B, Division A, Part II, para 5.
17 Ibid, Sch B, Division A, Part III, para 1 and the Stock Exchange (Listing) Regulations 1984, Sch 2, para 4.
18 The Stock Exchange: *Admission of Securities to Listing*, Section 1, Chapter 2, para 3.

admitted to listing only if the shares in question are already or simultaneously listed on the Stock Exchange or are dealt in on another regulated, recognised and regularly operating open market, such as the Unlisted Securities Market, but this condition does not apply if the Quotations Committee is satisfied that subscribers for the securities will have all the information necessary to form an opinion of the value of the shares in question.[19] The Stock Exchange rules repeat this condition,[20] but in practice the company issuing the debt securities will not be required to procure the immediate issue and listing of the shares into which the debt securities are convertible, or for which they may be exchanged, or which may be acquired by the use of the accompanying warrants, and it will suffice that the company which is to issue the shares at all times maintains sufficient unissued share capital to satisfy the rights of holders of the debt securities and that that unissued capital is appropriately increased if the company issues shares of the relevant class for other purposes.[1]

Conditions for the listing of debt securities issued by public authorities

The conditions which the Admission Directive requires to be satisfied if debt securities issued by a state or a regional or local authority or by a public international body (other than a member state of the European Community or a regional or local authority of a member state) are to be listed are as follows.

(1) The securities must be freely transferable, whether fully or only partly paid.[2] The Stock Exchange rules permit reasonable restrictions to be imposed on the transfer of all partly paid securities,[3] and in respect of partly paid debt securities issued by public authorities they appear to conflict with the Admission Directive. The point is of no practical importance, however, because both fully and partly paid debt securities issued by public authorities are in fact always freely transferable.

(2) If a public issue of the debt securities precedes the admission to listing, the listing may take effect only after the period for submitting applications to subscribe for the securities has expired, but this condition does not apply if there is no closing date for applications and the securities are consequently issued on tap as and when applications are made.[4] This condition will never apply in practice,[5] and so the Stock Exchange rules do not provide for it.

(3) The application for listing must extend to all debt securities issued

19 Admission Directive, Sch B, Division A, Part III, para 2 and the Stock Exchange (Listing) Regulations 1984, Sch B, para 5.
20 The Stock Exchange: *Admission of Securities to Listing*, section 1, Chapter 2, para 18.
1 Ibid, Section 9, Chapter 2, para 2.1(*b*), (*c*) and (*f*).
2 Admission Directive, Sch B, Division B, para 1.
3 The Stock Exchange: *Admission of Securities to Listing*, Section 1, Chapter 2, para 4.
4 Admission Directive, Sch B, Division B, para 2.
5 See p 34, above.

by the public authority which rank pari passu.[6] The same observations apply to this condition as apply to the corresponding condition for the listing of debt securities issued by a company.[7]

(4) The physical form of certificates for debt securities issued by a state or by a regional or local authority, or by an international public authority, is governed by an identical condition to that applicable on the listing of shares.[8]

Additional conditions for a listing imposed by the Stock Exchange rules

The extensions and modifications made by the Stock Exchange rules to the conditions for a listing of shares or debt securities imposed by the Admission Directive have already been noted in connection with those conditions. Additionally, the Stock Exchange rules impose certain independent conditions for a listing which are unconnected with the conditions in the Admission Directive, but are nevertheless valid because imposed in exercise of the Stock Exchange's power reserved by the directive to subject the grant of a listing to more stringent conditions.[9] These additional conditions are as follows.

(1) If a listing is sought for the debt securities of a company, it must have published or filed annual accounts for its five complete financial years preceding the application, or such less number of years as the company has been in existence, in the same way as if the application were for the listing of shares, but in exceptional cases the Quotations Committee may accept an application even though the company has filed or published annual accounts over a shorter period or not at all.[10]

(2) Whether a company seeks a listing of shares or debt securities, a listing will be refused if the relationship between it and a substantial corporate shareholder (ie one which controls 30 per cent or more of the voting power at general meetings, or which controls the appointment of a majority of the company's directors) could result in a conflict between the company's obligations to that shareholder and to its shareholders generally, and the possibility of that conflict makes the company unfit for listing.[11]

(3) If a fee or remuneration is paid by the company to a director, officer, technical adviser or promoter of the company which seeks a listing otherwise than in cash (eg in fully paid shares), a listing of the company's securities may be refused.[12]

(4) If a listing is sought for equity shares (ie any shares other than non-participating preference shares) which have been or are about to be

---

6 Admission Directive, Sch B, Division B, para 3.
7 See p 35, above.
8 Admission Directive, Sch B, para 4. See p 32, above.
9 Ibid, art 5(1).
10 The Stock Exchange: *Admission of Securities to Listing*, Section 1, Chapter 2, para 5. See p 30, above.
11 Ibid, Section 1, Chapter 2, para 6.   12 Ibid, Section 1, Chapter 2, para 7.

issued for cash, they must be offered in the first place rateably to the company's existing equity shareholders, unless a general meeting has otherwise resolved.[13] In the case of companies incorporated in the United Kingdom, this condition merely reflects the preferential subscription rights of equity shareholders conferred by the Companies Acts, which can only be waived by a special resolution passed by a general meeting.[14]

(5) If options or warrants are issued by the company which seeks a listing entitling their holders to subscribe for equity shares for cash, the total number of shares which may be so subscribed must not exceed ten per cent of the company's issued equity share capital (unless the options are given under an employees' share scheme),[15] and if the options or warrants are issued for cash otherwise than rateably among the company's existing equity shareholders, the issue must be approved by a general meeting.[16] This latter requirement again in the case of companies incorporated in the United Kingdom, merely reflects the existing equity shareholders' preferential subscription rights under the Companies Acts, which may only be waived by a special resolution passed by a general meeting.[14]

Wholly apart from these supplemental rules applicable to a company which seeks a listing, all the Stock Exchange rules relating to applications for the listing of debt securities issued by a public body apply to debt securities issued by member states of the European Community and their regional and local authorities, unlike the Stock Exchange (Listing) Regulations 1984, and the Admission Directive. Consequently, the conditions dealt with in the preceding section of this Chapter apply to such public authorities which seek a Stock Exchange listing for their securities insofar as the conditions are incorporated in the Stock Exchange's own rules.

OBLIGATIONS OF ISSUERS OF LISTED SECURITIES

The Admission Directive requires companies and other issuers to fulfil the obligations set out in the Directive once a listing for their securities has been granted, and these obligations differ depending on whether the listed securities are shares or debt securities.[17] These obligations may be supplemented by more stringent obligations imposed by the Stock Exchange's own rules,[18] and the Stock Exchange has in fact imposed supplemental obligations, most of which relate to giving publicity to information about the issuer. The obligations imposed by the Admission Directive do not apply to a member state of the European Community or to a regional or local authority of such a state which has obtained a listing for its debt securities.[19]

13 The Stock Exchange: *Admission of Securities to Listing*, Section 1, Chapter 2, para 15 and Section 5, Chapter 2, para 38a.
14 Companies Act 1980, s 17(1) and (11) and s 18(1); (now Companies Act 1985, s 89(1), s 94(2) and (5) and s 95(1)).
15 The Stock Exchange: *Admission of Securities to Listing*, section 1, Chapter 2, para 16.
16 Ibid, Section 1, Chapter 2, para 17.
17 Admission Directive, art 4(2) and Schedules C and D.
18 Ibid, art 5(2).
19 Ibid, art 1(2), the Stock Exchange (Listing) Regulations 1984, art 6 and Sch 2, para 1.

Obligations of the issuer of listed shares

The continuing obligations which the Admission Directive imposes on a company which has a listing for any class of its shares are as follows.

(1) If the company makes a further issue of shares of a class which is already listed, it must apply for the further shares to be listed within one year after they are issued or before they become freely transferable.[20] The Stock Exchange rules increase this obligation in exercise of the power to impose more stringent rules by requiring the application for a listing of the further issue of shares to be made within one month after they are issued.[1]

(2) The company must ensure that all shareholders who are in the same position are treated equally, and that in each member state where its shares are listed all necessary facilities and information are available to enable shareholders to exercise their rights; in particular shareholders must be informed of the holding of meetings and enabled to exercise their voting rights, the company must publish notices or send circulars to shareholders individually in respect of the declaration and payment of dividends and the issue of new shares, including arrangements for subscription, the allotment of shares, the renunciation of subscription rights and the exercise of conversion rights, and the company must appoint a financial institution as its agent to make dividend and other payments to shareholders unless it makes payment directly itself.[2] The Stock Exchange rules repeat the obligation imposed on a listed company to ensure equality of treatment for shareholders who are in the same position,[3] and this approximately expresses the legal rights of shareholders under the existing companies legislation and case law. Although the courts have never expressly accepted the principle of equality of treatment of shareholders of the same class as a positive rule of law, as the courts of France and Germany have done, they have achieved much the same result by invalidating alterations of a company's memorandum or articles of association which discriminate between shareholders[4] or which are not in the interests of the shareholders as a whole,[5] and schemes for the modification of shareholders' rights will be invalidated if they discriminate between shareholders of the same class[6] or are otherwise unfairly prejudicial to a section of shareholders of the same class;[7] again the acts of directors will be invalidated if they are done otherwise than for the benefit of the

---

20 Admission Directive, Sch C, para 1.
1 The Stock Exchange: *Admission of Securities to Listing*, Section 1, Chapter 2, para 9 and Chapter 5, para 2.
2 Admission Directive, Sch C, para 2.
3 The Stock Exchange: *Admission of Securities to Listing*, Section 5, Chapter 2, para 4(*a*).
4 *Brown v British Abrasive Wheel Co Ltd* [1919] 1 Ch 290; *Dafen Tinplate Co Ltd v Llanelly Steel Co (1907) Ltd* [1920] 2 Ch 124.
5 *Allen v Gold Reefs of West Africa* [1900] 1 Ch 656; *Greenhalgh v Arderne Cinemas Ltd* [1951] Ch 286.
6 *Re Consolidated South Rand Mines Deep Ltd* [1909] 1 Ch 491; *Re Holders Investment Trust Ltd* [1971] 2 All ER 289.
7 Companies Act 1948, s 72(1) and (3) (now Companies Act 1985, s 127(1), (2) and (4)).

shareholders as a whole,[8] and the statutory remedy of minority shareholders to petition the court for relief against the unfairly prejudicial conduct of the company's affairs or against individual acts which are unfairly prejudicial to them is intended in some measure to ensure equality of treatment.[9] The Stock Exchange rules also repeat the obligation imposed on listed companies by the Admission Directive to ensure that all necessary facilities and information are made available to enable shareholders to exercise their rights, in particular their rights to vote in person or by proxy and their rights on the issue of new shares, and the company must appoint a paying agent unless it pays dividends and other payments itself.[10] To a considerable extent the obligation to inform shareholders and to facilitate the exercise of their voting and subscription rights is already embodied in United Kingdom companies legislation.[11]

(3) A listed company must notify any intended alteration of its memorandum or articles of association or equivalent instrument to the Quotations Department not later than the date when it sends notices to its shareholders calling the general meeting to resolve on the alterations.[12] This obligation is not specifically mentioned in the Stock Exchange rules, but it is covered by the general obligation imposed on a listed company to send copies of all notices, circulars and other documents to the Company Announcements Office of the Stock Exchange at the time they are issued.[13]

(4) A listed company must make its annual accounts and directors' annual report available to the public as soon as possible, and if the annual accounts and directors' report do not give a true and fair view of the company's assets and liabilities and its financial position and profit or loss, the necessary additional information must also be given; a company which prepares its own annual accounts and consolidated accounts for the group of which it is the parent company, must make both its own and the consolidated accounts available to the public, unless the Stock Exchange permits it to publish only consolidated accounts.[14] The Stock Exchange rules require the obligation to publish annual accounts to be fulfilled within 6 months after the end of the company's financial year to which the accounts relate, and the rules permit a parent company to publish consolidated accounts alone unless its own accounts contain significant additional information.[15] It would seem that annual

---

8 *Charterbridge Corpn Ltd v Lloyds Bank Ltd* [1970] Ch 62; *Rolled Steel Products (Holdings) Ltd v British Steel Corporation* [1984] BCLC 466.
9 Companies Act 1980, s 75(1) and (3) (now Companies Act 1985, s 459(1) and s 461(1)).
10 The Stock Exchange: *Admission of Security to Listing*, Section 5, Chapter 2, paras 36, 37 and 38(*a*).
11 Companies Act 1948, s 132(1), s 133(2), s 134(*a*), s 136(1), s 140(1) and (2), s 141(1) and (2) and s 207(1); Companies Act 1976, s 1(6); Companies Act 1980, s 17(1), (6) and (7) (now Companies Act 1985, s 89(1), s 90(1) and (6), s 241(1), s 368(1) and (2), s 369(2), s 370(1), s 372(1), s 376(1) and (2), s 378(1) and (2) and s 426(2)).
12 Admission Directive, Sch C, para 3.
13 The Stock Exchange: *Admission of Securities to Listing*, Section 5, Chapter 2, para 35.
14 Admission Directive, Sch C, para 4.
15 The Stock Exchange: *Admission of Securities to Listing*, Section 5, Chapter 2, para 20.

accounts and the directors' annual report are not made available to the public in fulfilment of the obligation imposed by the Admission Directive if copies of them are merely sent to shareholders of the company and to the Registrar of Companies as required by companies legislation;[16] it would appear necessary that the accounts should additionally be published in the press or that copies of them be made available to the public generally on request.

(5) A listed company must inform the public as soon as possible of major new developments in its activities which are not already known by the public and which by reason of their effect on the assets, liabilities, financial position or general course of business of the company may result in substantial movements in the price of its shares; the company must also inform the public without delay of changes in the rights attaching to different classes of its shares and of changes in its major shareholders and their holdings as soon as the information comes to its notice.[17] The first two parts of this obligation are incorporated in the Stock Exchange rules,[18] and the obligation to publish changes in major shareholdings is covered by a requirement that all notifications received by companies incorporated in the United Kingdom of acquisitions, disposals and changes in interests held in five per cent or more of their shares carrying unrestricted voting rights[19] should be published.[20] The Stock Exchange rules merely require the company to notify the Company Announcements Office of the Stock Exchange of the information which the Admission Directive requires it to publish, and publication is then effected by that office.[1] In accordance with the Directive the Quotations Committee may dispense with the publication of information about major new developments in the company's activities if publication would be likely to prejudice the legitimate interests of the company[2] (eg by revealing its market tactics or success in obtaining orders to its competitors).

(6) A listed company must ensure that all information which it makes available about itself, its affairs and securities in a stock exchange in a member state of the European Community where its shares are listed, or the equivalent of such information is made equally available on all other stock exchanges in member states of the European Community where its shares are listed, and if its shares are listed on a stock exchange in a non-member state, it must ensure that any such information which it makes available on that stock exchange or equivalent information is made equally available on all

16 Companies Act 1948, s 158(1); Companies Act 1976, s 1(7) (now Companies Act 1985, s 240(1) and s 241(3)).
17 Admission Directive, Sch C, para 5.
18 The Stock Exchange: *Admission of Securities to Listing*, Section 5, Chapter 2, paras 5(a) and 12.
19 The notifications will be given to the company by the interested persons under the Companies Act 1981, s 63(1)–(3) (now Companies Act 1985, ss 198 to 200 and s 201(1).
20 The Stock Exchange: *Admission of Securities to Listing*, Section 5, Chapter 2, para 16(a).
 1 Ibid, Section 5, Chapter 2, paras 5, 12 and 16(a).
 2 Admission Directive, Sch C, para 5(a); The Stock Exchange: *Admission of Securities to Listing*, Section 5, Chapter 2, para 5.1.

stock exchanges in member states where its shares are listed.[3] The Stock Exchange rules impose this obligation to publish equivalent information in respect of information published on any stock exchange where the company's shares or other securities are listed, and requires equivalent information to be published on all such stock exchanges, whether within or outside the European Community.[4]

Obligations of companies issuing debt securities

The continuing obligations which the Admission Directive imposes on a company which has a listing for debentures or other debt securities issued by it are as follows.

(1) The company must ensure that all holders of debt securities which rank pari passu are given equal treatment in respect of the rights attached to the securities they hold, but this does not prevent the company from repaying certain debt securities before others if this is permitted by the law governing the securities; the company must also ensure that in each member state in which the debt securities are listed all necessary facilities and information are available to enable holders of the securities to exercise their rights, and in particular the company must publish notices or send circulars to holders of the securities individually in respect of meetings of holders, the payment of interest, the exercise of conversion, exchange and subscription rights and the repayment of the principal of the securities, and must appoint a financial institution as its agent to make interest and other payments to holders of the securities unless it makes payment directly itself.[5]

The Stock Exchange rules repeat the obligation to ensure equality of treatment for all holders of a class of debt securities which rank pari passu, but empowers the Quotations Committee to permit only overseas companies to repay certain securities of a series in advance of the others.[6] Under certain systems of law, particularly French law, the holders of debt securities of the same class or series automatically have equal rights because the legal definition of a class or series of debt securities involves each security having the same nominal value and carrying the same rights. This is not so under English law, where the rights of the security holders to equality of security and equality in other respects depend on the contractual terms of the securities themselves or the instrument which governs them, such as the trust instrument executed by the borrowing company before the securities are issued. A contractual provision that the securities of the series shall rank equally or pari passu in point of charge and that no security of the series shall have any priority over any other, is effective to ensure equality of distributions out of the proceeds of sale of property which is mortgaged or

3 Admission Directive, Sch C, para 6.
4 The Stock Exchange: *Admission of Securities to Listing*, Section 5, Chapter 2, para 3.
5 Admission Directive, Sch D, Division A, para 1.
6 The Stock Exchange: *Admission of Securities to Listing*, Section 5, Chapter 2, para 4(*b*).

charged to secure the series irrespective of the chronological order in which the securities are issued,[7] and this is so with regard to all securities of the series which are issued before steps are taken to realise the mortgage or charge.[8] Likewise, under such a pari passu clause a security holder who is indebted to the company must pay his debt in full into the company's assets (including debts owed to it) which are charged with the amount owing to all the security holders of the same series, and he cannot set the debt off against the amount owing to himself under the securities of the series he holds and claim a rateable payment of the net amount out of the company's assets.[9] On the other hand, the courts have held that a security holder can retain a payment made to him by the company on account of the principal and interest in respect of the securities held by him, or the amount received by him realising a collateral security given by the company, and he need not account to his fellow security holders of the same series and share the payment or amount realised with them unless the payment was made or the realisation was effected after steps had been taken to realise the assets of the company which are charged with the amount owing to all the security holders of the same series.[10]

It would seem that the obligation of a listed company under the Admission Directive and the Stock Exchange rules to ensure equality of treatment between the holders of securities of the same series goes no further than an obligation to ensure, so far as the company can, that the rights accorded to them all by the law or by a pari passu clause are satisfied, and in particular the company is free, unless the law governing the securities forbids it, to redeem some of the securities in advance of others[11] or to purchase securities of the series on the market from holders who wish to sell them. However, a listed company must at least observe equality of treatment if it purchases certain securities of the series by offering to purchase securities on the market from all holders, or by giving all holders an opportunity to tender a proportionate number of their securities, and if purchases are effected on the market, the price which the company pays must not exceed 105 per cent of the average of the middle market price for the securities over the preceding ten days.[12]

The obligation of listed companies to give holders of debt securities all necessary facilities and information for the exercise of their rights is repeated by the Stock Exchange rules,[13] which also require drawings of securities for redemption and any redemptions on the exercise of an option by the company to be notified to the

---

7 *Gartside v Silkstone and Dodworth Coal and Iron Co* (1882) 21 Ch D 762.
8 *Re Hubbard & Co Ltd* (1898) 69 LJ Ch 54.
9 *Re Rhodesia Goldfields Ltd* [1910] 1 Ch 239.
10 *Landowners West of England and South Wales Land Drainage and Inclosure Co v Ashford* (1880) 16 Ch D 411; *Re Midland Express Ltd* [1914] 1 Ch 41.
11 This would not seem permissible if the terms of issue of the securities provide for redemption of all the securities together on the same date, or by payment of equal instalments of the principal owing on all of them at intervals, or if the securities are redeemable by drawings at intervals.
12 The Stock Exchange: *Admission of Securities to Listing*, Section 9, Chapter 2, para 1.1.
13 Ibid, Section 5, Chapter 2, para 36.

Quotations Committee, so that the matter may be published by the Company Announcements Office of the Stock Exchange. Moreover, the trust deed or other instrument securing a series of debt securities issued by a company must provide for the calling of meetings of the holders of the securities by not less than 21 days' notice;[14] must authorise the holders of one-tenth in nominal value of the securities to requisition the calling of such a meeting; must make the quorum for such a meeting called to pass an extraordinary resolution (other than an adjourned meeting) the holders of a majority in nominal value of the securities of the series outstanding; must make the majority for passing such a resolution not less than three-quarters of the votes cast; must confer voting rights at such a meeting proportionate to the nominal value of the securities held; must enable security holders to appoint any persons as their proxies; and must provide for the issue of two-way proxy forms so that each security holder may authorise his proxy to vote either for or against each resolution proposed at such a meeting.[15]

(2)   A listed company must notify any intended alteration of its memorandum or articles of association or equivalent document, or of the instrument setting out the rights of holders of its debt securities, to the Quotations Committee for publication by the Company Announcements Office not later than the date when it sends notices to its shareholders calling the general meeting which will resolve on the alteration of the memorandum or articles, or the meeting of security holders which will resolve on or consent to the alteration of the instrument setting out their rights.[16] This obligation is covered in the Stock Exchange rules by the general obligation imposed on a listed company to send copies of all notices, circulars and other documents to the Company Announcements Office of the Stock Exchange at the time they are issued.[17]

(3)   The same obligation is imposed on companies whose debt securities are listed as on companies whose shares are listed to make their annual accounts and annual directors' report available to the public and as to the form and content of such annual accounts,[18] and the same observations therefore apply as were made above in respect of that obligation.[19]

(4)   A similar obligation is imposed on companies whose debt securities are listed to inform the public of major new developments in its activities as is imposed on a company whose shares are listed,[20] but the additional specific information which must also be communicated to the public relates not to the company's share capital, but to changes in the rights attaching to different classes of its debt

---

14 The Stock Exchange: *Admission of Securities to Listing*, Section 5, Chapter 2, para 11.
15 Ibid, Section 5, Chapter 2, para 37 and Section 9, Chapter 2, para 3.
16 Admission Directive, Sch D, Division A, para 2.
17 The Stock Exchange: *Admission of Securities to Listing*, Section 5, Chapter 2, para 35.
18 Admission Directive, Sch D, Division A, para 3.
19 See p 40, above.
20 See p 40, above.

securities, to further issues of debt securities by the company and guarantees and mortgages given to secure them, and of changes in the rights attached to classes of shares into which debt securities of the company are convertible, or for which they are exchangeable, or which may be subscribed for or purchased by holders of debt securities under warrants issued with them.[1] This obligation is incorporated in the Stock Exchange rules,[2] and the same observations apply to the manner of informing the public of the information as were made above about informing the public of matters relating to listed shares.[3]

(5) The same obligation is imposed on a company to ensure that equivalent information which it makes available on one of the stock exchanges in a member state of the European Community where the debt securities are listed is also made available on all other stock exchanges in other member states where the securities are listed, and that information which it makes available on a stock exchange in a non-member state where the securities are listed is also made available on all such stock exchanges in the member states, as is imposed on a company whose shares are so listed.[4] The Stock Exchange rules require an equivalence of information at all the stock exchanges where any of the company's securities is listed.[5]

Obligations of public bodies issuing debt securities

Only two obligations are imposed by the Admission Directive on a state or a regional or local authority or a public international body which has issued listed debt securities, namely, obligations equivalent to the first and fifth obligations imposed on companies which have issued listed debt securities.[6] These obligations are repeated in the Stock Exchange[7] rules, which apply to all states and regional and local authorities, and do not exclude member states of the European Community and their regional and local authorities, as does the Admission Directive.

Additional obligations imposed by the Stock Exchange rules

In addition to the obligations imposed by the Admission Directive, a listed company or other issuer must comply with the supplemental obligations imposed by the Stock Exchange's rules which go further than giving effect to the Directive. These obligations used formerly to be covered by the Listing Agreement which the company or other issuer entered into with the Stock Exchange at the time a listing for any of its securities was granted.[8]

---

1 Admission Directive, Sch D, Division A, para 4.
2 The Stock Exchange: *Admission of Securities to Listing*, Section 5, Chapter 2, paras 5(a), 9 and 12.
3 See p 41, above.
4 Admission Directive, Sch D, Division A, para 5. See p 41, above.
5 The Stock Exchange: *Admission of Securities to Listing*, Section 5, Chapter 2, para 3.
6 Admission Directive, Sch D, Division B, paras 1 and 2. See pp 42 and 45, above.
7 The Stock Exchange: *Admission of Securities to Listing*, section 5, Chapter 3, paras 2 and 3.
8 The Stock Exchange: *Admission of Securities to Listing* (1979 edn), Chapter 2 and Appendix, Sch VIII.

This agreement has been dispensed with in the latest edition of the Stock Exchange's manual, the *Admission of Securities to Listing*,[9] but the same conditions in a re-drafted form are imposed on issuers, with the sanction that if they are broken or disregarded, the listing may be suspended or terminated.

The most important additional obligations imposed by the Stock Exchange rules relate to the publication and circulation to holders of securities of information relating to events and transactions which substantially affect a listed company or the value of its securities. These are dealt with in Chapter 4 of this book in connection with listed companies' obligations in respect of continuing publicity and information. It suffices to note here the most important addition made by the Stock Exchange rules to the publicity requirements of the Admission Directive, namely the general obligation imposed on listed companies to notify to the Company Announcements Office of the Stock Exchange for publication all information necessary to enable holders of the company's listed securities and the public to appraise the position of the company and to avoid the establishment of a false market in the listed securities,[10] and the more specific obligation imposed on a company whose debt securities are listed to notify the Company Announcements Office of new developments in the company's activities which are not known to the public and which may significantly affect the price of its shares, or in the case of debt securities, its ability to meet its commitments,[11] and the obligations imposed on all listed companies to notify details of all substantial acquisitions and disposals of assets and holdings in other companies,[12] and of changes in directors' holdings of shares or debentures of the company or of other companies in the same group.[13] Besides the obligation to notify, circulate or publish information the Stock Exchange rules also require listed companies to conform to certain standards in respect of other matters, in particular, to adopt rules governing dealings by its directors in listed securities of the company and imposing restrictions which are no less exacting than those set out in the Stock Exchange's Model Code for Securities Transactions by Directors.[14]

ADMISSION PROCEDURE

The procedure for the admission of securities to listing is not regulated by the Stock Exchange (Listing) Regulations 1984, or by the directives to which the Regulations give effect, except in respect of the approval and publication of listing particulars and the date on which a listing takes effect. The remaining procedural steps are therefore regulated by the Stock Exchange's own rules, which apply to all issuers, including member and non-member states of the European Community and their regional and local authorities.

9 The Stock Exchange: *Admission of Securities to Listing*, Section 5, Chapter 1.
10 Ibid, Section 5, Chapter 2, para 1.
11 Ibid, Section 5, Chapter 2, para 5.
12 Ibid, Section 5, Chapter 2, para 14.
13 Ibid, Section 5, Chapter 2, para 17(*b*).
14 Ibid, Section 5, Chapter 2, para 45.

The application for the admission of securities to listing

An application for a listing of securities must be submitted to the Quotations Department of the Stock Exchange through a firm of sponsoring brokers who are members of the Exchange and through whom all negotiations concerning the application are channelled.[15] The sponsoring brokers must satisfy themselves that the applicant company is suitable for listing, that it can be expected to publish all necessary information for the market to be properly informed about the company and its securities, that its directors understand the obligations they and the company will undertake if a listing is granted and that they can be expected to honour those obligations.[16]

At least 14 days before the publication of the listing particulars in respect of securities of a company the sponsoring broker must lodge the drafts of certain documents at the Quotations Department for approval together with certain other documents.[17] The documents which must be lodged include four copies of the draft listing particulars, two copies of the company's memorandum and articles of association or equivalent instrument, and if the securities are debentures or other debt securities, two copies of the draft trust deed or other document setting out the terms of the loan and security for it,[17] together with a declaration by each director of the issuing company about all directorships held by him and his personal antecedents.[18] When the Quotations Department has approved the draft listing particulars and any trust deed or document setting out the terms of the loan and the security for it and has approved the other documents submitted, the listing particulars are published in the manner described below before the Quotations Committee sits to consider the application for listing.

At least two business days before the application for listing is considered by the Quotations Committee, the sponsoring broker must lodge further documents at the Quotations Department, including an application for admission in a standard form signed by a duly authorised officer of the company; these further documents comprise four copies of the listing particulars in their final form, one of which must be dated and signed by each director and proposed director of the company, unless the securities to which the application relates are of a class which is already listed; a copy of the trust deed or other document setting out the terms of the loan secured by debt securities to which the application relates; a certified copy of the resolution of the board of directors of the company authorising the issue of the securities to which the application relates, the making of the application for listing and the publication of the listing particulars; a copy of any resolution of a general meeting of the company relating to the issue of the securities (eg a resolution authorising the issue of shares or convertible debentures[19] or a resolution waiving shareholders' preferential subscription rights when ordinary shares or debentures convertible into ordinary shares

15 Ibid, Section 1, Chapter 1, paras 3 and 4.
16 Ibid, Section 1, Chapter 1, para 5.
17 Ibid, Section 2, Chapter 1, para 2.
18 Ibid, Section 2, Chapter 1, para 3 and Sch 4.
19 Companies Act 1980, s 14(1) and (10), (now Companies Act 1985 s 80(1) and (2)).

are issued for cash);[20] a certified copy of every letter, report, valuation, contract, resolution or other document referred to in the listing particulars; and a certified copy of any agreement under which the company has acquired or will acquire any assets, business undertaking or shares in consideration of the issue of the securities to which the listing application relates.[1]

If an application is made for listing of debt securities issued by a public body, including a member state of the European Community or a regional or local authority of such a state, the procedure is simplified. Public bodies for this purpose are taken to include: (a) companies which are governed by the law of a member state of the European Community and benefit from a state monopoly, and which are either regulated by special legislation or have their borrowings unconditionally and irrevocably guaranteed by a member state or one of its constituent regions if the member state is federal in form (eg a *Land* of the German Federal Republic); and (b) incorporated bodies (other than companies) which are governed by the law of a member state and were established under special legislation to raise funds by the issue of debt securities to finance production, and whose debt securities are treated by the law of the member state as equivalent to state securities or as guaranteed by the state (eg the Italian *Istituto per la Ricostruzione Industriale*).[2] A public body which applies for a listing must at least 14 days before the application is considered by the Quotations Committee, submit to the Quotations Department through its sponsoring broker four copies of a draft of the listing particulars or offer document it intends to employ, and (except in the case of HM Government) it must at least two business days before the application is considered by the Committee submit a formal application for a listing signed by a duly authorised official of the issuer together with four copies of the listing particulars or equivalent offer document in their final form, one copy of which must be signed by a duly authorised officer of the issuer.[3]

On the consideration by the Quotations Committee of the application for a listing of securities which are about to be issued, the listing particulars are taken as approved if the published version in no way departs from the draft listing particulars approved by the Quotations Department, and the Committee decides whether or not to grant the listing sought. A decision to grant a listing may be, and often is, conditional on certain steps being taken, or a certain level of subscriptions by the public being achieved so as to ensure that the securities are sufficiently widely held. A conditional grant of a listing becomes effective when the steps required by the Committee are fulfilled to the satisfaction of the Quotations Department, or when the results of allotments are reported to the Quotations Department and are found to accord with the marketing arrangements required by the Committee. If the securities for which a listing is sought have already been issued and an introduction on the Stock Exchange is sought for them, the

20 Companies Act 1980 s 18(1); (now Companies Act 1985, s 95(1)); The Stock Exchange: *Admission of Securities to Listing*, Section 5, Chapter 2, para 38.
 1 The Stock Exchange: *Admission of Securities to Listing*, Section 2, Chapter 1, para 5.
 2 Ibid, Section 2, Chapter 2, para 1. The definition of a public body is taken from the Listing Particulars Directive, art 6(3)(*b*) and (*c*), which enables member states to exempt certain bodies from the obligation to publish listing particulars.
 3 The Stock Exchange: *Admission of Securities to Listing*, Section 2, Chapter 2, para 6.

Quotations Committee usually makes an unconditional decision to grant or refuse a listing when it considers the application, because there are no further steps to be taken in order to market the securities and the Quotations Department will already have satisfied itself that the existing distribution of the securities is or will be sufficiently wide.

The publication of listing particulars and the effective date of listing

Listing particulars in respect of securities issued by a company may not be published until they have been approved by the Quotations Department (acting on behalf of the Quotations Committee) and approval can be given only if they comply with the Listing Particulars Directive, which is discussed on detail in Chapter 4.[4] The Listing Particulars Directive requires listing particulars to be published when approved by the national competent authority either by insertion in full in one or more newspapers circulating throughout the member states in which a listing is sought (ie a national daily newspaper), or in the form of a brochure made available to the public free of charge at the office of the stock exchange or exchanges on which a listing is sought, at the registered office of the issuing company and at the office of the financial institutions engaged by it as its paying agents in the member state where a listing is sought.[5] The same provisions apply to listing particulars in respect of securities of an issuer other than a company, but not to listing particulars or an offering document in respect of securities issued by a state or a regional or local authority of a state.[6]

The Stock Exchange rules require listing particulars in respect of securities of a company offered to the public generally to be published in at least two daily newspapers, but if the securities are being placed with the permission of the Quotations Committee instead of offered for subscription or purchase by the public generally, or if a placing would have been permissible because of the small size of the issue, the listing particulars may be published in one national daily newspaper and only a formal notice of the issue need be published in a second national daily newspaper.[7] If a company's securities are introduced on the Stock Exchange, only a formal notice need be published in two national daily newspapers if the company does not already have a Stock Exchange listing for any of its securities, or in one national daily newspaper if it does.[8] If a listed company makes a rights offer of securities, it must publish a formal notice in one national newspaper, but if the securities are of a class for which it already has a listing, no notice need be published in the press.[8] The same applies when a listed company issues securities in any other way than by a public offer, a placing or a rights offer.[8] If a formal notice is published, it must contain certain minimal information about the company and the securities, including a statement of the addresses where copies of the full listing particulars may be obtained by the public free of charge during a period of at least 14 days after the notice is published, and those addresses must include the

4 Listing Particulars Directive, art 18(2) and (3).
5 Ibid, art 20(1).
6 Ibid, art 1(2).
7 The Stock Exchange: *Admission of Securities to Listing*, Section 2, Chapter 3, paras 1 and 2.
8 Ibid, Section 2, Chapter 3, para 3.

registered office of the issuer, the offices of any paying agent engaged by the issuer in the United Kingdom and the Company Announcements Office of the Stock Exchange.[9] If formal notices only are published (ie where the securities are introduced on the Stock Exchange), this satisfies the requirement of the Admission Directive that the listing particulars shall be made available to the public in the form of brochures.[5]

Secondary advertisements published in conjunction with full listing particulars relating to securities issued by a company (ie abridged particulars, mini-prospectuses summarising the listing particulars and formal notices of the issue of securities) must be submitted to the Quotations Committee before publication, and it may require them to be modified or withdrawn if it considers them misleading or inadequate.[10] In practice drafts of such secondary advertisements are submitted to the Quotations Department at the same time as the draft listing particulars some 14 days before the Quotations Committee considers the application for a listing. All such secondary advertisements must contain the minimal information mentioned in the preceding paragraph in connection with formal notices, and in particular must set out the addresses where the public may obtain copies of the full listing particulars in the form of a brochure.[5]

The Stock Exchange rules governing the publication of listing particulars or offering documents in respect of the debt securities of a public body (including any member or non-member state of the European Community or a regional or local authority of such a state, a company governed by the law of a member state of the European Community which has a state monopoly and a corporation established under the law of a member state to raise finance for production where the company or corporation's borrowings are state guaranteed) require the listing particulars or offering document to be published in full in a national daily newspaper, or alternatively, formal notices to be published in two national daily newspapers.[11] A formal notice must give minimal information about the issuer and the securities for which a listing is sought, but it must also set out the addresses from which full copies of the listing particulars may be obtained by the public free of charge, and those addresses must include the registered or principal office of the issuer (if it is a corporation), the offices of the issuer's paying agents in the United Kingdom and the Company Announcements Office of the Stock Exchange.[12]

Whether listing particulars are published in full in newspapers or in the form of a brochure in the manner indicated above, the Stock Exchange must publish in the *Stock Exchange Weekly Intelligence* a copy of the particulars in full or at least a notice stating where they have been published and where copies of any brochure may be obtained.[13] This does not apply in the case of listing particulars for debt securities issued by a state or a regional or local authority.[14]

In certain circumstances the Stock Exchange rules may permit the complete or partial exemption of applicants for a listing of securities from

9 The Stock Exchange: *Admission of Securities to Listing*, Section 2, Chapter 3, para 6.
10 Listing Particulars Directive, art 22.
11 The Stock Exchange: *Admission of Securities to Listing*, Section 2, Chapter 4, para 3.
12 Ibid, Section 2, Chapter 4, para 5.
13 Listing Particulars Directive, art 20(2); The Stock Exchange (Listing) Regulations 1984, reg 6 and Sch 2, para 8.

the obligation to publish listing particulars. These exemptions are closely connected with the question of the obligatory contents of listing particulars, and are dealt with in Chapter 4 under the heading of modifications of the normal requirements in respect of listing particulars.

Listing particulars in respect of a company's securities must be published within a reasonable period before the listing granted in respect of them becomes effective, and in practice they are published before the Quotations Committee grants a listing, but the Committee may in exceptional circumstances permit the postponement of publication until after the listing becomes effective if the securities are of a class already listed and they are issued for a consideration other than cash.[15] If the admission of securities to listing is preceded by dealings on the Stock Exchange in preferential rights to subscribe for them (ie in letters of right or provisional letters of allotment in connection with rights issues), the listing particulars must be published within a reasonable period before such dealings commence, but exceptionally if the securities are of a class already issued and they are issued for a consideration other than cash, the Stock Exchange may permit the postponement of publication until after dealings in preferential rights commence.[15] These rules apply also to listing particulars in respect of securities of an issuer other than a company, but not to listing particulars or an offering document in respect of securities issued by a state or a regional or local authority of a state.[14] The Stock Exchange rules do not prescribe the minimum or maximum periods which must elapse between the publication of listing particulars and the date when the listing becomes effective and dealings in the securities or rights to subscribe for them may begin, and the date when the listing particulars are published and the later date when dealings commence are in practice fixed by arrangement with the Quotations Department. Strictly speaking the omission of provisions governing this matter from the Stock Exchange (Listing) Regulations and the Stock Exchange rules involves a failure by the United Kingdom to comply completely with the Listing Particulars Directive. In the case of listing particulars in respect of shares or debentures of a company offered for subscription by the public generally, there will at least be a minimum interval of three days between the publication of the listing particulars and allotment of the securities imposed by the Companies Acts,[16] unless the relevant provision of those Acts is excluded by the Stock Exchange (Listing) Regulations 1984.[17]

Procedure after a listing has become effective

As soon as possible after a listing has been granted for securities issued by a company, certain documents must be delivered to the Quotations Department by the applicant for a listing through the sponsoring brokers.[18] These documents are:

(a) if the securities were offered to the public generally or by an open

---

14 Listing Particulars Directive, art 1(2).
15 Ibid, art 21(1) and (2).
16 Companies Act 1948, s 50(1) (now Companies Act 1985, s 82(1)).
17 The Stock Exchange (Listing) Regulations 1984, reg 7(1)(*b*) (see p 20, above).
18 The Stock Exchange: *Admission of Securities to Listing*, Section 2, Chapter 1, para 7.

offer to the company's shareholders, a copy of the national daily newspaper which contains an announcement of the basis of allotment; the company is obliged to publish this information in the press before dealings in the securities begin;[19]

(b) if the securities were offered for subscription or sale by tender, a copy of a national daily newspaper containing an announcement of the striking price;

(c) if the securities were placed with jobbers or with institutional investors, or with the clients of placing brokers, a list of the names and addresses of the persons with whom they were placed;

(d) if the securities were offered under a takeover or other bid in exchange for the shares or debentures of another company with a cash alternative, the number of securities issued;

(e) if the securities were offered to a company's shareholders by way of rights, a statement of the issue price and the basis of allotments, the sale price realised for securities not taken up under the offer and the number of shares allotted in response to excess applications by shareholders and the basis of such allotments;

(f) if the shares or debentures were issued on a capitalisation of reserves or under a rights offer, a statement of the amount of fractional entitlements and the way in which the shares or debentures representing them were disposed of; and

(g) a statement of the opening price of the securities on the commencement of dealings.

---

19 The Stock Exchange: *Admission of Securities to Listing*, Section 5, Chapter 2, para 13.

CHAPTER 3

Listing Particulars

Listing particulars are the document containing information about an issuer and the securities it has issued, or is about to issue, which is used as the basis for admitting the securities to listing on the Stock Exchange, and when published is relied on by investors in deciding whether to invest in the securities for which a listing is sought or has been given. If the securities to which the listing particulars relate are newly created by the issuer, the listing particulars fulfil the function of a prospectus in inducing investors to subscribe for the securities and so provide fresh share or loan capital for the issuer. On the other hand, if the securities already exist or have been allotted to a person who wishes to dispose of them immediately (such as a vendor of a business to a company for shares which he immediately sells, or shareholders of an offeree company, the target of a takeover bid under which new shares of the offeror company are issued in exchange for shares of the target and are immediately disposed of by the allottees or by underwriters), the introduction of the securities on the Stock Exchange does not result in fresh capital being provided for the issuer, and the listing particulars are then published simply to induce investors to buy the securities from their existing holders or other investors. Whether the operation is one to raise money for the issuer of the securities or alternatively, one to market securities which have already been issued or agreed to be issued, the listing particulars must necessarily contain the same information so that investors may be equipped to make sound and well informed decisions whether to invest in the securities. The contents of listing particulars do differ according to the kind of securities to which they relate (shares, debt securities, or debt securities convertible into or carrying the right to subscribe for shares) and the manner in which they are offered for subscription or purchase (public offering, rights offer, capitalisation issue or takeover offer), but they do not vary according to the use to which the price paid by investors who take them is put.

Because listing particulars are vehicles for the information of investors at the time securities are marketed on the Stock Exchange and their purpose is to ensure that investors are fully and accurately informed about the issuer and the securities, the two key rules in the Listing Particulars Directive are not surprisingly that no securities shall be admitted to listing on the Stock Exchange unless listing particulars approved by the Quotations Committee of the Stock Exchange have been published,[1] and that listing particulars must 'contain the information which according to the particular nature of the issuer and of the securities for the admission of which application is being made, is necessary to enable investors and their investment advisers to make an informed assessment of the assets and liabilities, financial

---

1 Listing Particulars Directive, art 3.

position, profits and losses and prospects of the issuer and of the rights attaching to such securities'.[2]

This second general and overriding requirement is derived from the German Stock Exchange Law,[3] and imposes an obligation on the issuer and the Quotations Committee to ensure that approved listing particulars contain all the information which investors need to make informed investment decisions, and that that information is complete and accurate. The Listing Particulars Directive is largely taken up with setting out the heads and details of information which all listing particulars relating to the same kind of securities (shares, debt securities issued by companies and debt securities issued by public bodies) must contain, but these heads and details are necessarily general in terms and are designed to govern the standard or average issuer or rather, the features of issues of securities which are common to most issuers. The peculiarities and special features of each issuer and its securities cannot be wholly subsumed under such generally applicable rules, and so in addition to the detailed information which listing particulars must give about the features of the issuer and the securities which would figure in a prospectus issued by any company whatsoever, supplemental information must be given about the peculiarities and special features of the company and the securities offered. Moreover, the obligation to give all the information which investors require is overriding to the extent that, although information of a general character common to all companies which raise capital from the public must be given, the headings under which that information is classified in the Listing Particulars Directive need not be slavishly followed, and where the headings are inappropriate because of the issuer's area of activity (business activities or other functions) or its legal form, equivalent information may be given under a different arrangement.[4] Moreover, the information relevant to the particular issuer must be given 'in as easily analysable and comprehensible a form as possible',[5] so that varying emphasis should be given to the items of information included, in order to indicate their relative importance. The result of fulfilling the requirements of the Listing Particulars Directive should be to give a true and fair view of the issuer's financial position and prospects and of the securities which are to be dealt in on the Stock Exchange, in the same way as the annual accounts of a company should give a true and fair view of the state of its affairs and its profit or loss for the year.[6]

The Listing Particulars Directive applies only to securities issued by companies and other corporate and unincorporated issuers, but not to securities issued by collective investment undertakings of the open-ended kind[7] and states and their regional and local authorities.[8] No distinction is drawn between securities issued by member and non-member states and

---

2 Listing Particulars Directive, art 4(1).
3 *Börsengesetz* § 38(2).
4 Listing Particulars Directive, art 5(3).
5 Ibid, art 5(1).
6 Companies Act 1948, s 149(2) (as re-enacted by Companies Act 1981, s 1(1)) (now Companies Act 1985, s 228(2)).
7 See p 27, above, for the definition of collective investment undertakings of the open-ended kind; this definition is repeated in the Listing Particulars Directive, art 2(*a*).
8 Listing Particulars Directive, art 1(1) and (2).

their respective regional and local authorities, as is done in the Admission Directive; all such public authorities are excluded from the Listing Particulars Directive. On the other hand, state controlled corporations and companies enjoying the benefit of state monopolies, or whose borrowing is state guaranteed, fall within the directive. The Stock Exchange rules which apply and supplement the requirements of the Listing Particulars Directive likewise apply only to listing particulars in respect of securities of companies and other corporate and unincorporated issuers, except states and their regional and local authorities.[9] Nevertheless, the Stock Exchange has separate rules governing the contents of offering documents in respect of securities issued by states and their regional and local authorities, and these are dealt with in this Chapter after the listing particulars of companies. The Stock Exchange rules applicable to public authorities' offering documents do not form part of the law because they are outside the scope of the Listing Particulars Directive. Nor, it would appear, do the Stock Exchange rules which impose requirements supplemental to those in the Listing Particulars Directive. The supplemental requirements are imposed under the provisions of the Admission Directive which permits more stringent or additional conditions to be imposed on the grant of a listing than the directive imposes,[10] and while such supplemental requirements are thereby made lawful, they are not given the status of legislation and do not form part of the law.

The detailed requirements of the Listing Particulars Directive as to the contents of listing particulars are set out in Schedule A to the Directive when the listing particulars relate to shares, and in Schedule B when they relate to debt securities.[11] There is a third schedule to the Directive, Schedule C, which governs the contents of listing particulars relating to certificates for shares, such as the *certificaten* issued by the administrative offices of banks in respect of shares in Dutch companies and depositary receipts and certificates for shares issued by banks and stockbrokers in continental Europe and the United States, but as securities in that form cannot be listed on the Stock Exchange, Schedule C is inoperative in the United Kingdom.

The contents of listing particulars specified in Schedules A and B set a standard of disclosure which is appropriate for a company which seeks a first listing for its shares or non-convertible debentures on offering them to the public for subscription in cash. Listing particulars are, of course, published in connection with many other operations as well (eg the issue of convertible debentures, rights offers, takeover bids), and the Listing Particulars Directive makes appropriate modifications to the standard form of contents of listing particulars for such situations. The modifications are dealt with in this Chapter after the standard forms of listing particulars have been analysed.

The Stock Exchange rules supplement the Listing Particulars Directive by amplifying the detailed information which Schedules A or B of the directive require listing particulars to contain, and by calling for the

---

9 The Stock Exchange: *Admission of Securities to Listing*, Section 3, Chapter 1, para 1 and Section 3, Chapter 2, Heading.
10 Admission Directive, art 5(1).
11 Listing Particulars Directive, art 5(1).

disclosure of information which the directive does not require to be included or by imposing conditions not contained in the directive on the inclusion of certain items of information. The supplementary requirements of the Stock Exchange rules are largely taken from the 1979 edition of the Stock Exchange manual, *Admission of Securities to Listing*, which was in force up to 1 January 1985 when the present edition took effect.

The Quotations Committee (acting through the Quotations Department) has no general power to permit an issuer to omit any of the detailed information required to be included in listing particulars by Schedules A or B, although it can in appropriate cases authorise the omission of supplemental information which is called for by the Stock Exchange's own rules and not by the Directive.[13] Nevertheless, the Quotations Committee can waive or authorise the omission from any listing particulars of information included in Schedules A or B if the Committee considers either: (a) that the omission is of minor importance only and will not affect the assessment by investors of the assets, liabilities, financial position, profits or losses and prospects of the issuer; or (b) that disclosure of the information would be contrary to the public interest (eg national defence technology), or would be seriously detrimental to the issuer (eg confidential commercial information, or information the disclosure of which might prejudice the trading interests of the issuer in another country), but if an omission of information is sought to be authorised because of the possibility of serious detriment to the issuer, the omission must not be likely to mislead the public about facts and circumstances which it is essential for investors to know in order to make an assessment of the securities in question.[14] This provision for waivers or the authorisation of omissions is repeated in the Stock Exchange rules.[13] Waivers, or to use the expression employed by the Listing Particulars Directive, derogations, must be expressly and specifically requested of the Quotations Committee, even where the reason for the request is that the item of information in question is one which is inapplicable to the issuer or the information is a simple negative. The permission to omit information which would otherwise be required is then embodied in a letter of derogation from the Quotations Department.

LISTING PARTICULARS FOR SHARES

The obligatory minimum contents of listing particulars for shares called for by the Listing Particulars Directive are arranged in Schedule A under seven main heads, but listing particulars need not set the information out in that order.[15] However, the draft listing particulars submitted to the Quotations Department for approval must contain marginal annotations to indicate which of the items of Schedule A and the supplementary items of the Stock Exchange rules each item in the draft particulars covers.[16] The obligatory contents are as follows.

13 The Stock Exchange: *Admission of Securities to Listing*, Section 3, Chapter 1, para 1.5.
14 Listing Particulars Directive, art 7.
15 The Stock Exchange: *Admission of Securities to Listing*, Section 3, Chapter 1, para 1.3.
16 Ibid, Section 2, Chapter 1, para 2.1. This is done by referring to the paragraph numbers in Section 3, Chapter 2.

1. Information about the persons responsible for the listing particulars and about the auditors

The listing particulars must give the names and registered offices (if companies) of the persons who are responsible for the listing particulars or for parts of them, indicating which parts, and the particulars must contain a declaration by each such person, or by a responsible person on behalf of each such company, that to the best of his knowledge and belief (after the exercise of due care to verify it) the information in the particulars or the part of it for which he or it is responsible is in accordance with the facts and makes no omissions likely to affect the import of the listing particulars.[17] These requirements are repeated by the Stock Exchange rules, and a form of declaration by the persons responsible for the listing particulars is prescribed.[18] The persons responsible for the listing particulars are not defined by the Listing Particulars Directive, but will include all the directors of the company which seeks a listing, who must sign one copy of the final version of the listing particulars which must be delivered to the Quotations Department,[19] and the persons responsible will also include any experts (such as reporting accountants, valuers or engineers) whose reports, statements or opinions appear in the listing particulars. Such experts must give their written consent to the inclusion of statements and reports by them, and the fact that this has been done must be stated in the listing particulars.[20] If the listing particulars relate to shares which have been allotted to a financial institution with a view to them being offered to the public, directly or through the market, or if controlling shareholders are offering a block of their shares to the public for purchase through the market, it would seem that the financial institution or the controlling shareholders will also be persons responsible for the listing particulars, and they should make declarations about its accuracy and completeness accordingly. In fact, it would seem that anyone who could be sued for compensation under the Companies Acts[1] in respect of an untrue statement in a prospectus will be a responsible peson if the prospectus takes the form of listing particulars.

Listing particulars must state the names, addresses and qualifications of the company's auditors for the preceding three financial years, must confirm that the annual accounts for those years have been audited, and if the auditors have refused to report on any such accounts or have qualified any of their reports, the refusals or qualifications must be set out in full in the listing particulars with the reasons given by the auditors.[2] If any other information has been audited (eg the directors' annual reports) an indication must be given of the extent of the audit.[2] The Stock Exchange rules also require a statement to be included of the names and addresses, not only of the company's auditors, but also of its bankers, brokers and solicitors

---

17 Listing Particulars Directive, Sch A, paras 1.1 and 2.
18 The Stock Exchange: *Admission of Securities to Listing*, Section 3, Chapter 2, paras 1.6 and 7.
19 Ibid, Section 3, Chapter 2, para 5.4.
20 Ibid, Section 3, Chapter 2, para 1.8.
 1 Companies Act 1948, s 43(1) and (3) (now Companies Act 1985, s 67(1) and (2) and s 68 (3)–(5)).
 2 Listing Particulars Directive, Sch A, para 1.3.

and the solicitors who are acting in connection with any issue of securities to which the listing particulars relate.[3]

2. Information concerning the listing and the shares to be listed

The listing particulars must state whether the shares to which the listing particulars relate have already been issued and are to be introduced on the Stock Exchange, or whether they are to be issued and will be available to the public for subscription or for purchase from the financial institution to which they have been allotted or agreed to be allotted with a view to sale to the public.[4] To comply with the Stock Exchange rules this statement must be accompanied by a formal announcement that an application has been or will be made for the shares to be listed on the Stock Exchange.[5] There must then be set out the class of shares of the issuing company, their nominal value, the number of shares of each class which have been or will be issued, and the resolutions, authorisations and approvals by board or general meetings or otherwise for the issue of the shares.[6] If the shares have been or will be issued in connection with a merger or division of a company, or the transfer of the whole or part of its assets and liabilities, or a takeover offer, or in consideration of a transfer of assets other than cash, the listing particulars must state where the documents containing the terms and conditions of the transaction may be inspected by the public,[7] and by the Stock Exchange rules the documents must be available for inspection for at least 14 days at a named address in the City of London or in such other regional centre as the Quotations Committee permits, and also at the company's registered office and at the offices of its paying agents in the United Kingdom (if any).[8] The listing particulars must also contain a concise description of the rights attaching to the shares to which the listing particulars relate, including voting and divided rights and the right to participate in surplus assets in a liquidation, together with any relevant time limits for claiming dividends,[9] and if the company after the issue will have two or more classes of shares, the Stock Exchange rules require the rights attached to the other classes of shares also to be stated.[10] The particulars must state whether tax on dividends will be withheld in the country where the issuing company is resident or in the United Kingdom, and whether the company will withhold such tax at source.[11] The particulars must also state how the shares to which the listing particulars relate may be transferred, whether there are any restrictions on transferring them,[12] the entitlement of holders of shares to dividends (ie the first dividend distribution in which they will participate and the fixed dates (if

---

3 The Stock Exchange: *Admission of Securities to Listing*, Section 3, Chapter 2, paras 1.9 and 10.

4 Listing Particulars Directive, Sch A, para 2.1.

5 The Stock Exchange: *Admission of Securities to Listing*, Section 3, Chapter 2, para 2.1.

6 Listing Particulars Directive, Sch A, para 2.2.0.

7 Ibid, Sch A, para, 2.2.1.

8 The Stock Exchange: *Admission of Securities to Listing*, Section 3, Chapter 2, para 3.17.

9 Listing Particulars Directive, Sch A, para 2.2.2.

10 The Stock Exchange: *Admission of Securities to Listing*, Section 3, Chapter 2, para 2.9.

11 Listing Particulars Directive, Sch A, para 2.2.3.

12 Ibid, para 2.2.4.

any) for the payment of dividends),[13] all the stock exchanges on which a listing for the shares is being sought,[14] and the names and addresses of the company's paying agents in the United Kingdom (if any).[15]

Information must be given in listing particulars of the manner in which shares of the company for which a listing is sought have been issued during the preceding 12 months or are to be issued either by public or private offer or placing.[16] The listing particulars must state whether any preferential subscription rights of existing shareholders have been or will be exercised or have been waived, and if they have been waived or restricted, the reasons for this, the method of calculation of the issue price in cash and the persons who have or will benefit by the waiver or restriction; the total amount of shares of each class issued or to be issued on each offer or placing, and if blocks of shares have been or are reserved for marketing on the stock exchanges of two or more states, the amount so reserved;[17] the issue or placing price for the shares, their nominal value and any issue or share premium, and amount of any expenses charged to subscribers or placees, and the manner of payment of the issue price of the shares, including any part remaining unpaid;[18] the procedure for the exercise of preferential subscription rights, whether they may be or could have been renounced or transferred, and the way in which subscription rights not taken up have been or will be dealt with;[19] in the case of offers of shares for subscription, the date when subscription lists open and the agents of the company authorised to receive subscription applications;[20] the time when and the method by which share certificates will be or have been delivered by the company and any arrangements for the issue of temporary documents (letters of allotment or acceptance);[1] particulars of underwriters of the shares, and if the shares are not fully underwritten, the extent to which they are not;[2] a statement or estimate of the total of the expenses of the issue and listing and the amount per share, and particulars of the total amount of underwriting, placing and selling agents' commission and other intermediates' remuneration;[3] and the net proceeds of the issue or placing which the company has received or will receive and the intended application of those proceeds.[4]

The listing particulars must give detailed information about the marketing of the shares for which a listing is sought, namely, the number, nominal value and designation of the shares and (in the case of shares in bearer form) the dividend coupons attached to them;[5] if the shares have not

---

13 Ibid, para 2.2.5.
14 Ibid, para 2.2.6.
15 Ibid, para 2.2.7. The Stock Exchange rules refer to the company's registrars and paying agents (The Stock Exchange: *Admission of Securities to Listing*, Section 3, Chapter 2, para 2.16).
16 Listing Particulars Directive, art 2.3.
17 Ibid, paras 2.3.0, 2.3.1 and 2.3.2.
18 Ibid, para 2.3.3.
19 Ibid, para 2.3.4.
20 Ibid, para, 2.3.5.
 1 Ibid, para 2.3.6.
 2 Ibid, para 2.3.7.
 3 Ibid, para 2.3.8.
 4 Ibid, para 2.3.9.
 5 Ibid, para 2.4.0.

previously been issued or sold to the public and are to be made available to the public on the market by a placing, the number of shares which will be made available to the public and their nominal value, and, where applicable, the minimum sale or tender price;[6] the dates (if known) when newly issued shares will be listed and when dealings will commence;[7] if shares of the same class are already listed on any other stock exchanges, an indication of all such exchanges, or if shares of the same class are already dealt in on any other recognised and regulated, regularly operating markets (eg the Unlisted Securities Market), an indication of those markets;[8] particulars of any takeover offers made for the issuer's shares during the company's last preceding and current financial years, and particulars of any such offers made by the company for other companies' shares during the same period, including the price or exchange of securities offered and the outcome of the offer;[9] and finally, if simultaneously with the issue of new shares for which a listing is sought, the company is arranging for shares of the same class to be subscribed for or placed privately, details must be given of the private arrangements and of the number and particular features of the shares involved (eg if they carry a majority of votes exercisable at general or class meetings or a power to block special or extraordinary resolutions).[10]

In addition to the matters under the present head which the Listing Particulars Directive requires to be included in listing particulars, the Stock Exchange rules also require the inclusion of a statement by the directors of the issuing company that in their opinion the working capital available to it is sufficient, or if it is not, that the directors intend that additional working capital will be made available in the manner specified in the particulars;[11] a statement of any payment or benefit paid or given to a promoter so far as this is required by the general law,[12] and if the company does not already have a listing for any of its securities and the Quotations Committee so requires, a statement of the names of all or any of the promoters of the company (including persons who are directors) and the amount of any cash, securities or benefits paid, issued or given to any promoter within two years before the publication of the listing particulars, or proposed to be so paid, issued or given and the consideration given or to be given by him in return;[13] and where the shares for which a listing is sought are offered by way of rights or allotted on a capitalisation of profits or reserves, the listing particulars must specify the last day renounced letters of rights and letters of allotment will be accepted for registration of

---

6 Listing Particulars Directive, art 2.3, para 2.4.1.
7 Ibid, para 2.4.2.
8 Ibid, paras 2.4.3 and 2.4.4.
9 Ibid, para 2.4.5.
10 Ibid, para 2.5.
11 The Stock Exchange: *Admission of Securities to Listing*, Section 3, Chapter 2, para 2.19.
12 This information is required in prospectuses issued generally by the Companies Act 1948, Fourth Schedule, para 13 (now Companies Act 1985, Sch 3, para 10(1)(*a*)), but this requirement does not apply to listing particulars because of its exclusion by the Stock Exchange (Listing) Regulations 1984, reg 7(1)(*b*) (see p 143, above). The company and the promoters may nevertheless be obliged under the rules of equity to disclose this information to subscribers of the shares issued to enable the company to commence business (*Lagunas Nitrate Co Ltd v Lagunas Nitrate Syndicate* [1899] 2Ch 392; *Gluckstein v Barnes* [1900] AC 240).
13 The Stock Exchange: *Admission of Securities to Listing*, Section 3, Chapter 2, para 2.20.

the ultimate holder of them in the register of members, how the shares will rank for future dividends (ie the first dividend for which holders of the shares will qualify), whether the shares rank equally with other listed shares of the same class and, if the shares are issued by way of rights or on a capitalisation of profits or reserves, how fractional rights to shares will be treated, and in the case of a rights issue there must also be stated how shares not taken up will be dealt with and the period (not being less than 21 days) during which the rights offer may be accepted, and in the case of a capitalisation issue, the listing particulars must state whether the letters of allotment or other temporary documents issued to shareholders are or will be renounceable.[14]

3. Information about the issuing company and its capital

Listing particulars must set out the issuing company's name, registered office or principal administrative establishment (if different), the date of its incorporation and, if the duration of its corporate existence is limited by law or its consitution, the length of its corporate life, the legislation which governs the company and the corporate form it has assumed under that legislation (eg a public limited company, a French *société anonyme* or an American public corporation with limited liability), the company's objects or principal objects and a reference to the clause of its memorandum of association where they are set out (a rehearsal of the whole of the objects clause of its memorandum being unnecessary), the register in which the company is registered (eg the Companies Registry for a United Kingdom company) and its registration number and an indication of the address where the documents mentioned in the listing particulars are open to public inspection.[15]

There must also be set out in listing particulars a statement of the company's issued capital, the number and classes of shares which it has issued and the principal characteristics of each class (ie rights, privileges and subordination to other classes of shares), the amount of unpaid capital on issued shares and the number or nominal value of shares of each class of partly paid shares and the extent to which they have been paid up.[16] If the company has unissued shares comprised in its nominal capital or has undertaken to issue further shares (particularly to satisfy the conversion or subscription rights of the holders of convertible debentures or debentures with subscription warrants attached), the amount of such unissued shares or further shares and the duration of any authorisation for their issue must be stated, together with the persons who have preferential rights to subscribe for those shares and the terms on which they will be issued and the arrangements for their issue.[17] If the company has issued shares which are not comprised in its share capital, the number and characteristics of such shares must be stated;[18] this is not possible in the case of a United Kingdom company, all of whose shares can only be shares in its capital, but the requirement would apply to such shares as the founders' shares of a

14 Ibid, Section 3, Chapter 2, para 2.23.
15 Listing Particulars Directive, Sch A, paras 3.1.0 to 3.1.5.
16 Ibid, Sch A, para 3.2.0.
17 Ibid, Sch A, para 3.2.1.
18 Ibid, Sch A, para 3.2.2.

French company (*parts de fondateur*) or the shares (*Kuxe*) of an unincorporated German mining company. The listing particulars must also state the amount of issued debt securities which are convertible into or exchangeable for shares, and the amount of issued debt securities which have subscription warrants for further shares attached; and the conditions for the exercise of the conversion, exchange or subscription rights must be set out.[19] The conditions imposed by the company's memorandum or articles of association, or by the equivalent document if the company is a foreign one, for altering the company's share capital or the rights attached to the various classes of its shares must be stated if they are more onerous than the conditions imposed by law (eg if a United Kingdom company's nominal capital may be increased only by special resolution).[20]

Listing particulars must give summary descriptions of all operations and transactions during the three preceding years which have resulted in changes in the company's issued capital or the number or classes of shares which its issued capital comprises.[1] Also the particulars must indicate, so far as the company is aware, the person or persons who individually or together exercise, or can exercise, control over the issuing company and the fraction of the company's issued capital carrying voting rights which is held by them, but the voting shares of two or more persons are not to be aggregated for the purpose of ascertaining whether they have control of the company unless they have concluded an agreement under which they may adopt a common voting policy.[2] The listing particulars must further name any person or persons who are directly or indirectly interested in 5 per cent or more of the company's issued share capital, and must state the amount of their respective interests.[3] If the issuing company is a member of a group of companies, the listing particulars must give a brief description of the group and of the issuing company's position in it,[4] and if the company or another company in which the company holds more than 50 per cent of the issued capital, holds shares of the company directly or through a nominee, the number and nominal value of those shares must be stated together with the value at which they stand in the company's or subsidiary's books, but this information need not be given if it appears in the company's balance sheet.[5]

The Stock Exchange rules add to the foregoing requirements by requiring listing particulars to contain a statement that no material issue will be made of unissued shares carrying full voting rights within one year after the publication of the listing particulars (otherwise than by a rights offer made to existing holders of voting shares in proportion to their existing holdings) unless a general meeting approves the issue, but this does not apply if the unissued voting shares amount to less than ten per cent in nominal value of the total voting share capital of the company (issued and unissued), nor does it apply to unissued shares reserved for fulfilment of existing conversion rights and options to subscribe, and such reserved shares are not taken into account in determining whether ten per cent or more of the company's

---

19 Listing Particulars Directive, Sch A, para 3.2.3.
20 Ibid, Sch A, para 3.2.4.
 1 Ibid, Sch A, para 3.2.5.
 2 Ibid, Sch A, para 3.2.6.
 3 Ibid, Sch A, para 3.2.7; The Stock Exchange (Listing) Regulations 1984, reg 6 and Sch 2.
 4 Listing Particulars Directive, Sch A, para 3.2.8.
 5 Ibid, Sch A, para 3.2.9.

voting share capital is unissued.[6] Moreover, the Stock Exchange rules require certain further information to be disclosed than the Listing Particulars Directive calls for, namely, particulars of persons who hold options to subscribe for any share capital of the company or any of its subsidiaries together with the subscription price, the consideration given for the option and the duration of each option, but if the option has been given to all the shareholders or debenture holders of the same class or to employees under a share option or share subscription scheme, it suffices to state that fact without giving the names of the individual option holders.[7] Where relevant, because the company is or has been a close company, a statement must be included that appropriate indemnities have been obtained by the company against liability which it may incur for income tax on undistributed profits which the Inland Revenue has apportioned or may apportion among the shareholders of the company for tax purposes,[8] and unless similar indemnities have been given against the company's contingent liability for capital transfer tax when it is or has been a close company and has transferred any of its assets gratuitously or at an undervalue,[9] a statement must be included that the directors have been advised that no material liability is likely to fall on the company or any of its subsidiaries.[10] Listing particulars must also contain a summary of each material contract (not being one entered into in the ordinary course of business) entered into by the company or any of its subsidiaries within two years before the listing particulars are published, giving the dates, parties, terms and consideration passing to or from the company or its subsidiaries, unless the material contract has been available for public inspection during the last two years in connection with the publication of listing particulars or a prospectus, but the Quotations Committee may dispense with this requirement if it would involve the disclosure of important information to trade competitors with detrimental consequences to the company.[11] Finally, listing particulars must give an address in the City of London, or such other regional centre as the Quotations Committee permits, where the public may during a period of not less than 14 days inspect certain documents, namely the company's memorandum and articles, all reports, letters, balance sheets, valuations and statements by experts contained or referred to in the listing particulars, and the annual accounts of the company or consolidated accounts of the company and its subsidiaries for its two preceding financial years.[12]

---

6 The Stock Exchange: *Admission of Securities to Listing*, Section 3, Chapter 2, para 3.5.
7 Ibid, Section 3, Chapter 2, para 3.12.
8 Ibid, Section 3, Chapter 2, para 3.13. The liability of the company, if the shareholders do not pay the income tax on profits apportioned to them, arises under the Finance Act 1972, s 94(1) and Sch 16, para 6(2).
9 The value of the gift or the amount of the undervalue is apportioned among the shareholders, who are liable for capital transfer tax thereon, but if they do not satisfy their liability, the Inland Revenue may recover the tax payable by them from the company (Capital Transfer Tax Act 1984, s 94(1) and (2) and s 202(1)).
10 The Stock Exchange: *Admission of Securities to Listing*, Section 3, Chapter 2, para 3.14.
11 Ibid, Section 3, Chapter 2, para 3.16.
12 Ibid, Section 3, Chapter 2, para 3.17.

4. Information about the issuing company's activities

Listing particulars must give extensive information about the issuing company's principal business or other activities, namely, a statement of those activities and the main categories of the products which the company sells or of the services it performs or both, and also any significant innovations in its products or services;[13] a breakdown of the company's turnover during the last three financial years, both by the different categories of its activities and by the geographical location of its markets, and in this connection activities and markets must be classified by reference to the organisation of the sale of its main products and the provision of its main services, so that less important products and services will be dealt with as part of the major products or services to which they are most closely related,[14] whilst under the Stock Exchange rules the breakdown of turnover must be supplemented by such figures as are necessary, in terms of profits, losses, assets employed and other relevant factors, to indicate the relative importance of each of the company's main activities;[15] a statement of the location and size of the company's principal establishments (namely, all those which account for ten per cent or more of its turnover) and summary information about its land and buildings,[16] including (under the supplemental rules of the Stock Exchange in the case of United Kingdom companies) its tenure of lands and buildings, the rents and unexpired terms of leaseholds it holds and the address of its principal place of business in the United Kingdom;[17] if the company is engaged in mining, quarrying, the extraction of hydrocarbon oils or similar activities, a description of the main mineral deposits it is working, an estimate of the extent of its mineral reserves which can be exploited economically, their expected period of working, and the progress being made in working them and the duration and financial and other principal terms of the concessions under which they are being worked,[18] to which the Stock Exchange supplementary rules add (if the company does not already have a listing for any of its securities) the name, address, qualifications and experience of the company's technical advisers, a report by the technical advisers on the company's estimated mineral reserves, dealing (inter alia) with the company's current working, its proven and probable mineral reserves and its production policy, and statements of the estimated funding requirements and cash flow of the company over the next two years and of the interests of its promoters, directors and technical advisers in the promotion of the company or assets acquired by it;[19] finally, if any of the foregoing information indicates the influence of exceptional factors, that fact must be mentioned.[20]

The listing particulars must additionally give summary information about the extent to which the issuing company is dependent on patents, patent licences, industrial, commercial or financial contracts or new manu-

---

13 Listing Particulars Directive, Sch A, para 4.1.0.
14 Ibid, Sch A, para 4.1.1.
15 The Stock Exchange: *Admission of Securities to Listing*, Section 3, Chapter 2, para 4.4.
16 Listing Particulars Directive, Sch A, para 4.1.2.
17 The Stock Exchange: *Admission of Securities to Listing*, Section 3, Chapter 2, paras 4.5 and 6.
18 Listing Particulars Directive, Sch A, para 4.1.3.
19 The Stock Exchange: *Admission of Securities to Listing*, Section 10, Chapter 2, para 5.
20 Listing Particulars Directive, Sch A, para 4.1.4.

facturing processes where such factors are of fundamental importance to its business or profitability;[1] information about the company's policy in respect of research and the development of new products and processes over the last three years, if this is significant in relation to its activities;[2] information about any recent litigation or arbitration proceedings involving the company and any recent interruption of its business which may have had a significant effect on its financial position;[3] and a statement of the average number of persons currently employed by the company and any material changes in that number over the last three financial years, together with a breakdown of those numbers between the main categories of the company's business activities.[4] The listing particulars must also describe the main investments made by the company in other companies during the preceding three financial years and the current year, including the acquisition of shares and debentures of other companies, stating the amounts involved;[5] must give information about the company's principal investments currently being made (other than the acquisition of shares and debentures of other companies), including the geographical spread of the investments and the method of financing them (retention of profits or raising of funds externally);[6] and finally, must give information about the company's principal future investments (with the exception of acquisitions of shares and debentures of other companies) on which its board has made firm commitments (ie which the board has resolved or contracted to acquire).[7]

5. Information about the company's assets and liabilities, financial position and profits and losses

The listing particulars must under the Listing Particulars Directive include the balance sheets and profit and loss accounts of the issuing company for its last three financial years (ending not earlier than 18 months before the listing particulars are published) in the form of a comparative table setting out the figures for the individual items appearing in the annual accounts for each of those years.[8] If the company is the parent company of a group and it prepares both its own annual accounts and consolidated accounts for the group, the comparative table must comprise the figures from both sets of accounts, unless the Quotations Committee permits the company to include the figures from one of the sets of accounts only, because the other sets of accounts do not provide significant additional information; if the company prepares only consolidated accounts,[9] the

1 Ibid, Sch A, para 4.2.
2 Ibid, Sch A, para 4.3.
3 Ibid, Sch A, paras 4.4 and 4.5. The Stock Exchange rules equate recent with during the last 12 months (The Stock Exchange: *Admission of Securities to Listing*, Section 3, Chapter 2, paras 3.1.5. and 4.10).
4 Listing Particulars Directive, Sch A, para 4.6.
5 Ibid, Sch A, para 4.7.0.
6 Ibid, Sch A, para 4.7.1.
7 Ibid, Sch A, para 4.7.2.
8 Ibid, Sch A, para 5.1.0.
9 United Kingdom parent companies must prepare both their own and consolidated balance sheets, but they may dispense with their own profit and loss accounts if they prepare consolidated profit and loss accounts (Companies Act 1948, s 149(5), now Companies Act 1985, s 228(7)).

comparative table will comprise only the figures for the group of companies of which it is the parent company.[10] The Stock Exchange rules give effect to these requirements by calling for the inclusion in the listing particulars of an accountant's report giving the detailed information called for by Section 4 of the Stock Exchange's manual, *Admission of Securities to Listing*, in respect of the company's or group's assets and liabilities, financial record (ie profits or losses) and financial position for each of the preceding five complete financial years, but if any of the company's subsidiaries has had a listing for any of its securities on the Stock Exchange during the 12 months preceding publication of the listing particulars, the accountant's report need not deal with that listed subsidiary if the information relating to it is included in a comparative table showing the profits and losses, assets and liabilities and financial record and position of the group as a whole in each of the preceding five financial years.[11] Such a comparative table in respect of the issuing company, or the group of which it is the parent company, must be included in the listing particulars instead of an accountant's report, if the company already has a listing for any of its securities on the Stock Exchange, and the table must also include separate figures for any company which has become a subsidiary of the issuing company since the date to which its most recently published and audited annual accounts were made up.[12] The comparative table must be accompanied by the notes to the issuing company's latest published and audited annual accounts.[12] The listing particulars must also state that the annual accounts comprised in the accountant's report or the comparative table have been audited, and if any of the auditors' reports have been refused or are qualified, the reasons for the refusal given by the auditors or the terms of the qualifications must be reproduced in full.[13]

The Listing Particulars Directive also calls for a statement of the profits or loss per share of the company, or if it prepares only consolidated accounts, the group profits or loss attributable to each share of the parent company, for each of the preceding three financial years, with appropriate adjustments if the company or parent company's issued share capital has changed during those financial years.[14] The listing particulars must also state the amount of the dividend declared on each class of the company's shares in each of the three preceding financial years.[15] If more than nine months has elapsed since the end of the issuing company's last complete financial year, the listing particulars must include an interim financial statement covering at least the first six months of its current financial year, and if the Quotations Committee directs in the case of a parent company which prepares consolidated annual accounts, the listing particulars must also set out a consolidated interim financial statement in respect of the group of which the issuing company is the parent company; the interim financial statement need not be audited, but if it is unaudited, the fact must

10 Listing Particulars Directive, Sch A, para 5.1.1.
11 The Stock Exchange: *Admission of Securities to Listing*, Section 3, Chapter 1, para 3.1(*a*) and Chapter 2, paras 5.1 and 2.
12 Ibid, Section 3, Chapter 1, para 3.1(*a*) and Chapter 2, paras 5.2 and 5.5.
13 Ibid, Section 3, Chapter 2, para 5.3. This repeats the requirement of the Listing Particulars Directive, Sch A, para 1.3 (dealt with on page 57, above), but extends the period to be covered to the last 5 financial years.
14 Listing Particulars Directive, Sch A, para 5.1.2.
15 Ibid, Sch A, para 5.1.3.

be stated; the statement must describe any significant change which has taken place in respect of the company or its financial position since the end of its last complete financial year.[16] If the company's annual accounts or consolidated accounts do not give all the information required by law, or do not give a true and fair view of the company's financial position and profit or loss, the comparative table must be supplemented by additional information in the listing particulars to rectify this;[17] presumably, this obligation extends to all the accounts comprised in the accountant's report or summarised in the comparative table. Finally, a table showing the source and application of the company's funds over its last three financial years must be included.[18]

The financial information which must be given in listing particulars is extended beyond the issuing company and the companies of which it is the parent company by the obligation to disclose limited information about other companies in which the issuing company holds on a long term basis a percentage of the issued share capital which is likely to be significant in assessing its own assets and liabilities, financial position or profits or losses.[19] This information must in any case be given in respect of a shareholding in another company whose book value (ie acquisition price so far as not written off) represents at least ten per cent of the issuing company's capital and reserves shown in its latest annual accounts, or the earnings on a shareholding which accounts for at least ten per cent of the net profit or loss of the company shown in those accounts; if the issuing company is a parent company, the relevant percentages are of the consolidated net assets and the consolidated net profit or loss of the group as shown by the group's latest consolidated accounts.[19] The Stock Exchange rules also require certain information to be given if the issuing company holds on a long term basis 20 per cent or more in nominal value of the issued equity share capital carrying unrestricted voting rights of another company which is not its subsidiary.[20] The information which must be given about the other company comprises its name and registered office, the kinds of business activities in which it engages, its issued capital and reserves, its profit or loss after tax for its last financial year (excluding extraordinary items), the book value of the shares held by the issuing company in the other company, the amount (if any) unpaid on those shares, the dividends received on those shares during the issuing company's last complete financial year and the total amount of the indebtedness of the issuing company to the other company and of it to the issuing company.[19] In addition to this information about participations in other companies, the listing particulars must state the names and registered offices of companies in which the issuing company holds at least 10 per cent of the issued capital and the proportion of that capital which it holds, but this may be omitted if the shareholdings are of negligible importance in assessing the issuing company's financial position.[1]

If consolidated accounts are used in constructing the comparative table

16 Ibid, Sch A, para 5.1.4.
17 Ibid, Sch A, para 5.1.5.
18 Ibid, Sch A, para 5.1.6.
19 Ibid, Sch A, para 5.2.
20 The Stock Exchange: *Admission of Securities to Listing*, Section 3, Chapter 2, para 5.13.
 1 Listing Particulars Directive, Sch A, para 5.3.

of items in the issuing company's accounts for past financial years, there must be set out in the listing particulars a statement of the consolidation principles applied in preparing the consolidated accounts, the names and registered offices of the companies included in the consolidation if important in assessing the financial position of the issuing company, and a statement of the percentage or extent of shareholdings in each of those companies which are held by persons other than the issuing company and its nominees.[2] Furthermore, if the issuing company is a dominant undertaking (ie is able to exercise a controlling influence over other companies as a result of holding shares in them or otherwise), all the information required under head 4 above[3] and head 7 below[4] must be given on a consolidated basis for the issuing company and the other companies taken together as a group, but the Quotations Committee may authorise the omission from such information of matters relating to the issuing company or to the other companies if it is not material.[5] This requirement is made effective by heads 4 and 7 of the Stock Exchange rules being expressed in terms of the group of companies of which the issuing company is the parent company, instead of in terms of the issuing company itself, as in the Listing Particulars Directive.

The Stock Exchange rules contain only one requirement supplementary to the Listing Particulars Directive in respect of financial information in listing particulars, apart from the requirement of an accountant's report mentioned at the beginning of this section. The other supplementary requirement is that listing particulars for shares should give the same information about the company's borrowings as the Listing Particulars Directive requires in listing particulars for debt securities of a company,[6] namely, the total amount of the outstanding loan capital and term loans of the company and the group to which it belongs (distinguishing between guaranteed and secured and unguaranteed and unsecured indebtedness), the total amount of other borrowings of the company and the group (distinguished in the same way), the total amount of mortgages and charges created by the company and the group,[7] and the total amount of contingent liabilities and guarantees of the company and the group.[8]

6. Information in respect of management and administration

Listing particulars must give information in respect of directors of the issuing company, of the members of any supervisory board or council which the company has established to supervise the management of the company,[9] of any shareholders in the company who despite it being a limited company bear personal unlimited liability for its debts,[10] and of its

2 Listing Particulars Directive, Sch A, para 5.4.
3 See p 64, above.
4 See p 70, below.
5 Listing Particulars Directive, Sch A, para 5.5.
6 See p 76, below.
7 The total amount of mortgages and charges is not required by the Listing Particulars Directive.
8 The Stock Exchange: *Admission of Securities to Listing*, Section 3, Chapter 2, para 5.16.
9 Such as the *Aufsichtsrat* of a German *Aktiengesellschaft* or the *conseil de surveillance* of a French *société anonyme* which has opted for a two-tier structure.
10 This cannot apply in the case of a United Kingdom company, and relates to the little used

promoters if the company was incorporated less than five years before the publication of the listing particulars.[11] The required information relates to the names, addresses and functions of these persons and their principal activities outside the company if they are significant with respect to it (eg other directorships which they hold in companies active in the same or related fields).[11] The Stock Exchange rules extend this requirement so as to call for disclosure of all the outside business interests of the persons in question, and they empower the Quotations Committee to require disclosure of any former names of those persons, their present nationality (if not British) and their nationality of origin if it has been changed.[12]

Listing particulars must also disclose the interests of the directors and members of its supervisory board or council (if any) of the issuing company in it by stating the total remuneration paid and total benefits given to them during the company's last financial year as remuneration which is charged to overheads or to profit and loss account (including separate figures for remuneration provided by the issuing company's subsidiaries); the total number of shares in the issuing company held by such persons and the total number of such shares for which they have options to subscribe; information about the nature and extent of the interests of such persons in transactions entered into by the issuing company during its current and last preceding financial years and in transactions entered into earlier but which have not yet been completed, if the transactions were unusual in nature or terms (such as acquisitions of assets by the company of a kind it does not normally deal in or use, and the acquisition or disposal of fixed assets); and a statement of the total amount of loans made by the issuing company to its directors which remain outstanding and of the outstanding amount for which the issuing company has secured or guaranteed loans to its directors made by third persons.[13] The Stock Exchange rules again extend this requirement by requiring disclosure of any arrangements by which directors will waive their right to remuneration in the future and the extent to which they have waived remuneration for the last preceding financial year, and by calling for an estimate of the directors' remuneration payable by the issuing company or any of its subsidiaries for the current financial year;[14] by requiring particulars to be given of interests of directors and persons connected with them in shares or debentures of the issuing company or a company belonging to the same group if the interests have been notified to the company under the Companies Acts or entered in the register kept by the company under those Acts[15] or, in the case of a company not subject to United Kingdom companies legislation, the interests of each director and his spouse and children under 18 in the issued shares of the company or in options to subscribe for its shares;[16] and by requiring details to be given of existing and proposed service contracts between directors and the issuing

---

French *société en commandite par actions* and the German *Kommanditgesellschaft auf Aktien* or *Aktienkommanditgesellschaft*, where the managing directors who are also shareholders are personally liable for the company's debts.

11 Listing Particulars Directive, Sch A, para 6.1.
12 The Stock Exchange: *Admission of Securities to Listing*, Section 3, Chapter 2, para 6.1.
13 Listing Particulars Directive, Sch A, paras 6.2.0–6.2.3.
14 The Stock Exchange: *Admission of Securities to Listing*, Section 3, Chapter 2, para 6.3.
15 Companies Act 1967, ss 27, 29 and 31 (now Companies Act 1985, ss 324, 325 and 328).
16 The Stock Exchange: *Admission of Securities to Listing*, Section 3, Chapter 2, para 6.6.

company or its subsidiaries (other than contracts expiring or terminable by the employing company within one year without the payment of compensation), but this disclosure is unnecessary in the case of a service contract which has already been made available for inspection prior top the holding of an annual general meeting, unless the contract has since been varied.[17]

The Listing Particulars Directive finally requires information to be given of schemes involving the acquisition of interests in the share capital of the issuing company by its employees.[18] This covers share subscription and share option schemes set up by the issuing company for the benefit of all or some of its employees (including directors).

The Stock Exchange rules additionally call for the name and professional qualifications of the issuing company's secretary to be stated in listing particulars,[19] and for the inclusion of a summary of the provisions in the issuing company's articles of association, or equivalent document in the case of a foreign company, enabling directors to vote at board meetings on matters in which they are interested, enabling the board to vote remuneration, pensions or other benefits to directors in the absence of an independent quorum, conferring borrowing powers on directors, or providing for the retirement or non-retirement of directors on attaining a certain age.[20]

7. Information about recent developments and prospects of the company

Listing particulars must, unless the Quotations Committee grants a dispensation, contain general information about the trend of the issuing company's business since the end of the financial year for which it has last published annual accounts, and in particular, information must be given about significant recent trends in production, sales and holdings of stock and the level of orders placed with the company and recent trends in costs and selling prices.[1] Furthermore, unless the Quotations Committee waives the requirement, listing particulars must give information on the issuing company's prospects for the future, extending at least to the end of the current financial year,[2] but this need not include profit forecasts. The Stock Exchange rules amplify this by requiring information about the financial and trading prospects of the company and the group of which it is the parent company (if it has subsidiaries), together with any relevant material information, including all special trade factors and risks which are not mentioned elsewhere in the particulars, and which are unlikely to be known or anticipated by the general public, but which could materially affect the profits of the company or group.[3] The Stock Exchange rules also provide that if a profit forecast is included in listing particulars, the principal assumptions (including commercial assumptions) on which the

17 The Stock Exchange: *Admission of Securities to Listing*, Section 3, Chapter 2, para 6.4.
18 Listing Particulars Directive, Sch A, para 6.3.
19 The Stock Exchange: *Admission of Securities to Listing*, section 3, Chapter 2, para 6.2.
20 Ibid, Section 3, Chapter 2, para 6.9.
 1 Listing Particulars Directive, Sch A, para 7.1.
 2 Ibid, Sch A, para 7.2.
 3 The Stock Exchange: *Admission of Securities to Listing*, Section 3, Chapter 2, para 7.1.

directors have based the forecast must be stated; the accounting policies and calculations applied in making the forecast must be reported on by the reporting accountant and his report must be set out in the particulars; also the merchant bank or sponsoring brokers who are acting in connection with the marketing of the company's securities must report whether they are satisfied that the forecast has been made by the directors after proper careful enquiry, and that report too must be set out in the particulars.[4]

LISTING PARTICULARS FOR DEBT SECURITIES

Schedule B of the Listing Particulars Directive sets out under seven heads the detailed information which must be contained in listing particulars in respect of debt securities issued by a company or other issuer, except a collective investment undertaking of the open-ended kind or by a state or a regional or local authority of a state.[5] The arrangement and content of the information required by Schedule B follows the arrangement and content of Schedule A, and consequently the account of Schedule B which follows will concentrate on the points of difference between the two Schedules, namely, the information required under Schedule A which is not called for in listing particulars relating to debt securities under Schedule B, and conversely, the special or additional items of information which are called for under Schedule B (particularly in respect of the terms of issue of the debt securities, mortgages or charges over assets of the issuing company or any other person on which holders of the securities may rely and details of other debt securities of the issuer which are outstanding), but which have no equivalent under Schedule A. The Stock Exchange rules governing listing particulars relating to debt securities do not list their obligatory contents separately from those in listing particulars for shares, but certain of the requirements of the rules in respect of listing particulars for shares are excluded in their application to listing particulars for debt securities.[6] In the account given below the Stock Exchange requirements are dealt with only insofar as they add to the requirements of Schedule B in respect of listing particulars for debt securities. Because the Stock Exchange rules do not set out the obligatory contents of listing particulars for debt securities separately, it has been necessary for an eighth head to be added to them; this eighth part sets out the matters which must be included in listing particulars for debt securities, but not in listing particulars for shares.

As in the case of listing particulars for shares, the detailed information required in listing particulars for debt securities need not be set out in the order in which it appears in Schedule B,[7] but the draft listing particulars submitted to the Quotations Department for approval must contain marginal annotations indicating which of the items of Schedule B and the supplementary items of the Stock Exchange rules each item of information in the listing particulars is intended to cover.[8]

4 Ibid, Section 3, Chapter 2, para 7.2.
5 Listing Particulars Directive, art 1(1) and (2) and art 5(1).
6 The Stock Exchange: *Admission of Securities to Listing*, Section 3, Chapter 1, para 3.2(*a*).
7 Ibid, para 1.3.
8 Ibid, Section 2, Chapter 1, para 2.1. This is done by referring to the paragraph numbers in Section 3, Chapter 2.

1. Information about the persons responsible for the listing particulars and about the auditors

The information to be given under this head is identical to that which must be given under the same head in listing particulars relating to shares under both the Listing Particulars Directive and the Stock Exchange rules, and consequently the same observations as were made above in connection with listing particulars for shares apply equally here.[9]

2. Information concerning the listing and the debt securities to be listed

Like listing particulars for shares, listing particulars for debt securities must commence with a formal announcement that an application has been or will be made for the securities to be listed on the Stock Exchange, accompanied by an indication whether the securities have already been issued and are to be introduced on the Stock Exchange, or whether they are to be issued and will be available to the public for subscription or for purchase from the financial institution to which they have been allotted or agreed to be allotted with a view to sale to the public.[10]

Unless the securities are to be issued 'on tap', the listing particulars must set out the nominal amount of the loan secured by the issue of the debt securities, or if the amount is not fixed, a statement to that effect (eg if the total amount secured may be increased by the issuing company under a formula related to the current value of its net assets and the level of its profits, the possibility of such an increase must be mentioned); and the nature, number and numbering of the debt securities of the series and their denomination (the nominal value of each unit of the series) must be set out,[11] together with the issue and redemption prices and the nominal interest rate, or the formula by which a variable interest rate will be calculated (eg so many percentage points above the current London inter-bank offered rate (LIBOR) for three month deposits), or details of the periodic changes in interest rates if they are to increase or decrease over the term for which the loan will be outstanding.[12] The listing particulars must set out the procedure for allocating any other benefits which are to be given to holders of the debt securities (eg periodic distributions of a fraction of the issuer's profits),[13] must state whether tax will be withheld from interest or other income payments in the country where the issuing company is resident or in the United Kingdom, and whether the company will withhold such tax at source,[14] must describe the arrangements for the amortisation of the loan (eg by means of a sinking fund or market purchases) including the procedure for repaying the principal of the loan (eg by drawings over a period),[15] and must give particulars of the financial institutions which will act as the company's paying agents in the United

---

9 See p 57, above.
10 The Stock Exchange: *Admission of Securities to Listing*, Section 3, Chapter 2, para 2.1.
11 Listing Particulars Directive, Sch B, para 2.1.0.
12 Ibid, Sch B, para 2.1.1.
13 Ibid, Sch B, para 2.1.2.
14 Ibid, Sch B, para 2.1.3.
15 Ibid, Sch B, para 2.1.4.

Kingdom.[16] The listing particulars must also state the currency in which the loan is made and, if the loan is denominated in units of account (such as the European unit of account), the contractual provisions for ascertaining its equivalent in the currency of any countries in which the loan is repayable, together with any options given to holders of debt securities to receive payment of principal or interest in different currencies (eg a loan expressed in European units of accounts optionally repayable in sterling, Deutschemarks, French francs or Dutch florins).[17] The duration of the loan and any dates on which parts of it will become repayable, or on which the company will have an option to repay the whole or part of the loan, must be stated, and also the date from which interest will be calculated and the dates for the payment of interest, any time limit on claims for unpaid interest, and the procedure which will be followed for the issue of certificates for the debt securities and for the issue of temporary documents (such as letters of allotment).[18] Finally, the particulars must indicate the yield on the debt securities and the method by which it is calculated, but this is not necessary if the debt securities are issued 'on tap'.[19]

Listing particulars for debt securities must indicate the resolutions, authorisations and approvals which have been passed or given for the issue of the securities by the board or general meeting of the issuing company or otherwise, the kind of operation employed for the marketing of the securities (public offering, placing, offer for sale etc) and the number of securities which have been or will be issued on the publication of the listing particulars,[20] particulars of any guarantees, mortgages or charges or contractual commitments which have been or will be created or given as security for the payment of principal and interest on the loan and the places where the documents creating such guarantees etc may be inspected.[1] If there has been or will be an appointment of trustees or representatives of the holders of the debt securities to represent their interests, the fact must be stated in the listing particulars with the names addresses and qualifications of the trustees or representatives, a statement of the powers conferred on them, the conditions of their appointment and an indication of the address where the contract for their appointment and defining their powers and functions may be inspected by the public.[2] There must also be included in the listing particulars a note of any provision by which the debt securities will be subordinated to payments of principal or interest on other debt securities issued by the company,[3] of the law or legislation which will govern the debt securities and under which they have been created, and the court which will have jurisdiction to decide on claims under the debt securities,[4] an indication whether certificates for the securities will be in registered or bearer form,[5] and any restrictions which are imposed on the transfer of the securities by the terms on which they are issued.[6]

The stock exchanges on which a listing of the debt securities will be sought must be specified in the listing particulars,[7] and it must contain a statement of the stock exchanges on which debt securities of the same class

16 Ibid, Sch B, para 2.1.5.
17 Ibid, Sch B, para 2.1.6.
18 Ibid, Sch B, para 2.1.7.
19 Ibid, Sch B, para 2.1.8.
20 Ibid, Sch B, para 2.2.0.
 1 Ibid, Sch B, para 2.2.1.

2 Ibid, Sch B, para 2.2.2.
3 Ibid, Sch B, para 2.2.3.
4 Ibid, Sch B, para 2.2.4.
5 Ibid, Sch B, para 2.2.5.
6 Ibid, Sch B, para 2.2.6.
7 Ibid, Sch B, para 2.3.0.

are already listed[8] and of any recognised, regulated and regularly operating
markets (eg the Unlisted Securities Market) where dealings in such
securities take place.[9] Particulars of the persons who have agreed to
underwrite the issue of the debt securities must be given, together with a
note of the percentage of the securities which are not underwritten,[10] and if
the securities are being offered to the public or placed simultaneously on
the markets of two or more states, any reservation of a block of the
securities for a particular national market must be disclosed.[11] If the issue
of the securities is simultaneous with the listing or preceded it by not more
than 3 months, any preferential subscription rights for the debt securities
(eg under the terms of an existing series of debt securities) must be stated,
the procedure for the exercise of such rights must be set out and any right
to renounce or transfer such preferential subscription rights and the
arrangements for the disposal of securities for which preferential subscription rights were or are not exercised must be indicated.[12] If the issue is
simultaneous with listing or was made not more than three months
beforehand, the date for payment of the issue price of the securities or
instalments of it must be given,[13] the period during which applications for
the securities may be submitted (if they are offered otherwise than 'on
tap')[14] and the financial institutions which are authorised to receive
applications[15] must be specified, and a statement must be included that
applications for the securities may be reduced in the event of an over-
subscription if the power to reduce them is reserved.[16] Finally, an estimate
must be given of the net proceeds of the issue of debt securities after paying
issue expenses, commissions and fees,[17] and the intended application of
those proceeds must be stated.[18]

In addition to the matters which the Listing Particulars Directive
requires to be included in listing particulars relating to debt securities, the
Stock Exchange rules require the inclusion of the same information as in
listing particulars relating to shares in respect of the following matters: the
total amount of debt securities offered by public or private offers during the
preceding three months and the amount offered or to be offered by the
public or private offer to which the listing particulars relate;[19] a statement
by the directors that in their opinion the working capital of the company
and its subsidiaries (if any) is sufficient, or if it is not, the steps proposed to
be taken to make it sufficient;[20] and if the debt securities carry a fixed rate of
interest, particulars of the profit cover for interest payments (presumably

8 Listing Particulars Directive, Sch B, para 2.3.3.
9 Ibid, Sch B, para 2.3.4.
10 Ibid, Sch B, para 2.3.1.
11 Ibid, Sch B, para 2.3.2.
12 Ibid, Sch B, para 2.4.0.
13 Ibid, Sch B, para 2.4.1.
14 Ibid, Sch B, para 2.4.2.
15 Ibid, Sch B, para 2.4.3.
16 Ibid, Sch B, para 2.4.4.
17 Ibid, Sch B, para 2.4.5.
18 Ibid, Sch B, para 2.4.6.
19 The Stock Exchange: *Admission of Securities to Listing*, Section 3, Chapter 1, para 3.2(*a*)
   and Chapter 2, para 2.18(*b*) (see p 59, above).
20 Ibid, Section 3, Chapter 2, para 2.19 (see p 60, above).

based on the profits shown by the company's latest annual accounts) and the value of the net tangible assets of the company.[1]

3. Information about the issuing company and its capital

Listing particulars relating to debt securities must give the same information about the issuing company under this head as listing particulars relating to shares;[2] the information is set out in the first paragraph of the account given above of this third head in connection with listing particulars for shares.[3] The information which must be given about the issuing company's capital in listing particulars for debt securities is, however, less extensive than in listing particulars for shares, and only the following information need be included, namely, the amount of the company's issued share capital, the number of issued shares of each class, the principal characteristics of each class of shares, and the amount of capital unpaid on issued shares with details of the number or total nominal value of partly paid shares and the amounts unpaid on the shares of each class;[4] the particular must also state the amount outstanding of debt securities issued by the company which are convertible into, or exchangeable for, shares or which carry the right to subscribe for shares, together with a summary of the conditions for the exercise of these rights;[5] if the issuing company is a members of a group of companies, the particulars must contain a description of its position in the group,[6] and the number, nominal value and book value for accounting purposes of shares of the company held by it and other companies in which it holds more than 50 per cent of the issued capital, if those shares are not shown separately in the company's balance sheet and represent a significant percentage of its capital.[7]

The Stock Exchange rules additionally require listing particulars relating to debt securities to contain a summary of each material contract (not being one entered into in the ordinary course of business) entered into by the company or any of its subsidiaries within two years before the listing particulars are published, in the same way and with the same possibility of exemption by the Quotations Committee as in the case of listing particulars in relation to shares.[8]

4. Information about the issuing company's activities

The Listing Particulars Directive requires the same information to be given under this head in listing particulars relating to debt securities as in listing particulars relating to shares,[9] and the only items which do not have to be included are the company's net turnover for its three financial years

---

1 Ibid, Section 3, Chapter 2, para 8.9.
2 Listing Particulars Directive, Sch B, paras 3.10 to 3.1.5.
3 See p 61, above.
4 Listing Particulars Directive, Sch B, para 3.2.0.
5 Ibid, Sch B, para 3.2.1.
6 Ibid, Sch B, para 3.2.2.
7 Ibid, Sch B, para 3.2.3.
8 The Stock Exchange: *Admission of Securities to Listing*, Section 3, Chapter 1, para 3.2(*a*) and Chapter 2, para 3.16 (see p 63, above).
9 Listing Particulars Directive, Sch B, paras 4.1.0 to 4.7.2. For the obligatory contents of listing particulars for shares in this respect see p 64, above.

(its turnover for its last two financial years sufficing), a breakdown of the company's net turnover functionally and geographically for those years,[10] the company's policy on research and development over the last three financial years,[11] significant interruptions in the company's business in the recent past,[12] and the average number of employees of the company over the preceding three financial years.[13]

The Stock Exchange rules call for the same information under the present head in listing particulars for debt securities as the Listing Particulars Directive with no additions.

5. Information about the company's assets and liabilities, financial position and profits and losses

The Listing Particulars Directive requires the same information to be given under this head in listing particulars relating to debt securities as in listing particulars relating to shares,[14] but there need only be included in the comparative table of balance sheets and profit and loss account items in listing particulars for debt securities the figures taken from the annual accounts of the company for its last two financial years (as compared with its last three financial years in listing particulars for shares).[15] There may be omitted from listing particulars relating to debt securities a statement of the company's profits after tax and dividends declared for its last three financial years;[16] certain particulars of other companies in which the issuing company holds a percentage of issued share capital which is likely to have a significant effect on the assessment of its own financial position, namely, particulars of the other company's profit or loss for its last financial year, the book value of the issuing company's holding and the indebtedness of the issuing company and each company in which it has a holding to each other;[17] and the names and registered offices of other companies in which the issuing company holds at least ten per cent of the issued share capital and the percentage of capital held.[18] On the other hand, the directive requires listing particulars for debt securities to set out as at the most recent practicable date a statement of the total amount outstanding of loan capital issued by the company and by the other companies in the group of which it is the parent company (distinguishing between guaranteed and secured loans and unguaranteed and unsecured loans); the amount of the company's and group's other borrowings (distinguishing between guaranteed and secured debts and unguaranteed and unsecured debts), and the total amount of the company's contingent liabilities.[19] There is no definition of loan capital for this purpose in the directive. Presumably it means loans made for a substantial period (probably not less than seven years) which

10 Listing Particulars Directive, Sch A, para 4.1.1.
11 Ibid, para 4.3.
12 Ibid, para 4.5.
13 Ibid, para 4.6.
14 Ibid, Sch B, paras 5.1.0 to 5.5. For the obligatory contents of listing particulars for shares, see p 65, above).
15 Listing Particulars Directive, Sch B, para 5.1.0.
16 Ibid, Sch A, paras 5.1.2 and 5.1.3.
17 Ibid, Sch A, para 5.2, items (*f*), (*g*) and (*j*).
18 Ibid, Sch A, para 5.3.
19 Ibid, Sch B, para 5.1.4.

cannot be called in by the lender before the expiration of the loan period, except on the company's default.

The Stock Exchange rules as to the obligatory contents of listing particulars are similar in respect of the financial information which must be included to the corresponding rules governing listing particulars for shares.[20] In particular an accountant's report on the profits and losses, financial record and financial position of the company covering each of its five preceding financial years must be included if the company does not already have a listing for any of its securities, but items of concern only to investors in shares, namely, the dividends paid by the company for each of its last three financial years, arrangements for the waiver of future dividends and information about associated companies in which the issuing company holds ten per cent or more of the issued capital need not be given.[1]

6. Information in respect of management and administration

The only information required by the Listing Particulars Directive under this head in listing particulars relating to debt securities is of the names, addresses and functions of the directors of the issuing company, of the members of any supervisory board or council which the company has established to supervise the management of the company,[2] of any shareholders who, despite it being a limited company, are subject to unlimited liability for its debts,[3] and of the principal activities of all such persons outside the company if they are significant with respect to it (eg other directorships which they hold in companies active in the same or related fields).[4]

The Stock Exchange rules additionally require the disclosure of details of directors' existing and proposed service contracts with the company and its subsidiaries (except contracts which expire or are terminable within one year without the payment of compensation), but contracts which have previously been made available for inspection by the public prior to an annual general meeting of the company need not be included if they have not since been varied.[5]

7. Information about recent developments and prospects of the company

Both the Listing Particulars Directive[6] and the Stock Exchange rules[7] contain the same requirements as to the obligatory contents of listing particulars for debt securities under this head as they do in respect of the obligatory contents of listing particulars for shares, including the require-

---

20 The Stock Exchange: *Admission of Securities to Listing*, Section 3, Chapter 1, para 3.2(*a*) and Chapter 2, para 5.1.
1 Ibid, Section 3, Chapter 1, para 3.2(*a*) and Chapter 2, paras 5.1 and 5.6.
2 See footnote 11 on p 69, above.
3 See footnote 10 on p 68, above.
4 Listing Particulars Directive, Sch B, para 6.1.
5 The Stock Exchange: *Admission of Securities to Listing*, Section 3, Chapter 1, para 3.2(*a*) and Chapter 2, para 6.4.
6 Listing Particulars Directive, Sch B, paras 7.1 and 7.2 (see p 70, above).
7 The Stock Exchange: *Admission of Securities to Listing*, Section 3, Chapter 2, paras 7.1 and 7.2 (see p 70, above).

ments of the Stock Exchange rules when a profit forecast is included in the particulars. The same observations therefore apply as in connection with the corresponding part of listing particulars for shares.

LISTING PARTICULARS IN PARTICULAR CASES

The preceding account of the information which listing particulars must contain is based on the assumption that the issuing company has no listing on the Stock Exchange for any of its shares or non-convertible debt securities and that it intends to offer the shares or debt securities for which it seeks a listing to the public at large for subscription in cash, or that it has allotted or agreed to allot the securities to a merchant bank or other financial institution with a view to them being offered for sale to the public at large or placed through jobbers or dealers on the Stock Exchange. If the securities for which a listing is sought will be issued, or have already been issued, in any other way, the requirements of the Listing Particulars Directive and the Stock Exchange rules are modified so as to require the disclosure of information which is relevant to the kind of marketing operation in hand, but to dispense with the inclusion of information which would be relevant if a public offer of the securities were being made, but is unnecessary in the context of the marketing method actually being employed. The basic requirements of the Listing Particulars Directive and the Stock Exchange rules are also modified when the securities involved are of a particular character or carry special rights, such as the rights attached to convertible debt securities to convert them into, or exchange them for, equity shares and the subscription rights for shares conferred on the holders of debt securities issued with subscription warrants attached.

The particular cases which involve modifications of the normal requirements for listing particulars are (i) where the company already has a listing for securities other than those for which a listing is now sought; (ii) where the shares for which a listing is sought are offered to the existing shareholders of the company by way of a rights offer; (iii) where debt securities are convertible into or exchangeable for shares, or have warrants attached carrying the right to subscribe for shares; (iv) where the securities are debt securities guaranteed by a third person; (v) where the securities are introduced on the Stock Exchange; (vi) where the shares are issued on a capitalisation of profits or reserves, or on the exercise of conversion or exchange rights conferred by debt securities, or on the exercise of subscription rights conferred by warrants attached to debt securities; (vii) where small further issues are made of a class of shares which are already listed; (viii) where the debt securities issued are normally dealt in only by specialist dealers or financial institutions; (ix) where 'tap' issues of debt securities by credit institutions are the subject of the listing application; (x) where a listing is sought for shares issued to employees and shares of the same class are already listed; (xi) where a listing is sought for securities issued in connection with a takeover or merger; (xii) miscellaneous residual situations; and (xiii) where listing particulars require amendment after publication. The special provisions governing these cases will be dealt with in the order they are listed above.

1. Securities issued by a listed company

If a company seeks a listing for further shares and it already has a listing for any of its existing shares or debt securities, the listing particulars it must prepare and publish must contain the same detailed information under the Listing Particulars Directive as though it did not already have a listing, and the only reasons why it may in fact not have to include so much detail are:—
(a) the detail called for by Schedule A of the directive is somewhat less in the case of a listed company; (b) the Quotations Committee may be readier to authorise omissions from the listing particulars on the ground that the omitted material is of minor importance and is unlikely to affect the assessment of the company's financial position because it already has a listing, and this is particularly so when the information has already been published by way of circulars or press releases notified to the Company Announcements Office;[8] and (c) the information required to be inserted in listing particulars additional to that specified in Schedule A in order to enable investors and their advisers to make an informed assessment[9] will usually be less in the case of a listed company than an unlisted one.

The Stock Exchange rules, on the other hand, do permit a listed company seeking a listing for further shares to omit certain of the items which the rules normally require to be included in listing particulars in addition to the information called for by the directive.[10] These items are: the names and addresses of the company's bank, brokers and solicitors;[11] details of payments made or benefits given to promoters so far as the general law requires them to be disclosed;[12] the statement normally required in listing particulars if ten per cent or more of the company's shares carrying full voting rights remain unissued, namely, that further voting shares will only be issued during the year following the publication of the listing particulars if a general meeting approves the issue by ordinary resolution;[13] an accountant's report on the profits and losses, assets and liabilities, financial record and position of the company and the group of which it is the parent company covering the last five financial years (instead a comparative table setting out the items in the company's annual accounts and consolidated accounts for the last five years must be set out);[14] the other business activities of the company's directors, any former names they had, and their nationality and former nationality if it has been changed;[15] particulars of the company's secretary;[16] any waivers of remuneration by directors of the company for the last financial year and the current year;[17]

---

8 Listing Particulars Directive, art 7(*a*).
9 Ibid, art 4(1).
10 The Stock Exchange: *Admission of Securities to Listing*, Section 3, Chapter 1, para 2.1(*a*).
11 Ibid, Section 3, Chapter 2, para 1.10 (see p 57, above).
12 Ibid, Chapter 2, para 2.20. The additional matters mentioned in that paragraph need not be included either; they are cash paid, securities issued or transferred or benefits given to promoters during the preceding 2 years or proposed to be paid, issued or given to them (see p 60, above).
13 The Stock Exchange: *Admission of Securities to Listing*, Section 3, Chapter 2, para 3.5 (see p 62, above).
14 Ibid, Section 3, Chapter 2, paras 5.1 and 2 (see p 66, above).
15 Ibid, Section 3, Chapter 2, para 6.1(*b*) (see p 69, above).
16 Ibid, Section 3, Chapter 2, para 6.2 (see p 70, above).
17 Ibid, Section 3, Chapter 2, para 6.3(*b*) (see p 69, above).

an estimate of the directors' total remuneration for the current financial year;[18] and, finally, any provisions in the company's articles of association authorising directors to vote on matters in which they are interested at board meetings or to vote themselves remuneration at board meetings in the absence of an independent quorum, defining the borrowing powers of the board and providing how they may be varied, and prescribing the age limit at which directors must retire.[19]

If a company which has a listing for any of its shares or debt securities seeks a listing for debt securities carrying no conversion, exchange or subscription rights which it has issued or is about to issue, the Council of the Stock Exchange (acting through the Quotations Committee) may under the Listing Particulars Directive[20] permit the company to publish listing particulars which contain only the following items in Schedule B of the Directive: the information included in the first, second, sixth and seventh heads of the Schedule;[1] the name and the registered office or principal administrative establishment (if different) of the company;[2] an indication of the address where the documents referred to in the listing particulars are open to public inspection;[3] details of the issued capital of the company, the classes into which it is divided and the amount of capital remaining unpaid;[4] a brief description of the group to which the company belongs (if any) and of its position in the group;[5] particulars of significant pending and recent litigation or arbitration proceedings in which the company is involved;[6] if more than nine months has elapsed since the end of the financial year for which the company has last published annual accounts, an interim financial statement covering the first six months of the company's current financial year at least, with an indication that the statement has not been audited if that is so;[7] if the company's annual or consolidated accounts do not comply with the law or do not give a true and fair view of its financial position, further information to remedy the defect;[8] and a statement of the total loan capital of the company outstanding, distinguishing between guaranteed or secured loans and unguaranteed or unsecured loans, and the company's other borrowing and indebtedness and its contingent liabilities.[9] When published, the listing particulars must be accompanied by a copy of the company's annual accounts for its last financial year and, if it prepared consolidated accounts, a copy of those accounts for the same year, but the Quotations Committee may permit the company to dispense with one of these two sets of accounts if it furnishes no additional material information.[10]

---

18 The Stock Exchange: *Admission of Securities to Listing*, Section 3, Chapter 2, para 6.3(*c*) (see p 69, above).
19 Ibid, Section 3, Chapter 2, para 6.9 (see p 70, above).
20 Listing Particulars Directive, art 9(1).
 1 See pp 57, 58, 68 and 70, above.
 2 Listing Particulars Directive, Sch B, para 3.1.0 (see p 61, above).
 3 Ibid, para 3.1.5 (see p 61, above).
 4 Ibid, para 3.2.0 (see p 75, above).
 5 Ibid, para 3.2.2 (see p 75, above).
 6 Ibid, para 4.3 (see p 65, above).
 7 Ibid, para 5.1.2 (see p 66, above).
 8 Ibid, para 5.1.3 (see p 67, above).
 9 Ibid, para 5.1.4 (see p 76, above).
10 Listing Particulars Directive, art 9(2) and (3).

The Stock Exchange rules permit companies which already have a listing for any of their securities and seek a listing for an issue of debt securities which carry no conversion, exchange or subscription rights, to publish listing particulars in conformity with the minimum requirements of the Listing Particulars Directive.[11] Additionally, the Stock Exchange rules permit such listing particulars to omit the additional items of information which are required by the Stock Exchange rules in listing particulars for debt securities published by an unlisted company, but which may be omitted by a listed company from listing particulars for a further issue of shares.[11] In terms the Stock Exchange rules permit the omission from listing particulars for debt securities published by a listed company only certain of those additional items (namely, particulars of the company's bankers, brokers and solicitors, details of payments and benefits given to promoters and a description of the company's different business activities and the relative importance of each[12]), but the other items which must be included in listing particulars for shares published by an unlisted company, but which need not be included if the company has a listing, do not have to be included in listing particulars for debt securities published even by an unlisted company, and so the permission to omit certain items from the listing particulars does not need to authorise their omission expressly.

2. Rights offers

If a company or other issuer seeks a listing for shares issued or to be issued by way of a rights offer made to its existing shareholders, and the issuer does not have a listing for any of its other shares or debt securities, the listing particulars must contain the same information under the Listing Particulars Directive and the Stock Exchange rules as listing particulars for shares offered for subscription or purchase to the public at large, and no exceptions are made for any items of information. This is because the rights offered to the shareholders may be renounced or assigned by them to third persons who have had no previous connection with the company and therefore, as members of the general public, need to be as fully informed about it and its affairs as if the company were making a direct public offering of its shares; this is equally true whether the rights offer is made by means of letters of rights which call for an express subscription by each shareholder of the new shares offered to him, or by provisional letters of allotment which do not.

However, if a company which already has a listing on the Stock Exchange for any of its shares, makes a rights offer of further shares (not necessarily of the same class as those already listed) to its existing shareholders in satisfaction of their preferential subscription rights[13] or otherwise in strict proportion to their existing shareholdings, the Listing Particulars Directive and the Stock Exchange rules permit listing particulars in respect of the shares to omit certain items of information which would have to be included in listing particulars for a further issue of shares

---

11 The Stock Exchange: *Admission of Securities to Listing*, Section 3, Chapter 1, para 3.2(*b*).
12 Ibid, Section 3, Chapter 2, paras 1.10, 2.20 and 4.4.
13 For example, the preferential subscription rights for equity securities given to existing equity shareholders by the Companies Act 1980, s 17(1) and (2) (now Companies Act 1985, s 89(1)–(3)).

by a listed company when the shares are to be marketed by a public offering.[14] This facility to omit further items of information is available even though the rights offer is freely renounceable, so that members of the general public, as renounces, may acquire the shares immediately dealings in them begin, and even though the shares are of an entirely new class carrying rights or subject to burdens (such as subordination for the payment of dividends or the repayment of capital) which no existing class of shares has carried or borne. It is essential, however, that the new shares should be offered to existing shareholders in proportion to their existing shareholdings, although it is not necessary that the offer should extend to all classes of existing shareholders; a rights offer of preference shares made only to existing preference shareholders is therefore within the facility. The element of proportionality in the offer must nevertheless be maintained, and so an open offer to all existing shareholders on the understanding that if they apply collectively for more new shares than the number available, their subscriptions will be scaled down, is not within the facility and full listing particulars must be published.

Where the facility given by the Listing Particulars Directive to reduce the volume of information in listing particulars in connection with a rights offer is available, the listing particulars need only contain the following information under Schedule A of the Directive, plus such further information as is necessary to enable investors to make an informed assessment. The information required under Schedule A consists of:[15] the information called for by the first, second and seventh heads of Schedule A;[16] the name and the registered office of the company and its principal administrative establishment if different from its registered office;[17] the address where documents referred to in the listing particulars are open to public inspection;[18] the company's issued share capital and the classes of shares into which it is divided, together with details of unpaid capital;[19] particulars of the persons who can exercise control over the company;[20] the persons who directly or indirectly hold at least five per cent of the company's issued share capital;[1] a brief description of the group of companies to which the issuer belongs and its position in the group;[2] particulars of shares in the issuing company held by itself or by any other company in which the issuing company holds more than 50 per cent of the issued share capital;[3] information about the dependence of the company on patents and patent licences, on industrial, commercial or financial contracts and on new manufacturing processes if they are of fundamental importance;[4] particulars of pending and recent litigation or arbitration proceedings involving

14 Listing Particulars Directive, art 8(1); The Stock Exchange: *Admission of Securities to Listing*, Section 3, Chapter 1, para 3.1(*b*).
15 Listing Particulars Directive, art 8(1).
16 See pp 57, 58 and 70, above.
17 Listing Particulars Directive, Sch A, para 3.1.0 (see p 61, above).
18 Ibid, para 3.1.5 (see p 61, above).
19 Ibid, paras 3.2.0 and 3.2.1 (see p 61, above).
20 Ibid, para 3.2.6 (see p 62, above).
 1 Ibid, para 3.2.7; The Stock Exchange (Listing) Regulations 1984, Sch 2, para 9 (see p 62, above).
 2 Listing Particulars Directive, Sch A, para 3.2.8 (see p 62, above).
 3 Ibid, para 3.2.9 (see p 62, above).
 4 Ibid, para 4.2 (see p 64, above).

the company which have had or may have had a significant effect on the company's financial position;[5] information about interruptions in the company's business which have had or may have a significant effect on the company's financial position;[6] information on the principal investments currently being made by the company or intended to be made by it in the future under firm commitments (other than the acquisition of shares in other companies);[7] an interim financial statement covering at least the first six months of the current financial year if more than 9 months have elapsed since the end of the last financial year for which the company has published annual or consolidated accounts;[8] if the company's annual or consolidated accounts do not give a true and fair view of the company's financial position, or if they do not comply with the governing legal requirements, supplemental information to remedy the defect;[9] all the information called for under heads 4 and 7 of Schedule A in respect of the group of which the company is the parent company;[10] particulars of the company's directors, of members of its supervisory board or council (if any), of its shareholders with unlimited personal liability, and of its promoters if the company has been incorporated for less than five years;[11] the total amounts of remuneration paid and benefits given to directors and members of the supervisory board or council of the company by the company and its subsidiaries during its last financial year;[12] the total number of shares in the company held by the company's directors and members of its supervisory board or council, and the number of shares in the company for which they have subscription options;[13] information about the interests of directors and members of the supervisory board or council of the company in transactions of the company which are unusual in their nature or conditions;[14] and the total amount of outstanding loans made by the company to its directors and any guarantees or securities given by the company for such loans made by third persons.[15] When published, the listing particulars must be accompanied by a copy of the company's annual accounts for its last financial year.[16]

Under the Stock Exchange rules the listing particulars published by a listed company in connection with a rights offer of shares may omit the information called for by those rules in addition to that required by Schedule A of the Listing Particulars Directive if the supplemental information could be omitted from listing particulars in connection with a general offer of shares for public subscription or purchase.[17] Moreover, the listing particulars for a rights offer of shares by a listed company may omit two further items of supplemental information called for by the Stock Exchange rules, namely, a statement that appropriate indemnities have

5 Ibid, para 4.4 (see p 65, above).
6 Ibid, para 4.5 (see p 65, above).
7 Ibid, para 4.7.1 and 2 (see p 65, above).
8 Ibid, para 5.1.4 (see p 66, above).
9 Ibid, para 5.1.5 (see p 67, above).
10 Ibid, para 5.5 (see p 68, above).
11 Ibid, para 6.1 (see p 68, above).
12 Ibid, para 6.2.0 (see p 69, above).
13 Ibid, para 6.2.1 (see p 69, above).
14 Ibid, para 6.2.2 (see p 69, above).
15 Ibid, para 6.2.3 (see p 69, above).
16 Listing Particulars Directive, art 8(3) and (4).
17 See p 79, above.

been obtained for any income tax liability the company may incur on an apportionment by the Inland Revenue of the company's undistributed profits among its shareholders if it is, or has been, a close company, and appropriate clearances have not been obtained,[18] and a statement that, in the absence of appropriate indemnities, the directors have been advised that the company is not likely to incur a material liability for capital transfer tax on the transfer of any of its assets gratuitously or at an undervalue when the company is, or has been, a close company.[19]

3. Debt securities which are convertible or exchangeable or have subscription warrants attached

This category of debt securities comprises debentures, debenture stock, loan stock and notes which by their terms can be converted at the option of the holder into ordinary or other fully paid shares of the issuing company or another company; debentures etc which by their terms can be exchanged for ordinary or other fully paid shares which are held by trustees or nominees for the issuing or other company until the exchange option is exercised; and debentures etc accompanied on their issue by subscription warrants entitling the holder of the debentures, or if the terms of issue permit, a person to whom he transfers warrants separately from the debentures, to subscribe for a specified number of shares of the issuing or other company at a stated price.

In practice convertible, but not exchangeable, debentures are issued by United Kingdom companies. Exchangeable debt securities are issued principally by French companies, and the advantage of them is supposedly that the shares for which the debt securities can be exchanged exist from the time the debt securities are issued and can readily be transferred to holders of debt securities who exercise their option; in fact the advantage is more theoretical than real, because French companies which issue convertible debt securities can increase their share capital conditionally when the debt securities are issued, so that it is a mere formality for the directors to issue the requisite shares in satisfaction of the company's contractual obligation when holders of debt securities exercise the option to convert. The consideration given to the issuing or other company for the shares issued or transferred when the conversion or exchange option is exercised is the cancellation of the debt secured by the surrendered debt security, which by its terms of issue is deemed to become immediately due. Because the capital for the shares is paid up by the discharge of the company's indebtedness, the conversion or exchange ratio fixed by the terms of the debt securities must not result in the debt security holder acquiring shares with a paid up value greater than the paid up value of the debt securities which he surrenders; if this were done, the shares would be issued at a discount, and the company would be able to recover the amount of the discount in cash from the former holder of the debt securities to whom the shares have been issued or transferred.[20]

18 The Stock Exchange: *Admission of Securities to Listing*, Section 3, Chapter 1, para 3(1)(*b*) and Chapter 2, para 3.13 (see p 63, above).
19 Ibid, Chapter 2, para 3.14 (see p 63, above).
20 *Mosely v Koffyfontein Mines Ltd* [1904] 2 Ch 108; Companies Act 1980, s 21(1) and (2) (now Companies Act 1985, s 100(1) and (2)).

Debt securities with subscription warrants attached are issued by United Kingdom, European, American and Commonwealth companies. The debt security by its terms entitles its holder at certain periods to subscribe for a number of new shares in the issuing company or another company proportionate to the nominal value of the debt securities, and to pay an issue price for them which is fixed by the terms of the debt securities. The value of the subscription warrants lies in the difference between that pre-fixed price and the prospective market value of the shares at the time when the option to subscribe for them becomes exercisable. Provided that the issue price is not less than the nominal value of the shares, the fact that there is a difference between the issue price and the market price of the shares when the option to subscribe is exercised, does not mean that the shares are issued at a discount.[1]

General offers

Because investors in convertible or exchangeable debt securities or debt securities with subscription warrants attached are interested in the company both as holders of debt securities and as prospective or potential shareholders, listing particulars for such securities, whether already issued or about to be issued, must give the information which is needed to protect investors as debt security holders and also the additional information which they need as prospective shareholders. The Listing Particulars Directive consequently provides that the listing particulars must contain information as to the nature of the shares comprised in the conversion, exchange or subscription option and the rights attached to them; the information required under heads 3 to 7 inclusive of Schedule A of the directive;[2] the information required under head 2 of Schedule B of the directive;[3] the names addresses and qualifications of the auditors of the company's accounts for its last 3 financial years, a statement that those accounts have been audited, and if audit reports on them have been refused or qualified, the reasons given by the auditors for the refusal or the terms of the qualification, and an indication of other information mentioned in the listing particulars which has been audited;[4] and finally, a statement of the conditions and procedures for the exercise of the conversion, exchange or subscription options, and an indication of when and how they may be altered (eg with the consent of a special majority of the debt security holders).[5]

Whether the issuing company has or does not have a listing for any of its securities, if it seeks a listing for debt securities carrying conversion exchange or subscription rights which it has issued or is about to issue

---

1 *Hilder v Dexter* [1902] AC 474.
2 That is, the information required in listing particulars for shares in respect of the issuing company and its share capital, the company's business activities, the company's assets and liabilities, financial position and profits and losses, the company's management and administration and the company's recent development and prospects.
3 That is, the information required in listing particulars for debt securities in respect of the loan secured by the debt securities and the terms of those securities.
4 Listing Particulars Directive, Sch A, para 1.3 (see p 57, above). Curiously the other information called for under head 2 of Sch B need not be included, although it is required by the Stock Exchange rules (The Stock Exchange: *Admission of Securities to Listing*, Section 3, Chapter 7, para 3.3 (*a*) (iii)).
5 Listing Particulars Directive, art 14(1).

otherwise than by way of a rights offer, the information to be included in the listing particulars under heads 3 to 7 of Schedule A and head 2 of Schedule B of the Listing Particulars Directive will be the full information under those heads; this is because there are no exceptions to the requirement of that information in full merely because the company already has a listing.[6] On the other hand, some of the supplemental information required by the Stock Exchange rules need not be included in such listing particulars, and if the company already has a listing for any of its securities, more items of supplemental information may be omitted than if it has not. If the company does not already have a Stock Exchange listing, and the company has ten per cent or more of its share capital carrying full voting rights in the form of unissued shares, the listing particulars need not include a statement that the company will not make a material issue of those shares within the next 12 months (otherwise than by way of a rights offer) without the approval of a general meeting;[7] nor a statement that appropriate indemnities have been obtained against the company's potential liability for income tax on undistributed profits if the company is, or has been, a close company;[8] nor a statement that the directors have been advised that the company is not likely to incur any liability for capital transfer tax if no appropriate indemnities have been obtained.[9] The listing particulars must, however, contain an accountant's report on the company's profits, losses, assets and liabilities and on its financial record and present position for each of the preceding five financial years.[10] If the company already has a listing for any of its securities, the listing particulars may omit (in addition to the three items mentioned above) particulars of the company's bankers, brokers and solicitors;[11] a statement of payments and benefits made or given to promoters;[12] details of the outside business activities of the company's directors, members of its supervisory board or council and promoters;[13] particulars of the company's secretary;[14] particulars of any arrangement by directors of the company to waive future remuneration and an estimate of directors' total remuneration for the current financial year;[15] and finally, a summary of any provisions in the company's articles of association authorising directors to vote at board meetings on matters in which they are interested, or to fix their own remuneration in the absence of an independent quorum, or prescribing the borrowing powers of the company or an age limit for directors' retirement.[16] It will be noted that the items of information required by the Stock Exchange rules which may be omitted from listing particulars published by a listed company when it seeks a listing for debt securities carrying conversion, exchange or subscription rights, are rather less than the omissions permitted when the

---

6   See pp 79 and 80, above.
7   The Stock Exchange: *Admission of Securities to Listing*, Section 3, Chapter 1, para 3.3(a) and Chapter 2, para 3.5 (see p 62, above).
8   Ibid, Section 3, Chapter 2, para 3.13 (see p 63, above).
9   Ibid, Section 3, Chapter 2, para 3.14 (see p 63, above).
10 Ibid, Section 3, Chapter 2, para 5.1 (see p 65, above).
11 Ibid, Section 3, Chapter 1, para 3.3(*a*) and Chapter 2, para 1.10 (see p 57, above).
12 Ibid, Section 3, Chapter 2, para 2.20 (see p 60, above).
13 Ibid, Section 3, Chapter 2, para 6.1(*b*) (see p 69, above).
14 Ibid, Section 3, Chapter 2, para 6.2 (see p 70, above).
15 Ibid, Section 3, Chapter 2, para 6.3(*b*) and (*c*) (see p 69, above).
16 Ibid, Section 3, Chapter 2, para 6.9 (see p 70, above).

listing particulars relate to debt securities which carry no such rights.[17] This is, of course, because of the interest which investors in convertible etc debt securities have in obtaining information which an investor in shares of the company would require in order to make a proper appraisal of the shares.

If a company publishes listing particulars in respect of debt securities which carry the right to convert them into shares of another company, or to exchange them for such shares, or to subscribe for such shares, the Listing Particulars Directive requires the listing particulars to contain similar information to that required if the conversion, exchange or subscription rights were exercisable in relation to shares of the issuing company, but the information given under heads 3 to 7 of Schedule A and in respect of auditors and the audit of accounts[18] must be given in respect of the other company whose shares may be acquired by holders of the debt securities, and instead of limiting the information given in respect of the company issuing the debt securities to that called for by head 2 of Schedule B, all the information required by Schedule B must be included.[19] The reason why full information must be given under Schedule B is, of course, that the debt securities are, as regards the interests which the holders will have in the issuing company, the equivalent of ordinary debt securities of that company which carry no conversion, exchange or subscription rights. The information which must be included in the listing particulars under the directive will be the same whether the issuing company or the company whose shares may be acquired by the exercise of the conversion, exchange or subscription rights has or does not have a Stock Exchange listing for any of its securities. The Stock Exchange rules on the other hand, do make some concessions in respect of the supplemental information which must be included if the issuing company already has a listing. If it has no listing, the extent of the information to be included will be similar to that required if the company were issuing debt securities with conversion, exchange or subscription rights in relation to its own shares; all the information which would be required if the issuing company were issuing debt securities with no conversion, exchange or subscription rights must be included,[20] together with all the information about the other company (whose shares may be acquired by the exercise of the conversion, exchange or subscription rights) which would be required if it were issuing the convertible etc debt securities itself.[1] The supplemental information which must be included is basically the same whether the company which issues the convertible etc debt securities or the other company whose shares are subject to the conversion etc rights has a Stock Exchange listing for any of its securities or not, but with the modification that if the issuing company has a listing, the listing particulars need not include particulars of its bankers, solicitors or brokers,[2] nor information about payments made and benefits given to promoters,[3] and instead of an accountant's report on the

---

17　See p 80, above.
18　Listing Particulars Directive, Sch A, para 1.3 (see p 57, above).
19　Ibid, art 14(2).
20　That is, all the detailed information in listing particulars published by a company none of whose securities are already listed on the Stock Exchange (see pp 72 et seq, above).
 1　The Stock Exchange: *Admission of Securities to Listing*, Section 3, Chapter 1, para 3.3(*c*).
 2　Ibid, Section 3, Chapter 2, para 1.10 (see p 57, above).
 3　Ibid, Section 3, Chapter 2, para 2.20 (see p 60, above).

issuing company's financial record for the last five financial years, a comparative table of the figures in the company's annual accounts and consolidated accounts must be included.[4]

Rights offers by listed companies

When a company which already has a listing of any of its shares on the Stock Exchange seeks a listing for an issue by it of debt securities which carry conversion, exchange or subscription rights in respect of shares of the same or another company (whether listed or not), the Council of the Stock Exchange (through the Quotations Committee) may permit listing particulars to be published which omit certain information which the directive would otherwise require, but only if the debt securities are offered by the issuing company to its existing shareholders in satisfaction of their preferential subscription rights[5] or otherwise in strict proportion to their existing shareholdings.[6] When published, the listing particulars must be accompanied by a copy of the company's annual accounts for its last financial year and, if it prepared consolidated accounts, a copy of those accounts for the same year, but the Quotations Committee may permit the company to dispense with one of these two sets of accounts if it furnishes no additional material information.[7]

The information which such listing particulars in respect of a rights offer of convertible or exchangeable debt securities, or of debt securities with subscription warrants attached, must contain under the Listing Particulars Directive is the same as that required in listing particulars for such securities which are marketed otherwise than by a rights offer,[8] except that the information about the company whose shares are the subject of the conversion, exchange or subscription rights (whether the issuing company or another) is confined to that required by Schedule A of the Directive in listing particulars for a rights offer of shares of that company made by it to its own shareholders.[6] In respect of the debt securities as such, the listing particulars must contain the same information as would be required in listing particulars for convertible debt securities offered to the public generally, but in respect of the shares which may be acquired by the exercise of the conversion, exchange or subscription rights, the listing particulars must contain the same information as is required in listing particulars for a rights offer of those shares. The Stock Exchange rules repeat the requirements of the Listing Particulars Directive by detailing the items which listing particulars for a rights offer of convertible etc debt securities by a listed company must contain.[9] The supplemental information which the Stock Exchange rules require to be included in listing particulars but which may be omitted from listing particulars relating to a

---

4 The Stock Exchange: *Admission of Securities to Listing*, Section 3, Chapter 2, para 5.2 (see p 66, above).

5 For example, the preferential subscription rights for equity securities (including debentures carrying the right to convert into, or subscribe for, equity securities) conferred on existing equity shareholders by the Companies Act 1980, s 17(1), (2) and (11) (now Companies Act 1985, s 89(1)–(3) and s 94(2) and (5)).

6 Listing Particulars Directive, art 8(2).

7 Ibid, art 8(3) and (4).

8 See p 85, above.

9 The Stock Exchange: *Admission of Securities to Listing*, Section 3, Chapter 1, para 3.3(*b*).

rights issue of shares by a listed company, may also be omitted from listing particulars for a rights offer by such a company of convertible etc debt securities,[10] and because the listing particulars relate to debt securities, details of payments and benefits made or given to promoters may also be omitted.[11]

4. Guaranteed debt securities

When listing particulars relate to debt securities which are guaranteed by a third person (usually a bank or a financial institution), the listing particulars must contain the normal detailed information about the issuing company under Schedule B of the Listing Particulars Directive and also additional information in respect of the guarantor or surety, covering the matters which would be included in the listing particulars under heads 3 to 7 of Schedule B if the guarantor were the issuer.[12] Also the listing particulars must give particulars of the auditors of the guarantor, state whether its annual accounts have been audited (presumably for the last three financial years), set out the auditors' reasons for any refusal of auditors' reports by them or the qualifications they have included in their reports, and state whether any information about the guarantor included in the listing particulars (other than its annual accounts) has been audited.[13] If there are two or more guarantors, the information under Schedule B must be given in respect of all of them.[14] The contract of guarantee must be available for public inspection at the offices of the issuer and the financial organisations which will act as its paying agents.[15]

The information to be given about the guarantor is the same whether the guarantee is of the whole or part of the principal of the loan secured by the debt securities, and whether it extends also to unpaid interest or any other payments for which the issuer of the debt securities is liable. The terms of the guarantee affect the contents of the listing particulars only in that their nature and scope is one of the items of information which the listing particulars must contain,[16] and the existence and terms of the guarantee do not affect the information which the listing particulars must give about the issuing company. The content of this information will depend on whether the issuer already has a listing for any of its securities on the Stock Exchange, whether the debt securities are offered to the public generally or by way of a rights offer, and whether the securities carry the right for the holder to convert them into or exchange them for shares, or the right to subscribe for shares of the issuing company.

The Stock Exchange rules give effect to the provisions of the Listing Particulars Directive in respect of guaranteed debt securities by requiring the same information relating to the issuing company as though they were

---

10 Ibid (see p 83, above).
11 The Stock Exchange: *Admission of Securities to Listing*, Section 3, Chapter 2, para 2.20 (see p 60, above).
12 Listing Particulars Directive, art 13(1) (see pp 75 and 77, above).
13 Ibid, and Sch B, para 1(3) (see p 57, above).
14 Ibid, art 13(3).
15 Ibid, art 13(4). The Stock Exchange rules refer to the issuer's registrars and paying agents (The Stock Exchange: *Admission of Securities to Listing*, Section 3, Chapter 2, para 2.16).
16 Listing Particulars Directive, Sch B, para 2.2.1.

not guaranteed.[17] In respect of the guarantor, the Stock Exchange rules additionally require the same information to be given as if the guarantor were an issuer of debt securities none of whose existing securities were already listed, but the only information which need be given about the guarantor under the heading of information concerning the securities for which a listing is sought is a summary of the provisions of the guarantor's memorandum and articles of association governing alterations in its share capital and in the rights attached to classes of its shares.[18] If the guarantor has a listing for any of its securities, the listing particulars may omit details of its bankers, brokers and solicitors,[19] and of any payments made or benefits given to its promoters,[20] and the particulars need not contain an accountant's report on the guarantor's financial record for the last two financial years, but must include a comparative table of the figures in its annual accounts for those years.[1]

5. Securities introduced on the Stock Exchange

Listing particulars may be published in connection with an application for the listing of shares or debt securities which are offered for subscription or purchase simultaneously with the application, or for the listing of securities which have already been issued. In the latter situation the grant of the listing will result in the securities being introduced on the Stock Exchange, and the willingness of the Quotations Committee to admit them to listing will depend on whether the securities are already held by a wide enough range of investors for there to be a likelihood of active dealings in them and on whether there are arrangements for making a substantial fraction of the securities (ie 25 per cent of an issue of shares)[2] available for purchase by the public.[3]

If securities are to be introduced on the Stock Exchange, listing particulars must be published which contain the full information required by the Listing Particulars Directive when securities of an issuing company which has no listing for any of its securities are offered to the public for subscription or purchase.[4] In the unusual circumstance of the issuer already having a listing for some of its existing securities and seeking a listing for others of them which have already been issued, it suffices that the listing particulars contain the somewhat less extensive information required in listing particulars published when an issuer with a listing for its existing securities seeks a listing for further securities which are offered to the public for subscription or purchase.[5]

There are, however, certain situations where the publication of listing particulars on an introduction of securities on the Stock Exchange may either be dispensed with altogether by the Stock Exchange Council (acting

---

17 The Stock Exchange: *Admission of Securities to Listing*, Section 3, Chapter 1, para 4.2(*a*).
18 Ibid, Section 3, Chapter 1, para 4.2(*b*) (see p 62, above).
19 Ibid, Section 3, Chapter 2, para 1.10 (see p 57, above).
20 Ibid, Section 3, Chapter 2, para 2.20.
 1 Ibid, Section 3, Chapter 1, para 4.2(*b*) and Chapter 2, para 5.2.
 2 Ibid, Section 1, Chapter 2, para 8.
 3 Ibid, Section 1, Chapter 3, paras 3.1 to 3.3.
 4 See pp 57 and 72, above.
 5 See p 79, above.

through the Quotations Committee), or where the Committee may permit the publication of a shortened form of listing particulars. This is where not more than 12 months before the admission of the securities to listing a document has been published which in the opinion of the Quotations Committee contains information equivalent to that required in listing particulars (a) in connection with a public offering of the securities for subscription or purchase; or (b) in connection with a takeover offer by which the securities were offered in exchange for those of the company sought to be acquired; or (c) in connection with the issue of the securities to the holders of securities of another company, or in some cases to the other company itself, in exchange for the transfer of the whole or part of its undertaking to the issuer on a merger of the other company with the issuer, or on a division of the other company's undertaking between two or more companies, or on a transfer of the whole or part of the other company's assets and liabilities in exchange for the issue of securities by the acquiring company or a third company, or on a transfer of assets (other than cash) to the acquiring company in exchange for an issue of securities by it or a third company.[6]

Prior public offering

In the first of these situations the company or a merchant bank will have published a prospectus conforming to the requirements of the Companies Acts[7] (which are considerably less exacting than those of the Listing Particulars Directive), but if the prospectus was published in the United Kingdom and included additional material not required by the Companies Acts but sufficient to satisfy the Listing Particulars Directive, the Quotations Committee may permit the publication of further material which brings the information given in the prospectus up to date, and the document containing the further information will then serve the function of listing particulars. The original prospectus and the document containing the further material must be available for public inspection at the registered office of the company and at the offices of the financial organisations which act as its paying agents, and the further material must be published in the same way as listing particulars.[6] Furthermore, the Quotations Committee may require the actual publication of listing particulars containing the whole or part of the information in the original prospectus and the further information to bring it up to date, with or without supplemental information to correlate the two parts of the listing particulars.[6] The Stock Exchange rules require the publication of listing particulars in all cases, and unless the Quotations Committee requires the inclusion of supplemental information, the listing particulars will consist of the original prospectus and the additional material required to bring it up to date.[8] The listing particulars must state that an application has been made to the Stock Exchange for the securities in question to be admitted to listing, and also a declaration by the directors of the company that to the best of their

---

6 Listing Particulars Directive, art 6(1).
7 Companies Act 1948, s 38(1) and Fourth Schedule (now Companies Act 1985, s 56(1) and Sch 3).
8 The Stock Exchange: *Admission of Securities to Listing*, Section 3, Chapter 1, para 5(2).

knowledge and belief (after the exercise of due care to verify it) the information given in the listing particulars is in accordance with the facts and omits nothing likely to affect the import of it.[9]

Prior issue on a takeover or merger

Listing particulars will, as shown below,[10] have to be published in connection with a takeover if the offeror company offers an issue of its shares or the shares of a third company (eg its parent company) in exchange for the shares in the offeree company which it seeks to acquire, and a listing is sought for the new shares. Equally, if the acquiring company in a merger issues new shares for which a listing is sought in exchange for the undertaking of the other company it acquires, listing particulars will have to be published.[10] However, if a takeover or merger is effected by the issue of unlisted shares of the offeror or acquiring company (eg when the shares of the target or acquired company are themselves unlisted), the document which the offeror or acquiring company sets out the terms of its offer will not be a prospectus.[11] Even if a takeover offer is made for the shares of a public company or for the shares of a private company whose shares were listed or dealt in on the Unlisted Securities Market within ten years before the takeover offer is made, or dealings in whose shares were regularly advertised in a newspaper for at least six months during that ten year period, or which (while it was a public company) issued a prospectus during that ten year period, the offer document in connection with the takeover will only have to contain the information about the offeror company required by the Takeover Code,[12] which is far less than that required in listing particulars.

It is true that a circular issued to the shareholders of the company sought to be acquired offering them shares or other securities in the acquiring company in the case of a merger, or shares in the offeror company or a third company in the case of a takeover bid, will be an investment circular and it will only be lawful to send it out if this is done with the permission of the Secretary of State for Trade and Industry,[13] or by a dealer licensed by him,[14] or by an exempted dealer,[15] or by a member of the Stock Exchange,[16] and that a circular sent out by a licensed dealer must contain 'sufficient

---

9 The Stock Exchange: *Admission of Securities to Listing*, Section 3, Chapter 2, paras 1.7 and 2.1.

10 See p 103, below.

11 *Governments Stock and Other Securities Investment Co Ltd v Christopher* [1956] 1 All ER 490. But if made by a private company, it may be a public offering of its shares in breach of the Companies Act 1980, s 15(1) (now Companies Act 1985, s 81(1)).

12 The City Code on Takeover and Mergers (1985 Edition), Introduction, para 3.

13 Prevention of Fraud (Investments) Act 1958, s 14(1) and (2).

14 Ibid, s 14(3) (*a*) (i). The dealer must hold a principal's licence issued under s 3(1) of the Act.

15 Prevention of Fraud (Investments) Act 1958, s 14(3)(*a*)(ii). An exempted dealer is one declared to be exempted from the restrictions imposed by the Act by an order of the Secretary of State on the ground that the dealer's main business consists of something other than dealing in securities, or of dealing in securities only by issuing prospectuses, placing or underwriting securities, or carrying out transactions with professional dealers (s 16(1) and (2)).

16 Prevention of Fraud (Investments) Act 1958, s 14(3)(*a*)(i) and s 26(1).

information about the investment to provide a person such as [those] to whom the offer is addressed with an adequate and reasonable basis for deciding whether or not . . . to accept the offer',[17] and that a circular sent out by any other person is expected to contain the same information.[18] Nevertheless, the level of information required in such a circular will not necessarily be equivalent to that in listing particulars, and if it is not, full listing particulars must be published when the securities issued by the acquiring or offeror company are later introduced on the Stock Exchange.

However, if the introduction on the Stock Exchange takes place not more than 12 months after the offer document or circular is published in the United Kingdom, and the Quotations Committee considers that the earlier document in fact contained information equivalent to that required in listing particulars, it may under the Listing Particulars Directive dispense with the publication of listing particulars when the securities issued under the takeover or merger are later introduced on the Stock Exchange, provided that a document containing further information bringing the earlier document up to date is also published as though it were listing particulars.[19] Copies of the earlier document and the document containing the further information must be made available for public inspection at the company's registered offices and at the offices of its paying agents.[19] Furthermore, the Quotations Committee may require the actual publication of listing particulars containing the whole or part of the information contained in the original document and the supplemental information to bring it up to date, with or without supplemental information to correlate the two parts of the listing particulars.[19] The Stock Exchange rules extend the requirements of the Listing Particulars Directive by making it necessary to publish listing particulars in all cases, and the rules governing their content and form are the same as for listing particulars when securities are introduced on the Stock Exchange within 12 months after a prospectus is published offering them for subscription or purchase by the public.[20]

Prior issue on a division or transfer of assets

The concessions made by the Listing Particulars Directive and the Stock Exchange rules when securities are introduced on the Stock Exchange within 12 months after the publication of a document in connection with a takeover or merger giving information equivalent to that required in listing particulars, extend also to introductions of securities within the same

---

17 The Licensed Dealers (Conduct of Business) Rules 1983 (SI 1983/585), para 9(1)(a).
18 If a takeover offer is made by an offeror who holds less than 50 per cent of the equity share capital carrying voting rights of a private company which is not within the City Takeover Code (see footnote 12 above), and the offer is conditional on acceptance by sufficient shareholders of the offeree company that the offeror will, if the offer is successful, hold more than 50 per cent of the equity share capital of the offeree company carrying voting rights, the offer document may be circulated without the specific permission of the Secretary of State and need only contain limited information about the offeror and the offer, but this is so only if the offer is recommended by the board of the offeree company and the offeror makes copies of various relevant documents, accounts and reports available to shareholders of the offeree company (General Permission No 3 dated 20 April 1983, issued under the Prevention of Fraud (Investments) Act 1959, s 14(2)).
19 Listing Particulars Directive, art 6(1).
20 The Stock Exchange: *Admission of Securities to Listing*, Section 3, Chapter 1, para 5.2.

period if the securities were issued under certain similar operations in connection with which such a document was published.[1] The other operations are a division of a company (that is the transfer of parts of its undertaking to several different companies in return for the issue of shares of those companies or other companies to shareholders of the original company), the transfer of the whole or part of a company's assets and liabilities to another company in exchange for that company or a third company issuing shares or other securities to the original company or its shareholders (eg the transfer of a company's undertaking to a subsidiary of another company in return for an issue of the other company's shares), and the transfer of assets other than cash to a company in return for the issue of shares or other securities by that company or another company to the transferor company or its shareholders (eg the transfer of shares in a company to another company in return for an issue of its shares).

Divisions or demergers of companies have increased in number over recent years, but they usually involve private companies or public companies which do not have or seek a Stock Exchange listing, or which, if they have a listing, transfer parts of their undertakings to unlisted companies (eg on a management buy-out). There is then usually no desire to obtain a listing for the shares of the successor companies immediately, and it is unlikely that the securities issued by them will be introduced on the Stock Exchange within the following 12 months. It is also uncommon in practice for listed companies to transfer their undertakings in return for an issue of shares or other securities to themselves or their shareholders, and for that reason mergers in the form of a transfer of assets are far less common than takeovers or mergers by the acquiring company taking transfers of the shares in the acquired company. In fact, the only operations of this kind which are at all common are the transfer by a parent company of a group of part of its undertaking to a newly created subsidiary in return for the issue of the subsidiary's shares to it; the similar operation of the transfer of the whole or part of a subsidiary's undertaking to another subsidiary in the same group, whether newly formed or not, in return for the issue of shares by the acquiring subsidiary to the disposing one or to the parent company; and, finally, the hiving down of a profitable part of the undertaking of a company in receivership or liquidation by the transfer of that part of its undertaking to a newly formed subsidiary with a view to the sale of the subsidiary's shares to a purchaser. In none of these cases is there usually any intention to seek a listing on the Stock Exchange for the newly issued shares and no document is published which is comparable to listing particulars; this is so even if the parent company or the company whose undertaking is hived down already has a Stock Exchange listing for its shares.

However, although divisions and acquisitions of undertakings in return for the issue of securities for which a Stock Exchange listing is sought are not frequent, they are occasionally met with, and it is a useful facility that the introduction of the securities on the Stock Exchange within 12 months of the issue of an offer document or similar document may be effected upon the publication of a truncated, supplementary form of listing particulars.[1]

---

1 Listing Particulars Directive, art 6(1); The Stock Exchange: *Admission of Securities to Listing*, Section 3, Chapter 1, para 5.2.

Moreover, the extension of the facility to all acquisitions of undertakings or assets (including shares or other securities of companies) in exchange for the issue of securities of the acquiring company means that it is unnecessary to have a strict definition of a takeover or merger in the Listing Particulars Directive or the Stock Exchange rules. If a company acquires shares in another company from their holders in exchange for an issue of its own or another company's shares or other securities, the publication of truncated listing particulars may be permitted by the Quotations Committee when those shares or other securities are introduced on the Stock Exchange, whether the acquisition of the shares in the other company was made under a takeover offer in the narrow sense (ie one under which the offeror or acquiring company obtained voting control in the other company), or whether the bid was made to consolidate control over the other company which the offeror already had (ie an offer to acquire outstanding minority shareholdings), or whether the bid would in no case result in the offeror having control over the other company (eg a partial offer designed deliberately to result in the offeror holding less than 50 per cent of the voting power at general meetings of the other company).

6. Capitalisation, conversion, exchange and subscription rights issues

The Listing Particulars Directive authorises the Stock Exchange Council (acting through the Quotations Committee) to dispense with the obligation to publish listing particulars, or to permit the publication of listing particulars which do not contain all the information normally required under Schedule A, if the shares for which a listing is sought are issued in certain limited circumstances, namely: (a) the shares are issued free of charge to the holders of shares already listed on the Stock Exchange, that is, the shares are issued as bonus shares on a capitalisation of profits or reserves or by applying capital reserves (share premium account or capital redemption reserve)[2] to pay up their nominal value; (b) the shares are issued on the conversion of convertible debt securities, or in exchange for the surrender of exchangeable debt securities, and shares of the issuing company are already listed on the Stock Exchange; (c) the shares are issued in consequence of the exercise of rights conferred by warrants (eg warrants attached to debt securities giving their holders the right to subscribe for a proportionate number of shares of the issuing company), and shares of the company which issued the warrants are already listed on the Stock Exchange; and (d) the shares are issued in substitution for shares already listed on the Stock Exchange and the issue of the substituted shares does not involve an increase in the company's issued share capital.[3]

It is a condition of exemption from publishing listing particulars, however, that the information about the shares for which an admission is sought and about their admission to listing which would normally be required in listing particulars,[4] are, where appropriate, published in the

---

2 Companies Act 1948, s 56(2) and Companies Act 1981, s 53(3) (now Companies Act 1985, s 130(2) and s 170(4)).
3 Listing Particulars Directive, art 6(2).
4 See pp 57 and 72, above.

same way as listing particulars.[3] This means that if the Quotations Committee were to require the publication of truncated listing particulars, this information would have to be included in it. However, the Stock Exchange rules dispense with the publication of listing particulars altogether where shares are issued in these circumstances, and the information about the new shares and about their admission normally required in listing particulars[4] need merely be published by notifying it to the Company Announcements Office and, if the Quotations Committee requires, by publishing it in the form of a brochure made available free of charge to the public for 14 days at the registered office of the issuing company and the offices of the company's paying agents in the United Kingdom, but the brochure must in any case be available to the public for at least two days immediately following the publication of the information at the Company Announcements Office.[5] It is questionable whether the Stock Exchange rules fully conform to the Listing Particulars Directive in respect of the necessary publicity. The Directive requires the information about the shares and their admission to listing to be published in the same way as listing particulars where appropriate (that is, presumably, where investors need the information for a proper appraisal), and unless it be accepted that there are no situations where this is so, it should be obligatory to publish the information in the form of a newspaper advertisement or a brochure available to the public[6] unless the Quotations Committee gives a dispensation in the particular case. The Stock Exchange rules do not call for any publicity beyond notification to the Company Announcements Office, however, unless the Quotations Committee specifically calls for the publication of a brochure.[5]

The present complete or partial exemption from the publication of listing particulars calls for a number of observations. Where shares are issued by a listed company by way of a capitalisation of profits or reserves, or by appropriating amounts from share premium account or capital redemption reserve, it is necessary that the existing shares whose holders receive the bonus shares should be listed on the Stock Exchange, and it does not suffice that the issuing company has another class of shares or debt securities which are listed.[3] On the other hand, if shares are issued on the conversion of convertible debt securities, or on the exchange of exchangeable debt securities, or on the exercise of subscription rights under warrants issued by the company, it is not necessary that the shares issued should be of the same class as shares for which the company already has a listing.[3] Consequently, if a company has a listing for its ordinary shares but not for its preference shares none of which has yet been issued, and the company issues preference shares in satisfaction of convertible debenture holders' conversion rights, whether the debentures are listed or not, it is possible to obtain a listing for the new preference shares without publishing full listing particulars. The same applies if warrants are issued entitling their holders to subscribe for preference shares, and a listing is applied for when the subscription rights conferred by the warrants are exercised. In this connection it should be noted that the warrants do not have to be attached to debt securities, so that shares of a class as yet unlisted may be

5 Listing Particulars Directive, art 6(2); The Stock Exchange: *Admission of Securities to Listing*, Section 3, Chapter 1, para 5.3.
6 Listing Particulars Directive, art 20(1) (see p 49, above).

issued on the exercise of pure subscription options and a listing obtained for them without the publication of full listing particulars if the issuing company already has a listing for another class of its shares.

If the facility to publish truncated listing particulars is used when shares are issued in substitution for shares already listed on a stock exchange, the issue will usually take place on a consolidation or sub-division of the nominal value of the shares or on a variation of the rights attached to them. In British practice these operations do not require the issue of substituted shares; the original shares are simply consolidated or sub-divided, or the rights attached to them are altered, but the shares do not lose their identity and no new substituted shares are issued.[7] It is only exceptionally that it is necessary to cancel existing shares and to issue new ones in their place,[8] and consequently, the facility for obtaining a listing for substituted shares without publishing full listing is hardly ever likely to be invoked in the United Kingdom. It is conceived that the operation by which a company which has suffered losses reduces its capital by cancelling some of its issued shares and immediately issues new shares for cash to make good the loss does not fall within the facility. The company's issued share capital after the issue of the new shares may be no greater than before the reduction, but the new shares are not issued to replace the cancelled shares, but in order to raise fresh share capital. Moreover, there is no certainty if the company has a Stock Exchange listing that the new shares will be subscribed by holders of the cancelled shares, and investors who subscribe for the new shares therefore require the protection of full listing particulars.

7. Small further issues of a class of listed shares

The Listing Particulars Directive authorises the Stock Exchange Council (acting through the Quotations Committee) to give a complete or partial exemption from the obligation to publish listing particulars when a listing is sought for new shares of the same class as existing shares which have already been admitted to listing on the Stock Exchange, if the number, nominal value or estimated market value of the new shares is less than ten per cent of the number or corresponding value of already listed shares of the same class, and information about the number and kind of new shares to be admitted to listing and the circumstances in which the shares have been issued is published in the same way as listing particulars.[9] It is necessary, however, that the issuer should have complied with the Stock Exchange publicity requirements in the past (presumably this means its requirements, in conformity with the Directive, for the publication of listing particulars and similar documents on the admission of any of its securities to listing), and should have produced annual accounts and

---

7 See Companies Act 1948, s 61(1) (*b*) and (*d*) (now Companies Act 1985, s 121(1) and (2)(*b*) and (*d*)) and Companies Act 1980, s 32(1)–(5) (now Companies Act 1985, s 125(1)–(5)).

8 For a situation (unlikely to occur nowadays) where the issue of substituted shares may be necessary, see *Re County Palatine Loan and Discount Co, Teasdale's Case* (1873) 9 Ch App 54. In that case new shares with varying amounts credited as paid up were issued in place of existing shares on which a uniform amount had been paid up; the total amount credited as paid up on the new shares was the same as that paid up on the surrendered ones, but was redistributed unequally between the new shares.

9 Listing Particulars Directive, art 6(3)(*a*).

reports and interim reports[10] which the Quotations Committee considers adequate.[9] The Stock Exchange rules do not repeat this condition in the directive in the restatement in those rules of the concession for small further issues of shares, and (as is permissible under the terms of the directive) the Stock Exchange rules give general permission for listing particulars not to be published on the admission of the new shares to listing without requiring authorisation by the Quotations Committee in each case; the rules, nevertheless, do require that information about the number and kind of shares which are to be admitted and the circumstances in which they are being or have been issued to be published in the form of a brochure, copies of which must be made available to the public free of charge at the registered office of the issuing company and at the offices of its paying agents in the United Kingdom for a period of 14 days and also for a period of two days following the publication of the information at the Company Announcements Office.[11] Furthermore, if the small further issue of shares is made in consideration of an acquisition of assets by the company, the Quotations Committee may require further information to be included in the brochure.[11] The Stock Exchange rules contain a reminder that it may also be necessary to issue a circular explaining the issue of shares to the existing shareholders of the issuing company.[12]

The concession in the Listing Particulars Directive for a small further issue of shares of a class which is already listed will result in a useful saving of cost when a small further issue is made within a reasonable time after the issuing company last published full listing particulars, not necessarily in connection with the listing of shares of the same class. There is no limit on the interval between such a publication and the later listing of a further issue of shares, but the information in the last published listing particulars is intended to be kept up to date by fulfilment of the condition in the Directive (which does not appear in the Stock Exchange rules) that the issuer must have complied with the Stock Exchange's own publicity rules and have produced satisfactory annual accounts and reports and interim reports, and by the exercise of the Quotations Committee's power (again, not mentioned in the Stock Exchange rules) to require the publication of listing particulars in a truncated form so as to set out up-dating information.[9] The insistence of the Quotations Committee on the publication of truncated listing particulars giving up-dating information has the further advantage that the issue of shares will then be made under listing particulars approved by the Committee, and even if the shares are offered to the public or a section of the public so as to constitute a prospectus within the Companies Acts[13] the prospectus provisions of those Acts will not apply,[14] as they may do if merely formal information about the shares were made available to the public in a brochure. The danger of complete exemption from the publication of listing particulars being given by the Stock Exchange rules is that any document published by the company which can be construed as offering the shares to a wide enough range of

10 The interim reports must comply with the Interim Reports Directive (see p 113, below).
11 The Stock Exchange: *Admission of Securities to Listing*, Section 3, Chapter 1, para 5.4.
12 Ibid (see p 117, below).
13 Companies Act 1948, s 55(1) and s 455 (now Companies Act 1985, s 59(1) and s 744).
14 The Stock Exchange (Listing) Regulations 1984, reg 7(1)(*b*) (see p 19, above).

persons to amount to an offer to the public or a section of the public, will be a prospectus,[13] and because no listing particulars are concurrently published, there is nothing to prevent the prospectus provisions of the Companies Acts applying to it.

The concession for small further issues of shares may be employed whether the further shares are issued for cash or for a consideration other than cash, and it may also be used in place of another less generous facility (eg where a document has been published within the preceding 12 months in connection with a public offering of the issuer's shares or other securities or in connection with a takeover bid made by it), provided that the number of further shares issued is less than ten per cent of the existing shares of the same class.[15] The calculation of the ten per cent limit for further issues should present no difficulty, whichever of the alternative bases of number, nominal value or estimated market value of the existing shares of the same class mentioned in the Listing Particulars Directive,[9] are taken, because each of the existing and the new shares will have the same nominal and market values; the Stock Exchange rules in fact use the basis of the number of shares. There is the possibility of abuse of the concession by its repeated use, however, and this is not prevented by the Listing Particulars Directive. For example, a company which has a listing for 100,000 shares of a particular class may use the concession to obtain a listing for 9,900 further shares of the same class and then later to obtain a listing for yet another 10,900 further shares (ten per cent of all the listed shares of the same class when the second further issue is made). This is combatted by the Stock Exchange rules providing that a series of issues of shares in connection with a single transaction or a series of transactions will be treated as a single issue, and the number of shares issued will be aggregated for comparison with the number of shares already issued.[16]

8. Debt securities dealt in by specialist dealers and financial institutions

Where an application is made for the listing of debt securities nearly all of which, because of their nature, are normally bought and traded by only a limited number of investors who are particularly knowledgeable in investment matters, the Stock Exchange Council (acting through the Quotations Committee) may approve listing particulars for such securities omitting any part of the information required by Schedule B of the Listing Particulars Directive or may permit its inclusion in summary form, but only if the information is not material from the point of view of the investors concerned.[17] In the context of the United Kingdom market this power given to the Quotations Committee to relax the normal requirements governing listing particulars for debt securities is important only in respect of the international bond market; in that market all the participants are specialist dealers and institutions acting on their own behalf or on behalf of their clients in subscribing for and dealing in bonds, notes and other debt

---

15 This is pointed out by the last sentence of para 5.3 of the Stock Exchange: *Admission of Securities to Listing*, Section 3, Chapter 1.
16 The Stock Exchange: *Admission of Securities to Listing*, Section 3, Chapter 1, para 5(4)(*a*).
17 Listing Particulars Directive, art 10.

securities issued to secure medium and long-term loans raised by overseas governments, regional or local authorities and companies, particularly companies operating on a nation wide or international scale (such as foreign banks) and companies which the national government controls or in which it has a substantial interest. Many such loans are raised by syndication between the specialist institutions (usually banks and their subsidiaries) who collectively provide the loans, and the syndicate members either retain the securities issued in connection with the loan until maturity or transfer the securities by private negotiation to their clients or other specialists. It follows that the market in many international bond issues is a limited one, and even if a Stock Exchange listing is obtained for an international bond issue (which often is not done), transactions in the bonds will in practice be confined to specialist dealers and institutions which concern themselves in that kind of security, and the general investor will not participate. Because the investors in such debt securities are specialists who are able from their own knowledge and experience to protect themselves, the protection provided by full listing particulars is unnecessary and the requirements of the Listing Particulars Directive can be correspondingly relaxed.

International bonds are nowadays dealt in on the so called Euro-currency Security Market, which comprises securities denominated in United States dollars and Japanese yen as well as in sterling and the European currencies. The Stock Exchange rules recognise that this is a market for knowledgeable specialists, and concede that listing particulars need contain only information essential to the specialist by permitting the omission of much of the information called for by Schedule B of the Listing Particulars Directive.[18] In any case Schedule B applies only when the debt securities are issued by a company or by an issuer other than a sovereign state or by its regional or local authorities.[19] Space does not permit a full treatment of the differences between listing particulars for Euro-currency securities and for ordinary debt securities, but the following examples may be illustrative. The listing particulars for Euro-currency securities must contain particulars of dealing and settlement arrangements for Stock Exchange bargains, which will be different from those for other debt securities;[20] particulars of material contracts included in the listing particulars may be confined to contracts concerning the loan and the issue of debt securities, such as the loan or subscription agreement, the paying agency agreement and the syndication agreement (if there is one);[1] a report by accountants on the financial position and record of the issuer is not required, and in its place there must be set out the profit and loss accounts of the issuer for the last five years, the issuer's latest balance sheet and the auditors' report thereon and any interim financial statement published since the end of the last financial year;[2] instead of a detailed statement of the secured, unsecured and guaranteed loan capital and borrowing of the issuer and its subsidiaries, the particulars need only contain a summary statement

18 The Stock Exchange: *Admission of Securities to Listing*, Section 3, Chapter 1, para 5.1 and
      Section 7, paras 6.3 and 4.
19 Listing Particulars Directive, art 1(2).
20 The Stock Exchange: *Admission of Securities to Listing*, Section 7, para 6.3(*c*).
  1 Ibid, Section 7, para 6.3(*d*).
  2 Ibid, Section 7, para 6.3(*e*).

of loans outstanding and general indebtedness;[3] and the information required about the terms of the debt securities may omit information about the interest yield, profits cover for interest, the terms of any agreement under which a trustee or representative for bondholders is appointed and the closing of subscription lists.[4]

9. Tap issues of debt securities by credit institutions

The Listing Particulars Directive authorises member states to limit the information required in listing particulars published by credit institutions in connection with the issue of debt securities in a continuous or repeated manner.[5] If the issuing credit institution regularly publishes its annual accounts (which it is bound to do if it is registered as a company in the United Kingdom, or if it is an overseas company which has established a place of business there)[6] and the credit institution was formed or is governed by special legislation or under such legislation, or is subject to public supervision to protect savings, the contents of listing particulars it publishes in connection with such a continuous or repeated issue of debt securities may be confined to the names and addresses of the persons responsible for the listing particulars of parts of them[7] and information about the loan secured by the debt securities to which the particulars relate and the nature and terms of the debt securities,[8] together with information about important events relevant to the assessment of the securities which have occurred since the end of the financial year for which the issuer last published annual accounts.[5]

The kind of debt securities to which this relaxation of the normal requirements of the Listing Particulars Directive applies are securities which are not issued at one time under an offer open to acceptance by investors only immediately or within a limited period, but securities which are issued (usually up to a stated maximum amount) under a continuous offer extending over a long period or indefinitely, or under a succession of offers made at fairly regular intervals (eg weekly or monthly). This method of issuing debt securities is known as a 'tap issue' in the United Kingdom, where it is used only for issues of Government Stocks. The kinds of debt securities which are susceptible of issue in this way by non-public issuers in the United Kingdom, namely, banks, licensed deposit takers such as hire purchase and industrial finance companies, and specialised institutions such as building societies, are based on the deposit of money at interest for a fixed or indefinite period, and the debt securities issued in respect of such deposits may take the form of depositary receipts, certificates of deposit or credit entries in a pass book. Needless to say, such deposits and the debt securities representing them are never listed on the Stock Exchange, even if they are certificates for term deposits of substantial sums, which like

3 Ibid, Section 7, para 6.3(*f*).
4 Ibid, Section 7, para 6.4(1)(*a*).
5 Listing Particulars Directive, art 12.
6 Companies Act 1976, s 1(6) and (7) and s 9(2) (now Companies Act 1985, s 241(1) and (3) and s 700(2)).
7 Listing Particulars Directive, Sch B, para 1.1.
8 Ibid, Sch B, paras. 2.1.0 to 2.4.6.

Treasury bills, are treated as money market instruments and not securities suitable for dealings on the Stock Exchange. The same applies to the equivalent European debt securities, such as the French *bons de caisse* issued by the banks or the German *Schuldscheine* issued by banks and other financial institutions. But there are other tap securities issued by other financial institutions in Europe, can be and sometimes are listed on a stock exchange, such as the German *Hypothekenpfandbriefe*, which secure term deposits on a portfolio of land mortages held by a bank.

Because tap securities are not listed on the Stock Exchange in the United Kingdom, the Stock Exchange rules make no special provision for listing particulars in respect of tap issues. If debt securities issued on tap were to be listed on the Stock Exchange, normal listing particulars would have to be published. The only modifications of the normal Stock Exchange rules which are at present made for securities issued on tap (and this is merely to comply with the Listing Particulars Directive) are that the period during which tap securities are open for subscription need not be stated in listing particulars offering them,[9] nor need the issue and redemption prices and the nominal rate of interest payable,[10] nor the yield on the securities.[11]

10. Allotments to employees of shares of a class already listed

The Listing Particulars Directive authorises the Stock Exchange Council (acting through the Quotations Committee) to give complete or partial exemption from the obligation to publish listing particulars in connection with the listing of shares allotted to employees if shares of the same class have already been admitted to listing, and the fact that the shares allotted to employees differ from the other shares only in respect of the date when they first entitle their holders to dividends does not mean that they belong to a different class.[12] Information about the number and kind of shares to be admitted to listing and the circumstances in which the shares have been issued to employees must be published in the same way as listing particulars.[12] The Stock Exchange rules give effect to the facility provided by the Directive by dispensing with listing particulars altogether when a listing is sought for shares allotted to employees and shares of the same class are already listed, but a brochure containing information about the number and kind of the shares allotted to employees and the circumstances of their issue must be made available free of charge to the public at the issuing company's registered office and at the offices of its paying agents in the United Kingdom for a period of 14 days and also for two days following the publication of the same information at the Company Announcements Office.[13] Even if fuller documents are issued in connection with the offer or allotment of shares to employees (eg a circular sent to employees setting out the terms of an employees' share subscription scheme), they will not qualify as prospectuses under the Companies Acts, and so will not be subjected to the rules relating to prospectuses in those Acts. This is because

9 The Stock Exchange: *Admission of Securities to Listing*, Section 3, Chapter 2, para 2.18.
10 Ibid, Section 3, Chapter 2, para 8.3.
11 Ibid, Section 3, Chapter 2, para 8.8.
12 Listing Particulars Directive, art 6(3)(*d*).
13 The Stock Exchange: *Admission of Securities to Listing*, Section 3, Chapter 1, para 5.4.

the offer will either be made to the employees personally so that they cannot renounce it in favour of anyone else, or because renunciations are permitted, but only in favour of other employees.[14]

Neither the Listing Particulars Directive nor the Stock Exchange rules state whether the present facility applies only when shares are allotted to employees of the issuing company, or whether it applies also when shares are issued to employees of companies in the same group, or of associated companies, or of any companies, so that the only relevant qualification is that the allottee is an employee; whether the facility applies only when the employees to whom the shares are allotted subscribe for them for cash (eg under a share option or share subscription scheme), or whether it also applies when the shares are allotted gratuitously and are paid for out of the issuing company's profits or reserves (eg under an employees' profit-sharing scheme); and whether the facility applies only when shares are allotted directly to employees (even though they may renounce or assign their rights to the shares to other persons), or whether it extends also to the allotment of shares to nominees or trustees for employees (as beneficiaries of a share option or profit sharing scheme). It would appear that the concession should be interpreted widely in view of the generality of the terms in which it is expressed, and that provided the shares are allotted because the allottees, or the persons for whom they are trustees or nominees, are employees, and not because they fall into some other category (eg existing shareholders of the company, including employee-shareholders), it is immaterial that they are not employees of the issuing company, that they do not pay the issue price of the shares themselves and that the shares are allotted under a scheme by which they are held in trust for employees.

11. Securities issued in connection with a takeover or merger

If a listing is sought for shares or debt securities issued in connection with a merger or a takeover, or in connection with a division of a company's undertaking between two or more companies or as consideration for the transfer of the assets and liabilities of an undertaking or for the transfer of assets other than cash, the Listing Particulars Directive requires the documents setting out the terms and conditions of the transaction and a balance sheet of the acquiring company drawn up in connection with the transaction (if the acquiring company is a newly formed one which has not prepared its first annual accounts) to be made available for inspection by the public at the registered office of the company issuing the securities and at the offices of the financial organisations which act as its paying agents.[15] This obligation does not affect the issuing company's obligation to publish listing particulars, which will be in the form and contain the information which would be appropriate if the securities were issued for cash (eg listing particulars in respect of shares or debt securities or convertible debt securities offered in exchange for the existing shares of a company which is the target of a takeover offer).[16] However, in appropriate circumstances the

14 Companies Act 1948, s 55(2) (now Companies Act 1985, s 60(1)).
15 Listing Particulars Directive, art 15(1).
16 See pp 55, 72 and 84, above.

obligation to publish listing particulars at all or to publish full listing particulars may be dispensed with by the Quotations Committee (acting on behalf of the Council of the Stock Exchange) (eg when shares of a class already listed are issued in connection with a takeover offer, but the new shares are less than ten per cent of those already listed).[17] Under the Listing Particulars Directive the documents setting out the terms of the takeover or other transaction do not need to be reproduced or summarised as such in the listing particulars, but their principal contents will figure in the particulars in order to satisy the specific requirements of Schedule A or B of the directive and the general obligation to ensure that the particulars contain all the information necessary for investors to make an informed assessment of the issuing company's financial position and prospects and of the securities.[18]

The Stock Exchange rules expand the requirements of the Listing Particulars Directive considerably in respect of listing particulars connected with takeovers and mergers. If the target company will become part of the issuing company's group on the completion of the intended merger or the takeover offer succeeeding, and the issuing company does not already have a listing for any of its securities on the Stock Exchange, the information required in the listing particulars in respect of the issuing company and its subsidiaries, their business activities, financial position, capital structure, management and future development[19] must include corresponding information about the target company and its subsidiaries.[20] If the issuing company already has a listing for any of its securities and is issuing new shares or debt securities to effect the acquisition or consolidation of control over the target company by merger, takeover, scheme of arrangement or contractual transfer of assets and liabilities, it is obliged to include information about the target company and its subsidiaries in the listing particulars corresponding to the information it must give about itself and its subsidiaries[21] only if the target company is already a subsidiary of the issuing company (ie the issuing company is making a consolidation bid for minority holdings in its own subsidiary). Even if this is not so, the listing particulars must include the following: (i) a statement whether the directors of the issuer consider that the working capital of the issuer and the target company and their collective subsidiaries will be adequate after the completion of the acquisition by the issuer, and if not, what steps will be taken to remedy the situation;[1] (ii) a statement of the outstanding loan capital and term loans (distinguishing between secured, guaranteed and unsecured loans), the outstanding amount of all other borrowing and indebtedness, particulars of mortgages and charges and the total amount of contingent liabilities of the group comprising the issuing company, the target company and their collective subsidiaries;[2] (iii) the names of persons who will after the completion of the acquisition or the full acceptance of the takeover offer be interested directly or indirectly in 5 per cent or more of the issuing company's issued share capital as increased to effect the

17 See p 97, above.   18 Listing Particulars Directive, art 4(1).
19 See pp 58–71 and 72–78, above.
20 The Stock Exchange: *Admission of Securities to Listing*, Section 3, Chapter 1, para 4.1(*a*).
21 Ibid, Section 3, Chapter 2, para 4.7 (*b*).
 1 Ibid, Section 3, Chapter 2, para 2.19.
 2 Ibid, Section 3, Chapter 2, para 5.16.

acquisition or takeover;[3] (iv) particulars of the interests which directors of the issuing company and their spouses and minor children will have in listed shares and debt securities of the company upon the completion of the acquisition or the full acceptance of the takeover offer, if those interests are notifiable to the company under the Companies Acts;[4] and (v) information about the target company and its subsidiaries corresponding to that which the issuing company must give to its own shareholders in a circular relating to the acquisition required by the Stock Exchange rules.[5] The issuing company may obviously have difficulty in obtaining all the information about the target company which it requires to satisfy the Stock Exchange rules, unless the directors of the target company support the issuing company's offer. To assist an issuing company which already has a listing for any of its securities, the Quotations Committee may permit it to publish the information about the target company mentioned above after a listing has been granted for the shares or other securities it proposes to issue to the target company's shareholders, instead of having to include the information in the listing particulars, but this can be done only if the directors of the target company do not recommend the issuing company's offer or proposals to their shareholders.[6] There is no similar concession where the issuing company does not have a listing for any of its existing shares or other securities, and where therefore the listing particulars it publishes must contain full information about the target company as though it were already part of the issuing company's group.

A company which makes a takeover offer must send to the holders of shares and debt securities of the target company which it seeks to acquire an offer document setting out the terms of its offer together with information about the offeror company and the securities which it offers in exchange for those it seeks to acquire.[7] This offer document is distinct from the listing particulars which the offeror company must publish in order to obtain a listing for the shares or debt securities which it proposes to issue under the takeover offer, and the contents of the offer document are governed by the Stock Exchange rules and not by the Listing Particulars Directive. Nevertheless, a single document may incorporate both the offer document and the listing particulars, in which case their contents must be set out in separate sections.[8] Alternatively, the offer document and the listing particulars may be contained in separate documents, but in that case copies of the listing particulars and the offer document must be sent at the same time to the holders of the shares and debt securities of the target company which the offeror company seeks to acquire.[8]

To satisfy the Listing Particulars Directive listing particulars for securities issued in connection with a merger or takeover must be published in full in a national daily newspaper, or by brochures containing the particulars being made available to the public.[9] The Stock Exchange rules

3 Ibid, Section 3, Chapter 2, para 3.9.
4 Ibid, Section 3, Chapter 2, para 6.6.
5 Ibid, Section 3, Chapter 1, para 4.1(*b*). For the contents of the circulars which must be sent to shareholders of the acquiring company, see p 127, below.
6 The Stock Exchange: *Admission of Securities to Listing*, Section 6, Chapter 2, para 5.6.
7 Ibid, Section 6, Chapter 2, para 3.
8 Ibid, Section 6, Chapter 2, para 5.2.
9 Listing Particulars Directive, art 20(1).

governing publication of the listing particulars relax the normal requirement of the rules for more extensive publicity for listing particulars than the Directive requires by obliging the issuing company merely to make copies of the listing particulars in the form of a brochure available to the public at the registered office of the issuing company and the offices of its paying agents in the United Kingdom for a period of 14 days from the date when copies are sent to the holders of the shares or other securities of the target company.[10] However, if the issuing company offers a new class of its shares or debt securities to security holders of the target company, it must also publish a formal notice setting out basic information about the issuing company, the amount and title of the securities offered and the addresses where copies of the listing particulars may be obtained (including the Company Announcements Office) in two national daily newspapers, or if the issuing company already has a listing for any of its securities, in one such newspaper.[11] The formal notice must state that the public may obtain copies of the listing particulars from the registered office of the issuing company or the offices of its paying agents in the United Kingdom during the 14 days following the publication of the notice, or from the Company Announcements Office during the two days following publication.[11] The formal notice must be published at the same time as the issuing company's offer document is sent to the holders of the shares or other securities of the target company to which the offer relates.[12]

During the course of a takeover bid it may be necessary for the offeror company to send supplementary documents to the holders of shares and securities of the target company. If such documents merely contain additional or corrective information (eg revised profits or dividend forecasts), they must be published in the same way as the original listing particulars after they have been approved by the Quotations Department.[13] On the other hand, if the supplementary document entails the preparation of new listing particulars, because the rights attached to the shares or securities offered by the issuing company are changed, or because different securities from the original ones are offered either as an alternative to, or instead of, the originally offered securities, new listing particulars must be published.[14] If new listing particulars are necessary, they need not repeat information contained in the original particulars which remains unchanged.[14] This is because the original listing particulars will have been published in connection with a takeover bid within 12 months before the new listing particulars, and the Stock Exchange Council is therefore empowered to give partial exemption from the obligation to publish full new listing particulars; any material changes in the information given in the original listing particulars must, of course, be incorporated in the new ones.[15] Revised or new listing particulars must be published in the appropriate manner at the same time as the supplementary document is

---

10 The Stock Exchange: *Admission of Securities to Listing*, Section 2, Chapter 3, para 7 and Section 6, Chapter 2, para 5.5.
11 Ibid, Section 2, Chapter 3, paras 3 and 6 and Section 6, Chapter 2, para 5.5.
12 Ibid, Section 6, Chapter 2, para 5.6.
13 Listing Particulars Directive, art 23; The Stock Exchange: *Admission of Securities to Listing*, Section 3, Chapter 1, para 2.2 and Section 6, Chapter 2, para 5.7(*c*).
14 The Stock Exchange: *Admission of Securities to Listing*, Section 6, Chapter 2, para 5.7(*d*).
15 Listing Particulars Directive, art 6(1).

sent by the offeror to the security holders whose shares or debt securities are the subject of the takeover bid.[16]

During the currency of a takeover bid the offeror and the target company are required by the Stock Exchange rules to make available at an address in the City of London or, if either company has regional connections, at an address in a regional centre approved by the Quotations Committee, copies of the following documents, namely, the company's memorandum and articles of association or equivalent documents in the case of an overseas company; the company's audited annual or group accounts for its last two financial years; director's service contracts of more than one year's duration; all reports, valuations or other documents referred to in the offer document in respect of the takeover offer or in any supplementary document; the written consents of experts to the inclusion of reports, valuations or opinions by them in the offer document; and copies of all material contracts entered into by the company within the preceding two years (other than contracts entered into in the ordinary course of business).[17]

If a takeover offer or a merger proposal is made under which the shares or debt securities of another company than the offeror are offered to the holders of shares or securities of the target company, the rules set out above apply with the substitution of the other company as issuing company in place of the offeror. This may occur when a takeover bid is made by a subsidiary company, but the new shares or debt securities offered by it will be issued by its parent company.

Normally, a listing will be sought for shares or debt securities issued under a takeover offer or a merger at the time the offer or proposals for a merger are made, and this is particularly so if the company which makes the offer or proposals already has a listing for its securities. However, it may happen that securities issued under a takeover or merger are initially unlisted, but that an application is later made for them to be admitted to listing on the Stock Exchange by way of an introduction. The power of the Quotations Committee to dispense with the publication of listing particulars, or to permit the publication of truncated listing particulars, if the shares or securities issued under the takeover or merger are admitted to listing within 12 months after the offer document or document containing the merger proposals was published, has already been dealt with.[18] It remains to note here that when the application for the admission of the securities issued under the takeover or merger is made, the offer document in connection with the takeover or the proposals for the merger and any balance sheet prepared by a newly incorporated acquiring company, must be made available for public inspection at the registered office of the issuing company and at the offices of its paying agents in the same way as if the application for a listing were made concurrently with the takeover or merger, but the Quotations Committee may dispense with this requirement if the takeover or merger was completed more than two years before the securities are admitted to listing.[19]

16 The Stock Exchange: *Admission of Securities to Listing*, Section 6, Chapter 2, para 5.6.
17 Ibid, Section 6, Chapter 2, para 6.
18 Listing Particulars Directive, art 6(1); The Stock Exchange: *Admission of Securities to Listing*, Section 3, Chapter 1, para 5.2 (see p 93, above).
19 Listing Particulars Directive, art 15(1) and (2) (see p 103, above).

12. Miscellaneous situations

There are a number of residual situations where the Listing Particulars Directive modifies or allows dispensations from the normal rules governing the contents of listing particulars and their publication. Most of these situations are unlikely to involve the issue or marketing of securities by companies governed by United Kingdom law, but they may be of significance if issuers established in other countries of the European Community seek a listing for their securities on the Stock Exchange. The Listing Particulars Directive empowers the Council of the Stock Exchange (acting through the Quotations Committee) to give complete or partial exemption from the obligation to publish listing particulars in two cases,[20] namely, where a listing is sought for:

(i) debt securities issued by a company or corporation which is a national of a member state of the European Community and which holds a state monopoly in respect of its business (eg the German brandy monopoly) and is either established or governed by national legislation, or has its borrowings unconditionally and irrevocably guaranteed by a member state or, if it is a federal state, one of its component members (eg a *Land* of the German Federal Republic);[1]

(ii) debt securities issued by a corporation (other than a company) which is a national of a member state of the European Community and was established by special legislation of that state which governs its activities and confines them to raising loans under state control by the issue of debt securities and financing production by means of the proceeds of such issues and money provided by the state, but it is also necessary that the debt securities of the corporation should be treated by the legislation which governs it as issued or guaranteed by the state.[2]

The Stock Exchange rules apply the provisions of the Listing Particulars Directive by enabling companies or corporations which fall within either of the above categories to omit from listing particulars in respect of their debt securities the following information which is normally required to be included, namely, information about the issuer's registered or head office, the date of its incorporation and its duration, the legislation under which the issuer operates and its legal form under that legislation, the place where

---

20 There are three other cases where a dispensation may be made, but they are not of practical significance in the United Kingdom. They are where the securities for which a listing is sought are already listed on another stock exchange in the same member state (an impossibility in the United Kingdom), where the shares sought to be admitted were issued upon the renunciation by the directors of a company who are personally liable for the company's debts by law (eg a French *société en commandite par actions* or a German *Kommanditgesellschaft auf Aktien*) of their statutory right to a share of its profits; where supplementary *certificaten* in respect of fractions of shares are issued by a Dutch company in substitution for original listed *certificaten*, but without an increase in the company's capital (Listing Particulars Directive, art 6(3), (*f*) and (*g*)). No companies with personally liable directors have listings on the Stock Exchange, and *certificaten* for fractions of Dutch companies' shares cannot be admitted to listing.
1 Listing Particulars Directive, art 6(3)(*b*).
2 Ibid, art 6(3)(*c*).

the issuer is registered and its registration number;[3] more importantly, the issuer may omit all of the information normally required about the issuer's capital and financial position,[4] other than particulars of litigation or arbitration proceedings in which it is or has recently been involved and which have had or may have a significant effect on its financial position, a statement that certain documents of importance to investors or copies of them may be inspected at an address in the City of London and the offices of its paying agents in the United Kingdom, and (if applicable) a statement that bearer instruments representing the debt securities have not been printed from engraved steel plates.[5]

The Stock Exchange rules make the same concessions for listing particulars published by companies which are established or governed by special legislation and which have power to levy charges on consumers (eg a water supply company).[6] Insofar as this allows such companies to omit information required by the Listing Particulars Directive from listing particulars in respect of their securities, it would appear not to be in conformity with the directive; such companies may have an exclusive right to supply a service in a limited locality, but they do not have a state monopoly.

13. Amended listing particulars

If after listing particulars are approved by the Quotations Committee and published a significant new factor arises which is capable of affecting the assessment of the securities to which the particulars relate, and dealings in the securities on the Stock Exchange have not begun, a supplement to the listing particulars must be submitted to the Quotations Committee for approval, and on approval being given must be published in the same way as the original listing particulars.[7] The Stock Exchange rules repeat this provision, require a draft of the supplement to the listing particulars to be submitted to the Quotations Department for approval by the Committee, and provide that the securities in question will be admitted to listing only after publication of the supplement.[8]

The obligation to submit for approval and to publish supplements to listing particulars applies only if significant new factors arise between the publication of the original listing particulars and dealings commencing in the securities to which they related. There is no obligation imposed on the issuer or the persons responsible for the listing particulars to keep the information in the particulars up to date after dealings have begun. Moreover, it is not every event or change in circumstances occurring after the publication of the original listing particulars which makes it necessary to publish a supplement, even though the event or change results in information given in the particulars no longer being correct or complete. A supplement is called for only if the event or change is a significant factor in making an assessment of the issuer and the securities which are to be listed,

3 The Stock Exchange: *Admission of Securities to Listing*, Section 3, Chapter 1, paras 5.5 and 5.6(*b*).
4 Ibid, Section 3, Chapter 2, paras 3.1 to 3.18 and paras 5.1 to 5.16.
5 Ibid, Section 3, Chapter 2, paras 3.15, 3.17 and 3.18 (see pp 61 and 65, above).
6 Ibid, Section 3, Chapter 1, para 5.6(*a*).
7 Listing Particulars Directive, art 23.
8 The Stock Exchange: *Admission of Securities to Listing*, Section 3, Chapter 1, para 2.2.

for example, a profit forecast becoming clearly and substantially over-optimistic, the commitment of the issuer to action which will substantially affect its assets, liabilities or future profits, or the notification of an intended takeover offer to the board of the issuing company. Probably a sound test for the need to publish a supplement to listing particulars is whether the new factor is so material that a contract to subscribe for securities comprised in the listing particulars could be rescinded by the subscriber in equity for misrepresentation if the issuer failed to correct the information already supplied by it to subscribers.[9]

OFFERING DOCUMENTS OF PUBLIC AUTHORITIES

The Listing Particulars Directive does not apply to documents published in connection with the listing of securities issued by a state (whether a member state of the European Community or not) or by a regional or local authority of a state.[10] The Stock Exchange rules governing the contents of such documents are therefore simply its own requirements for the admission of such securities to listing, and in imposing and enforcing those requirements, the Quotations Committee (representing the Council of the Stock Exchange) does not act as the competent authority designated by the law under the Stock Exchange (Listing) Regulations 1984, nor as a public authority. Instead it retains its former status as a private law institution applying its own internal rules.

Offering documents in respect of securities issued or to be issued by states or regional or local authorities (whether United Kingdom or overseas) must contain certain basic information specified in the Stock Exchange rules, and must also contain additional information which the Quotations Committee considers appropriate having regard, particularly in the case of government and local authorities in the United Kingdom, to information already generally available about the issuer and its financial, economic and political status.[11] The drafting of offer documents for issues of securities by public authorities involves a degree of discussion and negotiation with the Quotations Department about the extent of disclosure as well as the details of the information to be included, whereas in preparing listing particulars for companies' securities the extent of disclosure is largely prescribed by Schedules A and B of the Listing Particulars Directive and the Stock Exchange's own specific rules.

The basic information which all offer documents in respect of securities issued by public authorities must contain are the name of the issuer; a statement that an application has been made to the Stock Exchange for the securities to be admitted to listing; the amount and name of the securities and a statement of the legal authority for their issue; the names and addresses of the issuer's bankers, brokers, London agents and the trustees of any trust deed executed to secure the issue; details of the state, regional, local or other revenues which will be charged with the amounts payable to

---

9 *Traill v Baring* (1864) 33 LJ Ch 521; *With v O'Flanagan* [1936] 1 Ch 575.
10 Listing Particulars Directive, art 1(2).
11 The Stock Exchange: *Admission of Securities to Listing*, Section 3, Chapter 3, Introductory paragraph.

holders of the securities and of the revenue which will be available for interest payments; the terms and conditions of issue of the securities, in particular, the rights of holders of the securities as regards income and capital, details of any sinking fund arrangements, any right reserved to the issuer to redeem or re-purchase any of the securities before the maturity date; particulars of any investments or other securities on which the amounts payable to holders of the securities are charged; the dates on which payments of interest or principal will accrue due to the then holders of the securities; the price at which the securities will be issued, or have been issued or agreed to be issued (eg to a financial institution as an intermediary engaged to market the securities); a statement whether the securities will be issued as fully paid, and if not, the instalments of the issue price remaining unpaid and the dates when they will fall due.[12]

12 Ibid, Section 3, Chapter 3, paras 1 to 7.

CHAPTER 4

Continuing Obligations

When a company or other issuer has obtained a listing for its securities on the Stock Exchange, it comes under a series of obligations which it must fulfil in order to maintain the listing. Some of these obligations are imposed by the Admission Directive as given effect in United Kingdom law by the Stock Exchange (Listing) Regulations 1984.[1] Other obligations are imposed by the Stock Exchange rules in exercise of the power conferred by the Admission Directive on the Council of the Stock Exchange (as the competent authority) to impose more stringent or additional obligations on listed issuers than those imposed by the Directive itself.[2] Yet other obligations have no connection with the Admission Directive, but are imposed by the Stock Exchange rules in place of the contractual obligations which were formerly undertaken by an issuer in the Listing Agreement it entered into with the Stock Exchange when its securities were admitted to listing.[3] Issuers no longer enter into listing agreements, but are nevertheless bound by the Stock Exchange rules as a condition for maintaining a listing for their securities. It would appear that these obligations derived from the former listing agreement, like those imposed by the Stock Exchange in addition to the obligations contained in the Admission Directive, do not form part of United Kingdom law, but are nevertheless lawful because imposed with lawful authority, and have the same status in law as the rules of a private law association.[4] Finally, an obligation is imposed on companies whose shares are listed on the Stock Exchange to prepare and publish interim reports for the first half of each of their financial years. This is a legal obligation imposed by the Interim Reports Directive as given effect in United Kingdom law by the Stock Exchange (Listing) Regulations 1984.[1] The obligations imposed on a listed issuer by the Admission Directive have been dealt with already in Chapter 2, and differ according to whether the issuer is a company or a state (other than a member state of the European Community) or a regional or local authority of such a state, and whether in the case of a company the listed securities are shares or debt securities.[5] This Chapter is therefore concerned with the remaining obligations imposed on a listed issuer, namely, the obligations imposed by the Interim Reports Directive and the obligations imposed by the Stock Exchange rules which are derived from the former listing agreement.

---

1 The Stock Exchange (Listing) Regulations 1984, reg 3(1) and (2).
2 Admission Directive, art 5(2).
3 See the Stock Exchange: *Admission of Securities to Listing* (1979 edn), Sch VIII, Part A.
4 See p 26, above.
5 Admission Directive, para 4(2) and Schedules C and D; The Stock Exchange (Listing) Regulations 1984, reg 6 and Sch 2, para 1.

INTERIM REPORTS

The Interim Reports Directive applies to companies whose shares are admitted to listing on the Stock Exchange, but not to investment companies other than those of the closed-end type[6] (ie the Directive does not apply to unit trusts, American mutual funds, French *sociétés d'investissement à capital variable* and *fonds d'investissement* or German *Kapitalanlagegesellschaften* which issue *Investmentfondsanteile* representing fractions of their investment funds). The Directive also does not apply to central banks, whether the Bank of England or the central bank of a foreign or Commonwealth country, whether a member state of the European Community or not.[7]

The Interim Reports Directive requires companies subject to it to prepare and publish reports on their activities and their profits or losses during the first six months of each financial year.[8] The half-yearly report must show the company's net turnover and its profit or loss before or after the deduction of tax for the relevant six months as calculated in accordance with the Fourth Directive issued by the Council of Ministers of the European Community to harmonise the laws of the member states in respect of the annual accounts of certain kinds of companies.[9] If the company has paid or proposes to pay an interim dividend, the half-yearly report must show the first six months' profit or loss after the deduction of tax and the interim dividend paid or proposed.[10] The report must also show the corresponding figures for net turnover and profit or loss for the first six months of the preceding financial year.[11] In addition to the financial results of the company for the six month period, the half-yearly report must contain an explanatory statement about the company's activities during those six months, including all significant information to enable investors to make an informed assessment of the company's activities and its profit or loss for the period and indicating any special factors which have influenced those activities and that profit or loss, and the statement must enable a comparison to be made with the company's activities and results in the first six months of its preceding financial year.[12] Moreover, the explanatory statement must, as far as possible, deal with the company's likely future development during a period covering at least the remainder of its current financial year.[12]

If the figures in a company's half-yearly report have been audited, the auditor's report must be reproduced in the half-yearly report in full, including any qualifications to the auditor's report.[13] If a company prepares consolidated annual accounts (which it will normally do if it is the parent

---

6 Interim Reports Directive, art 1(1) and (2).
7 Ibid, art 1(3) and The Stock Exchange (Listing) Regulations 1984, reg 6 and Sch 2, para 10.
8 Interim Reports Directive, art 2.
9 Ibid, art 5(1) and (2). The Fourth Council Directive (78/660), published in the Official Journal dated 14 August 1978 (No L 222/11), was given effect to in this respect by the Companies Act 1981, s 1 (substituting a new Companies Act 1948, s 149 and Sch 8) (now Companies Act 1985, s 228 and Sch 4).
10 Interim Reports Directive, art 5(4).
11 Ibid, art 5(5).
12 Ibid, art 5(6).
13 Ibid, art 8.

company of a group of companies),[14] it may prepare its half-yearly report in consolidated or unconsolidated form.[15] If it chooses the former, the figures given will be the net turnover and profit or loss of the group as a whole; if it chooses the latter, the figures will relate to the parent company alone and the profits or losses of its subsidiaries will be reflected only in the dividends which the subsidiaries have paid during the half year. However, the Stock Exchange may require the figures given to be supplemented by the report showing the alternative figures as well.[15]

The Stock Exchange rules amplify the requirements of the Interim Reports Directive by requiring the half-yearly report to contain, or to set out in a separate preliminary profits statement, a number of figures for the first six months of the current financial year in addition to the net turnover and the profits of the company or group before taxation and before taking extraordinary items (ie non-recurrent profits or losses) into account.[16] The additional items are separate figures for United Kingdom and overseas taxation on the company or the group of which it is the parent company; taxation on the reporting company's and its subsidiaries' interests in associated companies;[17] the extent of minority interests in the profits of the company's subsidiaries; the net profit or loss attributable to the company's shareholders before taking account of extraordinary items (ie the net attributable profit after tax); the amount of extraordinary profits or loss net of taxation; the profit or loss attributable to the company's shareholders after taking extraordinary items into account; the rates of dividend paid or proposed and the cost of paying them (including advance corporation tax); the amount of earnings per ordinary share calculated on the company's profits after taxation; and finally, comparative figures for the first six months of the preceding financial year in respect of net turnover and profits or losses and all the foregoing items.[18] The figures in the half-yearly report or preliminary profit statement must be shown on a consolidated basis if the company has subsidiaries, and the amount of earnings per ordinary share must be taken as the amount in pence obtained by taking the consolidated profits of the reporting company and its subsidiaries after tax for the six month period (excluding extraordinary items) less the part of those profits attributable to minority interests in subsidiaries and the cost to the company of paying preference dividends for the period, and dividing

14 Companies Act 1948, ss 151 and 152 (as substituted by the Companies Act 1981 s 2) now Companies Act, 1985, ss 229 and 230.
15 Interim Reports Directive, art 6.
16 The Stock Exchange: *Admission of Securities to Listing*, Section 5, Chapter 2, para 25(*a*) and (*b*) (i) and (ii).
17 An associated company is one in which the company (the investing company) and its subsidiaries have a long-term substantial interest (which is presumed if they hold equity shares in the other company carrying at least 20 per cent of the voting rights exercisable by its equity shareholders), but an associated company may also have that status if the position of the investing company is effectively that of a partner in a joint venture or consortium; in either case the investing company must be in a position to exercise a significant influence over the associated company, which means that it participates in making commercial and financial policy decisions of the associated company through representation on its board or otherwise (Statement of Standard Accounting Practice No 1, paras 13 to 16).
18 The Stock Exchange: *Admission of Securities to Listing*, section 5, Chapter 2, para 25(*b*) (iii) to (x).

the consolidated profit figure by the number of the company's issued ordinary shares qualifying for a dividend for the period.[19]

The Quotations Committee may exceptionally allow the half-yearly report or preliminary profit statement to contain estimated figures if the company does not have a quotation for any of its securities on a stock exchange other than the Stock Exchange.[20] If the figures in the report or statement have not been audited, that fact must be stated, and since the report or statement qualifies as an abridged set of accounts under the Companies Acts, the report or statement must also state that it does not contain full accounts of the company and that full accounts have not been delivered to the Registrar of Companies.[1] Again, the Quotations Committee may authorise the omission of any of the requisite figures from the report or statement if the disclosure of that information would be contrary to the public interest or seriously detrimental to the company, but in the latter case, the omission must not be likely to mislead the public about matters which are essential to an assessment of the shares.[2] The omission of of any such figures in the circumstances mentioned is permitted by the Interim Reports Directive provided that an authorisation is given for the purpose by the Quotations Committee (acting on behalf of the Stock Exchange Council),[3] and under the Stock Exchange rules, which go further in this respect than the directive, the Committee may also authorise the omission of any of the requisite figures from the half-yearly report or preliminary profits statement 'if they consider the omission otherwise necessary or appropriate'.[2] In practice authorisations to omit information from interim reports or to avoid or defer publicity for any information required to be disclosed under the Stock Exchange's own rules are given, not by the Quotations Committee, but by the Quotations Department acting on its behalf, and requests for waivers or deferment of publicity are dealt with by the chairman's panel (comprising the two chairmen of the Quotations Committee and the two vice-chairmen) or by the Quotations Committee only if the listed company objects to the initial decision of the Quotations Department.

The contents of the half-yearly reports called for by the Stock Exchange rules (apart from the turnover, profit, dividends and earnings figures mentioned above) are exactly the same as those specified in the Interim Reports Directive,[4] and the same powers to authorise omissions from the report are conferred on the Quotations Committee by the directive[3] and the Stock Exchange rules[2] as are conferred on it in respect of the figures for turnover etc.

If a company governed by the law of a country other than a member state of the European Community publishes a half-yearly report in its own country, the Quotations Committee may under the Interim Reports

---

19 Ibid, Section 5, Chapter 2, para 25(*b*) (ix); Statement of Standard Accounting Practice No 3, para 10.
20 The Stock Exchange: *Admission of Securities to Listing*, Section 5, Chapter 2, para 25.1. This is permissible under the Interim Reports Directive, art 5(3).
1 The Stock Exchange: *Admission of Securities to Listing*, Section 5, Chapter 2, para 25(*d*); Companies Act 1981, s 11(6) (now Companies Act 1985, s 255(3)).
2 The Stock Exchange: *Admission of Securities to Listing*, Section 5, Chapter 2, para 25.3.
3 Interim Reports Directive, art 9(4) and (5).
4 The Stock Exchange: *Admission of Securities to Listing*, Section 5, Chapter 2, para 25(*c*).

Directive, as given effect by the Stock Exchange rules, authorise it to publish the same report in the United Kingdom (translated into English if necessary) instead of a half-yearly report conforming to the rules dealt with above, but the published report must contain equivalent information.[5] This facility is particularly useful in the case of United States companies with a Stock Exchange listing, which may publish the half-yearly report which they are required to make to the US Securities and Exchange Commission in place of the half-yearly report called for by the Directive.

The Interim Reports Directive and the Stock Exchange rules require a listed company to publish its half-yearly report within four months after the end of the six months covered by the report, unless the Quotations Committee extends the four month period in exceptional circumstances.[6] The Directive requires the report to be published either in full in one or more national newspapers, or by copies being made available to the public at addresses mentioned in an announcement of the publication of the report inserted in one or more national newspapers, but the Quotations Committee (acting on behalf of the Stock Exchange Council) may authorise an alternative equivalent means of publication.[7] The Stock Exchange rules require publication in the same way as the Directive, but if the report is not published in full in two national daily newspapers the company must send copies of the report to the holders of all its listed securities, whether shares or debt securities, and in that case it must also make copies available to the public at its registered office and the offices of its paying agents in the United Kingdom.[8] Because of the stricter requirements of the Stock Exchange rules, it is not possible for a company to publish its half-yearly report by simply making copies available to the public at certain addresses, but on the other hand, if it adopts the alternative of sending copies of the report to the holders of its listed securities, it does not under the Stock Exchange rules have to advertise the availability of copies in the press. In practice United Kingdom companies whose shares are listed on the Stock Exchange will publish their half-yearly reports in the same way as their annual accounts are required to be published by the Companies Acts,[9] namely, by sending copies to the registered holders of their shares and debentures, and because of the prevalence of shares and debentures in registered form among United Kingdom companies and the rarity of shares and debentures in bearer form, it is unlikely that they will publish their half-yearly reports in full in the press.

The Interim Reports Directive requires a listed company to send a copy of its half-yearly report to the competent authority of each member state of the European Community where its shares are listed simultaneously with its publication in the country whose law governs the company.[10] The Stock Exchange rules repeat this requirement, and in particular require a copy of the report to be sent to the Company Announcements Office.[8]

5 Interim Reports Directive, art 9(6); The Stock Exchange: *Admission of Securities to Listing*, Section 5, Chapter 2, para 25.4.
6 Interim Reports Directive, art 4(1) and (2); The Stock Exchange: *Admission of Securities to Listing*, Section 5, Chapter 2, para 24.
7 Interim Reports Directive, art 7(1).
8 The Stock Exchange: *Admission of Securities to Listing*, Section 5, Chapter 2, para 24.
9 Companies Act 1948, s 158(1) (now Companies Act 1985, s 240(1)).
10 Interim Reports Directive, art 7(3).

OTHER OBLIGATIONS OF LISTED COMPANIES

The continuing obligations of a company which has a listing for its shares or debt securities (other than the obligation to prepare and publish a half-yearly report) are imposed either by the Admission Directive, Schedules C or D, as implemented by the Stock Exchange's own rules which give effect to or supplement the Admission Directive, or are independent requirements unconnected with the Admission Directive and largely derived from the former standard listing agreement which listed companies entered into. The continuing obligations imposed by the Admission Directive and the Stock Exchange rules supplementing them have already been dealt with in Chapter 2, and so only the independent Stock Exchange requirements need be dealt with here.

The most numerous additional requirements of the Stock Exchange rules relate to the publicity which listed companies must give to various events and items of information and the obligation imposed on them to notify holders of securities of the company individually in certain cases. Additionally, the Stock Exchange rules require listed companies to do or abstain from doing certain acts in order to protect the interests of security holders; the most important of these further rules are those which relate to the action which listed companies must take when they make substantial acquisitions or realisations of assets.

Notification of current information to the Stock Exchange and security holders

A listed company is under a general obligation to notify the Company Announcements Office of the Stock Exchange of any information necessary to enable holders of the company's listed securities and the public to appraise the company's position and avoid the establishment of a false market.[11] This obligation is particularly important when the information is not available to investors generally from another source (eg preliminary profit figures, dividend to be recommended), or is confidential information, and in either case the information is price-sensitive, that is, its disclosure on the market or to the public would be likely to have a material effect on the current dealing price of the securities. Such information must be notified to the Company Announcements Office as soon as practicable so that no particular investors are privileged to have the information when others are not, but this does not prevent the company maintaining confidentiality (eg in respect of the state of negotiations for a substantial contract or for a takeover or merger in which the company will or may be involved), provided that any discovered breach of confidentiality or the likelihood that it may occur is followed by a warning notice given by the company indicating the fact that negotiations are progressing or a development is taking place and that fuller information will be notified later.[12] If a listed company intends to disclose price-sensitive information at a meeting of holders of its securities, it must simultaneously notify that information to

---

11 The Stock Exchange: *Admission of Securities to Listing*, Section 5, Chapter 2, para 1 (see p 46, above).
12 Ibid, Section 5, Chapter 2, paras 1.1 and 1.2.

the Company Announcements Office.[13] In appropriate circumstances (particularly where a takeover offer is likely to be made) the company may request a temporary suspension of dealings in its securities until a fuller announcement can be made, and if the company does not request a suspension the Quotations Committee may impose it.[14] On the other hand, if the disclosure of information would normally be called for, but its release or premature release might prejudice the company's legitimate interests, the Quotations Department may be notified instead of an announcement being published by the Company Announcements Office, and the Quotations Committee may permit the company not to disclose the information or to defer disclosure.[15] Dealings in the company's securities will not then be suspended.

The Stock Exchange rules calling for the earliest possible disclosure of information which may affect the dealing price of listed securities are intended to ensure that dealing prices are realistic (ie that the market is not a false one), and that persons who have privileged access to price-sensitive information may not make use of it by dealing in listed securities with other persons who do not have such access. The Stock Exchange rules requiring disclosure are buttressed by the requirement that each listed company shall adopt its own rules restricting dealings by its directors in listed securities of the company in terms no less strict than those of the model code set out in the Stock Exchange rules,[16] and by the provisions of companies legislation which make dealing in listed securities of a company a criminal offence if the accused is connected with the company and is in possession of unpublished price-sensitive information concerning it or transactions concerning it at the time.[17]

A listed company must notify the Company Announcements Office of several specific events and matters which concern it, whether they are likely to have an effect on dealing prices for its listed securities or not. The principal items among these events and matters are major new developments in the company's business activities which may lead to substantial movement in the price of its shares or, if it has issued listed debt securities, which may affect its ability to meet its commitments;[18] board decisions to pay or pass dividends or interest payments on listed debt securities;[19] changes in the company's issued share or loan capital;[20] the basis of allotment of shares or debt securities offered to the public generally for cash, whether the issue has been over-subscribed, fully subscribed or under-subscribed;[1] information required to be notified to the Stock Exchange by the City Code on Takeovers and Mergers in connection with

---

13 The Stock Exchange: *Admission of Securities to Listing*, Section 5, Chapter 2, para 1.9.
14 Ibid, Section 1, Chapter 1, para 15.
15 Ibid, Section 5, Chapter 2, para 1.10.
16 Ibid, Section 5, Chapter 2, para 45.
17 Companies Act 1980, s 68(1) and (2) and s 73(1) and (2) (now Company Securities (Insider Dealing) Act 1985, s 1(1) and (2)).
18 The Stock Exchange: *Admission of Securities to Listing*, section 5, Chapter 2, para 5. This rule repeats the requirement of the Admission Directive, Sch C, para 5(*a*) and Sch D, para 4(*a*) (see pp 41 and 44, above).
19 The Stock Exchange: *Admission of Securities to Listing*, Section 5, Chapter 2, para 7.
20 Ibid, section 5, Chapter 2, para 10.
 1 Ibid, section 5, Chapter 2, para 13.

takeover and other general offers made by the company for the shares or other securities of another company, or by another company for its shares or other securities;[2] information given to the company in fulfilment of legal obligations to notify it of interests in 5 per cent or more of any class of issued shares of the company carrying unrestricted voting rights and of interests held by directors and their families in shares or debentures of the company or of companies in the same group;[3] purchases by the company of its own listed shares or debt securities;[4] changes in the general character or nature of the business of the company or of the group of which it is the parent company;[5] and changes in the composition of the company's board of directors.[6]

Communications between a listed company and its shareholders or debenture holders are by circular sent to the addresses entered in the company's register of members or debenture holders. The company must accompany notices of general meetings or meetings of a class of shareholders with explanatory circulars dealing with the purpose and effect of the measures proposed, but if the meeting is an annual general meeting, the explanatory material may be incorporated in the directors' annual report and it need not deal with routine items of business, such as laying and approving the company's annual accounts, declaring dividends and re-electing directors and auditors.[7] Circulars must also be sent to shareholders in connection with substantial acquisitions and disposals of assets by a listed company and takeovers and mergers involving it.[8] Whether circulars are sent to the holders of listed shares in compliance with Stock Exchange rules or voluntarily by the company, they must first be submitted in draft to the Quotations Department for approval, but circulars sent to the holders of listed debt securities only require such approval if they are in respect of proposals to alter the rights attached to their securities.[9] If circulars are sent to the holders of a particular class of shares or debt securities, copies or summaries of the circulars must also be sent to the holders of all other listed securities of the company, unless the matters dealt with in the circular do not affect the holders of those other securities.[10] Six copies of circulars sent by a listed company to holders of its shares or other securities must simultaneously be delivered to the Company Announcements Office.[11]

2 Ibid, section 5, Chapter 2, para 15; City Code on Takeovers and Mergers (1985 Edition), paras 8.1 and 17.1.
3 The Stock Exchange: *Admission of Securities to Listing*, Section 5, Chapter 2, para 16(*a*) and (*b*). The legal obligations to notify the company are imposed by the Companies Act 1967, s 27, Companies Act 1976, s 24 and Companies Act 1981, s 63 (now Companies Act 1985, ss 198 and 324). It is accepted that the company need not notify information it obtains as a result of its own investigations under the Companies Act 1981, s 74 (now Companies Act 1985, s 212) unless the information reveals that a person and his associates are interested in at least 5 per cent of the issued voting share capital of the company.
4 The Stock Exchange: *Admission of Securities to Listing*, Section 5, Chapter 2, para 17.
5 Ibid, Section 5, Chapter 2, para 18.
6 Ibid, Section 5, Chapter 2, para 42.
7 Ibid, Section 5, Chapter 2, para 32.
8 See p 127, below.
9 The Stock Exchange: *Admission of Securities to Listing*, Section 5, Chapter 2, para 31.
10 Ibid, Section 5, Chapter 2, para 39.
11 Ibid, Section 5, Chapter 2, para 35.

The circulation of annual accounts and reports

The Stock Exchange rules require listed companies to publish annual accounts and directors' reports to holders of their securities so that they are periodically kept fully informed about the company's financial position and the trends in its business activities and their profitability. These rules repeat in extended or stricter form obligations which are already imposed on listed companies by the Companies Acts.

A listed company must send copies of its annual accounts and directors' report to its shareholders and debenture holders and to the Registrar of Companies within six months after the end of the financial year to which the accounts and report relate.[12] If the company has subsidiaries, the accounts must be in consolidated form, and the company's own annual accounts must also be published if they contain significant additional information, but apparently not otherwise.[12] The annual accounts must give a true and fair view of the company's affairs and its profit or loss, and must be supplemented by more detailed or additional information if this is required to give such a true and fair view.[12] These provisions largely reflect the company's obligations under the Companies Acts.[13] However, the Stock Exchange rules shorten by one month the time within which a listed company must publish its annual accounts,[14] and apparently dispense with the publication of both the balance sheet and profit and loss account of a parent company if it publishes consolidated annual accounts, whereas the Companies Acts dispense only with the profit and loss account in that case.[15]

A listed company must include in its directors' annual report sent to its shareholders and debenture holders and to the Registrar of Companies various detailed items of information, some of which are required by the Companies Acts and others only by the Stock Exchange rules themselves. The directors' annual report must in addition to its general contents contain the following information: (i) if there are significant departures in the company's annual accounts from the applicable current standard accounting practices, the reasons for the departures,[16] (ii) an explanation of the company's trading results if they differ materially from any published forecast of profits or losses by the company,[17] (iii) a geographical analysis of the company's or group's net turnover and of the contribution to trading profits or losses of trading operations carried on outside the United Kingdom and Ireland,[18] (iv) the name of the principal country where each of the reporting company's subsidiaries operates,[19] (v) in respect of each associated company of the reporting company (not being a subsidiary) in

---

12 The Stock Exchange: *Admission of Securities to Listing*, Section 5, Chapter 2, para 20.
13 Companies Act 1948, s 149(1)–(3) and Companies Act 1976, s 1(1)–(4), (6) and (7) (now Companies Act 1985, s 227(1)–(3) and s 228(1)–(4)).
14 Companies Act 1976, s 6(1) and (2) (now Companies Act 1985, s 242(1) and (2)).
15 Companies Act 1948, s 149(5) (now Companies Act 1985, s 228(7)).
16 The Stock Exchange: *Admission of Securities to Listing*, Section 5, Chapter 2, para 21(*a*). The current standard accounting practices are in part set out in the Statements of Standard Accounting Practice issued by the principal accountancy bodies in the United Kingdom and Ireland.
17 The Stock Exchange: *Admission of Securities to Listing*, Section 5, Chapter 2, para 21(*b*).
18 Ibid, Section 5, Chapter 2, para 21(*c*).
19 Ibid, Section 5, Chapter 2, para 21(*d*).

which that company and its subsidiaries hold at least 20 per cent of the issued equity share capital, a statement of the country where the associated company principally operates, particulars of its issued share capital and debt securities and the percentage of each class of its debt securities in which the reporting company has an interest,[20] (vi) a statement as at the end of the company's financial year of the outstanding amount of bank loans and overdrafts owing by it and, in respect of other borrowing by the company, the aggregate amount repayable within one year or on demand, between one and two years, between two and five years, and after five years or more,[1] (vii) the amount of interest for the financial year on loans to and indebtedness of the reporting company or group if the interest has been treated as part of the capital cost of acquiring or producing fixed assets,[2] (viii) in the case of a United Kingdom company, a statement of the interests of each director in the issued share capital of the reporting company and other companies in the same group at the end of the financial year and of options held by each such director at the end of the year to subscribe for or purchase shares in those companies, together with a note of changes in each director's interests and options during the year,[3] (ix) in the case of a United Kingdom company, a statement of interests of persons in five per cent or more of any class of the reporting company's issued share capital carrying unrestricted voting rights if the interests have been notified to the company under the Companies Acts,[4] (x) a statement whether the reporting company is a close company for the purposes of corporation tax, capital gains tax and capital transfer tax and whether there has been a change in its status in that respect since the end of the financial year,[5] (xi) details of any substantial contract entered into by the reporting company or any other company in the same group which was subsisting (ie was not fully carried out) during or at the end of the financial year and in which any director or substantial shareholder of the reporting company is or was interested; a substantial contract is one involving an amount or value equal to one per cent or more

20 Ibid, Section 5, Chapter 2, para 21(*e*). This supplements the information about the percentage interest of the reporting company in each class of the issued equity and other share capital of the associated company required in the reporting company's accounts by the Companies Act 1967, s 4(1) (now Companies Act 1985, s 231(1) and Sch 5, para 7). The Companies Acts apply when the reporting company and its subsidiaries hold at least 10 per cent of the other company's equity share capital.
 1 The Stock Exchange: *Admission of Securities to Listing*, Section 5, Chapter 2, para 21(*f*). This goes further than the accounting rules in the Companies Acts, which require bank loans and overdrafts to be segregated from debenture loans and the aggregates of both such classes of loans to be sub-divided according to whether they fall due for repayment within 1 year or more than one year; the notes to the annual accounts must also segregate both such classes of loans so that the aggregate amount repayable within 5 years is shown separately from the aggregate amount repayable after 5 years (Companies Act 1981, s 1(2) and Sch 1, Balance Sheet Formats and para 48(1) (now Companies Act 1985, s 228(1) Balance Sheet Formats and para 48(1)).
 2 The Stock Exchange: *Admission of Securities to Listing*, Section 5, Chapter 2, para 21(*g*).
 3 Ibid, Section 5, Chapter 2, para 21(*h*). This requirement coincides with that in the Companies Act 1967, s 16(1)(*e*) (now Companies Act 1985, s 235(3) and Sch 7, para 2), which also applies to directors' interests in debentures issued by the reporting company and other companies in the same group.
 4 The Stock Exchange: *Admission of Securities to Listing*, Section 5, Chapter 2, para 21(*i*). The notification given to the company is made obligatory by the Companies Act 1981, s 68(1) and (3) and s 82(2) (now Companies Act 1985, s 198(1) and (2) and s 199(2)).
 5 The Stock Exchange: *Admission of Securities to Listing*, Section 5, Chapter 2, para 21(*f*).

of the reporting company's net assets, or if it is a current trading transaction, one per cent or more of the company's purchases, sales, payments or receipts; a substantial shareholder is one entitled to exercise or control the exercise of at least 30 per cent of the voting power at general meetings of the company, or to control the composition of the board of directors,[6] (xii) details of contracts for the provision of services for the reporting company or any of its subsidiaries by a substantial shareholder (defined as above), but disclosure is unnecessary if the contract was for services which it is the principal business of the substantial shareholder to provide and the contract is not substantial (as defined above),[7] (xiii) particulars of any arrangement for the waiver of a director's remuneration or for the waiver of a shareholder's right to payment of dividends,[8] and (xiv) in the case of a United Kingdom company, details of any authorisation by a general meeting for the company to purchase shares in itself which existed at the end of the financial year, and the names of the sellers of shares in the company purchased or proposed to be purchased by it during the financial year, except where the shares have been or will be purchased on the market or under a tender or proportionate offer made to all shareholders of the company.[9]

The Stock Exchange rules contain particular provisions in respect of the annual accounts of listed companies which are not governed by United Kingdom law. Such companies must each year send copies of their annual accounts and directors' report in English to all holders of their securities whose registered addresses are in the United Kingdom, and the accounts and report must be made up to a date not earlier than six months before their circulation and must normally cover a period of 12 months.[10] The annual accounts must be audited by a practising accountant of good standing who is independent of the company, and his report must be annexed to the accounts and circulated with them and must be to the same effect as the auditor's report on the annual accounts of a United Kingdom company.[11] If the annual accounts do not conform to the international accounting standards published by the International Accounting Standards Committee, any significant departure from those standards must be disclosed and explained.[12] The annual accounts or report must disclose the interests of directors and their families in the shares of the company and also the interests of persons interested in five per cent or more of the issued share capital, and details of options to subscribe for or purchase shares in the company held by any such persons must be given.[13] If any of the shares or debt securities of the company are in bearer form, a notice must be published in two daily newspapers published in the United Kingdom giving an address in the City of London (or elsewhere in the United Kingdom if the Quotations Committee approves) where copies of the accounts and report in English may be obtained free of charge.[14]

6 The Stock Exchange: *Admission of Securities to Listing*, Section 5, Chapter 2, para 21(*k*) and (*l*) and para 21.9.
7 Ibid, Section 5, Chapter 2, para 21(*m*).
8 Ibid, Section 5, Chapter 2, para 21(*n*) and (*o*).
9 Ibid, Section 5, Chapter 2, para 21(*p*).
10 Ibid, Section 5, Chapter 2, para 23(*a*).
11 Ibid, Section 5, Chapter 2, para 23(*b*) and (*c*).
12 Ibid, Section 5, Chapter 2, para 23(*e*).
13 Ibid, Section 5, Chapter 2, para 23(*f*).
14 Ibid, Section 5, Chapter 2, para 23(*g*).

Other rules for the protection of security holders

The Stock Exchange rules contain a number of provisions which are intended to protect the interests of holders of the shares or debt securities of a listed company or to enable them to exercise their rights effectively. Some of these provisions repeat or extend obligations or restrictions imposed by the Companies Acts, whereas others impose obligations which have no parallel in those Acts.

If directors of a listed company call a general meeting to resolve on an increase in the company's nominal capital, they must state in the explanatory circular accompanying the notice of the meeting whether they have any present intention to issue any part of that increased capital,[15] and if after the increase 10 per cent or more of the share capital carrying voting rights will remain unissued, the explanatory circular must state that no issue of shares will be made which would effectively alter control over the company without the prior approval of the shareholders by an ordinary resolution passed at a general meeting.[16] These rules supplement the provisions of the Companies Acts which require the authorisation of the shareholders by an ordinary resolution of a general meeting for the directors to issue any unissued share capital, but such an authorisation may only be given for a period not exceeding five years in advance;[17] the Stock Exchange rule therefore becomes important when the directors come to exercise their power to issue unissued shares, because it will then be necessary for them to obtain a further authorisation by ordinary resolution if the issue will result in an effective alteration of control of the company. The Stock Exchange rules do not define an effective alteration of control, but it would appear to include situations additional to that where a person or group of persons increase their holdings from less than 50 per cent to more than 50 per cent of the company's issued voting share capital. If a substantial number of the issued voting shares are held by persons who have small holdings and who do not normally act together, the acquisition of voting shares which results in the acquirer or acquiring group holding 35 per cent of the voting power at general meetings may transfer effective control over the company. If this will be achieved by an issue of further voting shares or such an issue in combination with purchases of voting shares, the issue must be approved by a general meeting of shareholders before it takes place.

The Stock Exchange rules provide that if a listed company intends to issue any securities with an equity element for cash, it must first offer them to its existing equity shareholders in proportion to their holdings and, where appropriate, the offer must extend to other holders of securities with an equity element (eg debentures convertible into ordinary shares or carrying subscription rights for ordinary shares); the company may issue securities with an equity element in any other way (eg under an open offer to its shareholders, or by an offer to the public at large or by a placing on the Stock Exchange) only if its shareholders approve by resolution of a general meeting.[18] This rule reflects the statutory rights of equity shareholders

---

15 Ibid, Section 5, Chapter 2, para 33.
16 Ibid, Section 5, Chapter 2, para 34.
17 Companies Act 1980, s 14(1)–(3) (now Companies Act 1985, s 80(1)–(4)).
18 The Stock Exchange: *Admission of Securities to Listing*, Section 5, Chapter 2, para 38(*a*).

conferred by the Companies Acts to subscribe for further issues of equity securities for cash in proportion to their existing holdings, unless a general meeting of the company otherwise resolved by special resolution,[19] and in fact the statutory preferential subscription rights were preceded by provisions similar to the present Stock Exchange rule which were incorporated in the listing agreement formerly entered into by companies on being granted a listing.[20] There are, however, a number of differences between the Stock Exchange rules and the statutory preferential subscription rights, and where they differ the statutory provisions must prevail. In the first place the Stock Exchange rule requires a company to offer a further issue of equity securities for cash to both its existing equity shareholders and holders of other securities with an equity element issued by it, where this is appropriate.[18] This would require a proportionate offer to be made to holders of the company's debt securities which are convertible into ordinary shares or which carry subscription rights for such shares, even though the holders have not yet exercised their conversion or subscription rights,[1] whereas the Companies Acts require the offer to be confined to the company's existing equity shareholders, the holders of debt securities with an equity element who have not already exercised their right to acquire equity shares in the company being excluded.[19] Secondly, the Stock Exchange rule makes no provision for the exercise of preferential subscription rights over a further issue of equity shares of a particular class (eg preferred ordinary shares) so as to give existing shareholders of that class prior preferential subscription rights over the further issue before it is offered to equity shareholders generally; the Companies Acts, on the other hand, permit the company's memorandum or articles or association to confer such prior preferential rights.[2] Finally, the Stock Exchange rule does not exclude further issues of equity securities under an employees' share scheme so as to avoid the need to offer such securities to all the company's existing equity shareholders for subscription before allotting them exclusively to employees or trustees for them. The Companies Acts expressly cover this point, so that equity securities may be allotted directly under an employees' share scheme,[3] but it is probable that even before the statutory preferential subscription rights were introduced by the Companies Act 1980, the Stock Exchange standard form of listing agreement did admit an implied exception in favour of share option and profit sharing schemes for the benefit of employees.

The Stock Exchange rules extend the protection given to existing equity shareholders against the dilution of their fractional interests in the company's equity by requiring a listed company to obtain the approval of a

19 Companies Act 1980, s 17(1) and (4) and s 18(1) and (2) (now Companies Act 1985, s 89(1) and (4) and s 95(1) and (2)).
20 The Stock Exchange: *Admission of Securities to Listing* (1979 edn), Sch VIII, Part A, para 13(1). The statutory rights were not derived from this provision, but were created to give effect to the Second Directive of the Council of Ministers of the European Community (77/91/EEC) of 13 December 1976 in respect of the formation and capital of public limited liability companies (published in the Official Journal dated 31 January 1977, No L 26/1).
 1 The offer of further equity securities to such holders of debt securities would presumably be proportionate to the number of equity shares which they are entitled to take by exercising the conversion or subscription rights conferred by their debt securities.
 2 Companies Act 1980, s 17(2) and (3) (now Companies Act 1985, s 89(2) and (3)).
 3 Companies Act 1980, s 17(5) (now Companies Act 1985, s 89(5)).

general meeting of its shareholders before any major subsidiary of the company makes an issue of securities having an equity element for cash if the issue will materially dilute the percentage equity interest of the company in the subsidiary.[4] This provision has no parallel in the Companies Acts, which impose no obligation on a parent company to maintain its proportionate holding of equity shares in any of its subsidiaries; it may be, however, that it would be a breach of duty by the directors of the parent company not to take up equity shares offered under a rights offer made by a subsidiary if it was in the interests of the parent company to do so and the parent company had, or could obtain, the necessary resources to pay the issue price of the shares. The Stock Exchange rule applies to the parent company in all cases where the subsidiary in question accounts for 25 per cent or more of the consolidated net assets or pre-tax trading profits of the group, although a subsidiary may be a major one even though it does not attain these fractions.[5] The parent company's obligation applies whether the subsidiary takes the initiative and offers the further securities with an equity element to its existing equity shareholders by a rights offer (which it will normally have to do unless it is a private company whose memorandum or articles exclude the statutory preferential subscription rights of equity shareholders),[6] or whether the parent company must take the initiative to preserve its proportionate holding in the subsidiary (eg by opposing a resolution proposed at a general meeting of the subsidiary that the statutory preferential subscription rights shall not apply).[7] If a parent company does not take up equity securities under a rights offer made by a major subsidiary, it may instead of obtaining a resolution of approval from its own shareholders to the consequent material dilution of its interest in the subsidiary, offer to renounce its subscription rights to its own shareholders in proportion to their existing holdings, so that they and the parent company together will have the same percentage interest in the subsidiary's equity as the parent company had before.[8] The Stock Exchange rules do not define a material dilution of a parent company's interest in a subsidiary, but it is submitted that a five per cent or greater dilution would be a material one, as would any dilution which resulted in the subsidiary no longer being a subsidiary of the parent company, or in the parent company losing the power to block a special resolution at a general meeting of the subsidiary or any resolution requiring a particular majority under the terms of the subsidiary's articles of association.

The remaining requirements of the Stock Exchange rules designed to protect the interests of investors are of a diverse character.

The Stock Exchange rules supplement the obligation imposed on every company to inform its shareholders in notices calling general and class meetings of their right to appoint proxies to represent them and to vote in their place, and the obligation to recognise all proxy appointments notified to the company not less than 48 hours before the meeting is held.[9] The Stock Exchange rules require the company also to send with notices of all

---

4 The Stock Exchange: *Admission of securities to Listing*, Section 5, Chapter 2, para 38(*b*).
5 Ibid, para 38.3.
6 Companies Act 1980, s 17(9) (now Companies Act 1985, s 91(1)).
7 Companies Act 1980, s 18(1) and (2) (now Companies Act 1985, s 95(1) and (2)).
8 The Stock Exchange: *Admission of Securities to Listing*, section 5, Chapter 2, para 38.3.
9 Companies Act 1948, s 136(2) and (3) (now Companies Act 1985, s 372(3) and (5)).

meetings of holders of the company's securities (including debenture holders' meetings) proxy appointment forms which enable the security holders to indicate in respect of each resolution proposed whether their proxy is to vote for or against the resolution.[10] This does not mean that a system of postal voting is introduced; a proxy must still attend the meeting and cast the vote of the member he represents if it is to be counted. But the two-way proxy form does raise the question whether, as regards the company, the proxy's mandate is limited to casting a vote in the manner indicated in the form as completed by the member. If it does, it reduces the proxy's function to that of a messenger, and leaves him no discretion as to the way he will vote, whatever may have emerged in discussion before the vote is taken, and whatever amendments may have been made to the resolution before it is put to the vote.

Another provision in the Stock Exchange rules for the protection of investors by providing them with relevant information requires listed companies to make available copies of all directors' service contracts entered into for more than one year, or memoranda of such contracts if they are not in writing, for inspection by all interested persons at the company's registered office or at the office where transfers of securities issued by the company are registered during the period from the despatch of notices calling the annual general meeting to the holding of that meeting, and also to make these documents available at the place where the meeting is held for 15 minutes before it commences and during the meeting, and the times when the copies or memoranda will be available for inspection must be stated in the notice calling the annual general meeting.[11] Furthermore, the directors' report circulated in advance of the annual general meeting and presented to the shareholders at the meeting must disclose the unexpired period of any service contract of a director proposed for re-election if the contract was entered into for more than one year.[12] These requirements supplement those in the Companies Acts which oblige all companies to keep copies or memoranda of service contracts between their directors and the company or any of its subsidiaries available for inspection by members (but not debenture holders or other persons) at the registered office of the company or at the office where its register of members is kept;[13] however, the statutory obligation differs from the Stock Exchange rule in that it applies throughout the year, but only to contracts which still have at least one year unexpired and which cannot be terminated by the company within the next 12 months without the payment of compensation.[13]

A final group of obligations imposed on listed companies by the Stock Exchange rules facilitates dealings in their shares and debt securities. Listed companies must arrange for instruments of transfer of securities issued by them to be certified against the lodgement with the company or its transfer agents of share or debenture stock certificates or temporary documents (ie letters of allotment or acceptance) and for the return of certified transfers on the day the company or its transfer agents receive

10 The Stock Exchange: *Admission of Securities to Listing*, Section 5, Chapter 2, para 37.
11 Ibid, Section 5, Chapter 2, para 43(*a*) and (*b*).
12 Ibid, Section 5, Chapter 2, para 43(*c*).
13 Companies Act 1967, s 26(1), (2), (4) and (7), as amended by Companies Act 1980, s 61(1) (now Companies Act 1985, s 318(1)–(3), (7) and (11)).

them; the company must arrange also for the issue of split letters of allotment or acceptance on the lodgement of letters of allotment or acceptance for larger amounts of securities.[14] The company must issue certificates in respect of registered shares and debt securities without payment of a fee,[15] and certificates must be issued within 1 month after the right to renounce temporary documents expires or within 14 days after the lodgement of instruments of transfer for registration.[16] Finally, if share warrants to bearer or bearer share certificates are issued by the company, they must be issued in exchange for registered share certificates within 14 days after they are lodged for the purpose; registered share certificates must likewise be issued in exchange for warrants or bearer share certificates within 14 days after they are surrendered for the purpose; and instruments of transfer must be certified against the lodgement of warrants or bearer share certificates on the day they are received.[17]

Acquisitions and realisations of assets

The Stock Exchange rules require steps of varying complexity to be taken if a listed company acquires or disposes of a substantial amount of its assets (including its holdings of shares or securities issued by another company). At one extreme, if a director or substantial shareholder (ie any person who holds or has within the previous 12 months held 10 per cent or more of the issued share capital carrying unrestricted voting rights of the listed company or any other company in the same group as it)[18] or an associate of such a director or substantial shareholder is interested in the transaction, it will usually be necessary for a circular in respect of the transaction to be sent to the shareholders of the listed company and for the transaction to be approved by a general meeting of the company.[19] At the other extreme, if the transaction is one where the value of the assets acquired or disposed of compared with the value of all the assets of the listed company represents a fraction less than 5 per cent, and additionally the profits attributable to the assets acquired or disposed of compared to the profits attributable to the listed company's assets as a whole, the value of the consideration for the acquisition or disposal compared to the value of the listed company's assets as a whole, and the amount of any equity capital issued by the listed company for the acquisition compared to its previously issued equity capital, all represent fractions less than 5 per cent as well, no announcement

---

14 The Stock Exchange: *Admission of Securities to Listing*, Section 5, Chapter 2, para 26. A certification of an instrument of transfer states that the share or debenture stock certificate in respect of the securities has been lodged with the company or its transfer agents, and this enables a purchaser to complete a purchase of part only of the securities represented by the certificate without the certificate being delivered to him; after completion the purchaser delivers the instrument of transfer to the company, which registers it and issues a new certificate for the securities purchased to the purchaser and a balance certificate for the remaining securities represented by the original certificate to the seller. Split letters of allotment are issued when an allottee renounces or assigns his right to part only of the securities allotted to him under a single letter of allotment.

15 The Stock Exchange: *Admission of Securities to Listing*, Section 5, Chapter 2, para 27.

16 Ibid, Section 5, Chapter 2, para 28.

17 Ibid, Section 5, Chapter 2, para 30.

18 Ibid, Section 6, Chapter 1, para 1.2.

19 Ibid, Section 6, Chapter 1, para 6.1.

or circular sent to shareholders or shareholder approval is called for.[20]

The Stock Exchange rules divide acquisitions and realisations of assets by a listed company into five classes for the purpose of graduating the degree of publicity which must be given to the transaction and determining whether shareholder approval of it is required. The first four classes are determined by the percentage ratios mentioned in the preceding paragraph, and one of them is really a sub-class of one of the other classes where the ratio of the value of assets involved to total assets of the company is particularly high. The final class depends, not on ratios, but on the identity of the persons who are interested in the transaction, namely, directors and substantial shareholders of the company and their associates.

The ratios which are applied in the first four classes are, as indicated above, four in number, and the transaction falls into the class determined by taking the highest ratio resulting from applying all four of them. The first ratio is that between the value of the assets acquired or disposed of by the company and the value of all its assets before the acquisition or disposal; the second ratio is that between the net profits attributable to the assets acquired or disposed of according to the most recent audited annual accounts (or later unaudited accounts if there is a material difference) and the total profits similarly ascertained of the acquiring or disposing company, and in calculating the ratio net profits must be taken after deducting all charges (eg debenture interest) other than taxation and excluding extraordinary, non-recurrent items; the third ratio is that between the aggregate value of the consideration given or received by the company for the acquisition or disposal and its total assets before the acquisition or disposal; and the fourth ratio, which applies only on an acquisition in return for an issue of shares, is between the equity share capital issued by the company as consideration for the assets acquired and the issued equity share capital of the company immediately before the acquisition.[1] Obviously, these ratios could be kept artificially low by carrying out connected acquisitions or disposals separately, and to counteract this the Quotations Committee or its chairman may direct that acquisitions or disposals shall be aggregated if they have taken place since the publication of the last annual accounts of the company or the issue by it of the most recent circular to its shareholders in connection with an acquisition or disposal (whichever is later), but the value of assets acquired or disposed of in respect of which adequate information has already been issued to shareholders will be treated as part of the net tangible assets or profits of the company (as the case may be) and not as a component of the transaction which is compared with them.[2]

Class 1 transactions

If any of the ratios mentioned in the preceding paragraph is 15 per cent or more, the transaction falls into Class 1, but if the assets of the company include substantial intangible assets (eg investments, industrial property rights), the Quotations Committee may allow a higher percentage than 15

---

20 The Stock Exchange: *Admission of Securities to Listing*, Section 6, Chapter 1, paras 5.1 and 2.
 1 Ibid, Section 6, Chapter 1, para 3.1.
 2 Ibid, Section 6, Chapter 1, para 3.3.

per cent to be taken as the threshold, and if all the ratios other than the third (consideration/total assets) are materially less than 15 per cent and the consideration is calculated by reference to the market value of equity share capital (eg an issue of ordinary shares as consideration for the acquisition), the Quotations Committee may treat the transaction as falling into Class 2, and not Class 1.[1]

If a transaction falls into Class 1, the company must send six copies of an announcement concerning it to the Company Announcements Office for publication to the market and by the press as soon as possible after the terms of the transaction have been agreed.[3] The announcement must set out: (a) particulars of the assets acquired or disposed of; (b) a description of the business activities of any undertaking acquired or disposed of; (c) the aggregate value of the consideration and its components (eg cash or an issue of shares or debentures) and any arrangements for deferred payment; (d) the value of the assets acquired or disposed of; (e) the net profits attributable to the assets acquired or disposed of calculated in the same way as for applying the profit ratio; (f) the benefits expected to accrue to the company from the transaction; (g) details of any service contracts of proposed directors (eg directors of an acquired company who will become directors of the acquiring company); and (h) on a disposal of assets, the intended application of the proceeds of sale.[4] Additionally, the company must send a circular to its shareholders containing certain of the items of information required in listing particulars, and this must be done whether the company issues securities in connection with the transaction or not. The circular will not constitute listing particulars, and it is in no way governed by the Listing Particulars Directive; the items for inclusion in the circular are simply designated by reference to the corresponding items which would have to be included in listing particulars.

If the company is making an acquisition, the relevant items to be included in the circular are: the name of the company and its registered or head office; a statement that experts to whom statements or reports are attributed in the circular have given and not withdrawn their consents to the inclusion of the statements or reports; a statement that an application has been made to the Stock Exchange for any shares or debt securities of the acquiring company issued or to be issued as consideration for the acquisition to be listed (if appropriate); a statement by the directors of the acquiring company that the working capital of itself and other companies in the same group will be adequate after the completion of the acquisition, or if not, what steps will be taken to make the working capital adequate; the names of persons who are or will after the acquisition be individually interested in 5 per cent or more of the company's issued capital and the amount of their interests; the same statements in respect of potential income tax and capital transfer tax liability of the company as are required in listing particulars;[5] the same information in respect of litigation or arbitration proceedings in which the company or any other company in the same group is or has been involved, and as regards material contracts entered into by any such company, as is required in listing particulars;[6] a

---

3 Ibid, Section 6, Chapter 1 paras 2 and 3.8.
4 Ibid, Section 6, Chapter 1, para 4.2.
5 See p 63, above.   6 See pp 63 and 65, above.

statement of an address in the City of London where the company's memorandum and articles of association, any relevant debenture trust deed, particulars of the trustees of the deed and copies of directors' service contracts may be inspected; if the acquisition is in connection with a merger, or with a takeover or division of another company, or is an acquisition of the assets and liabilities of another undertaking, or involves a transfer of the whole or part of the assets of another undertaking, particulars of the consideration to be given and any consequential variation in directors' remuneration; a statement of any significant change in the financial or trading position of the acquiring company since the end of the last financial year for which it has published annual accounts or since the publication of its most recent interim report; particulars of the loan capital and borrowings outstanding of the acquiring company and other companies in the same group and of mortgages and charges on their assets; details of directors' actual and proposed service contracts with the acquiring company and other companies in the same group, and particulars of directors' interests in significant or unusual transactions with such companies if they have been entered into or were not wholly fulfilled at any time during or since the company's last complete financial year; each director's beneficial and other interests in shares or debentures of the acquiring company and other companies in the same group; information about the future prospects of the company and the group to which it belongs covering at least the current financial year; and finally, the basis on which any profit forecast included in the circular was prepared.[7] The circular containing these items of information must be accompanied by an accountant's report on the assets or undertaking which is being acquired, or in the case of a merger or takeover. the company which is being acquired, and the report must cover the last five financial years for which audited accounts have been published, but no such report is required if the acquiring company will obtain control of another listed company on the successful completion of the transaction.[8] The accountant's report must deal with all the matters included in the announcement about the acquisition which must be sent to the Company Announcements Office.[7]

If the company which engages in a Class 1 transaction is disposing of part of its assets or undertaking, the circular it must send to its shareholders must deal with the same matters as a circular relating to an acquisition falling under Class 1, but certain items are omitted (particularly details of the consideration to be given if the disposal is in connection with a merger or division or a transfer of the whole or part of the company's undertaking or assets, and any significant recent change in the financial or trading position of the company), and the circular must also deal with the matters included in the announcement about the disposal which must be sent to the Company Announcements Office.[7]

Major Class 1 transactions

Certain acquisitions or disposals of assets within Class 1 are treated as major Class 1 transactions, and form a class or sub-class of their own. This

7 The Stock Exchange: *Admission of Securities to Listing*, Section 6, Chapter 1, para 3.5.
8 Ibid, Section 6, Chapter 1, paras 3.5 and 3.6.

is so if the ratio between the value of the assets acquired or disposed of and the value of the assets of the acquiring or disposing company before the transaction equals or exceeds 25 per cent, or if the ratio between the net profits (after deducting all charges except taxation and excluding extraordinary items) attributable to the assets acquired or disposed of and the total net profits of the acquiring or disposing company equals or exceeds that percentage.[9] Additionally, an acquisition is a major Class 1 transaction if the ratio between the gross capital of the acquired undertaking or company and the gross capital of the acquiring company equals or exceeds 25 per cent; for this purpose the gross capital of the acquired undertaking or company is the value of the consideration to be given for it plus the outstanding debt securities and capital liabilities charged on or payable out of its assets (apportioned where necessary) plus the excess of its current assets over its current liabilities (again apportioned where necessary), plus the issued preference capital of the company or an apportioned part of it attributable to the undertaking; the gross capital of the acquiring company is taken to be the market value of its issued equity share capital immediately before the acquisition plus its issued and oustanding preference capital and debt securities (taken at market value if listed), plus its capital liabilities and any excess of its current assets over its current liabilities, plus minority interests in its subsidiaries.[9] If an acquisition or disposal is a major Class 1 transaction, the acquiring or disposing company must not only send an announcement of it to the Company Announcements Office and send a circular to its shareholders, but the company must also obtain the approval of the transaction by its shareholders by an ordinary resolution passed at a general meeting, and any contract for the acquisition or disposal must be made conditional on that approval being given.[9]

There is a further class or sub-class of major Class 1 transactions, namely very substantial acquisitions and reverse takeovers, which are subject to even more stringent rules. A Class 1 transaction is a very substantial acquisition if it is an acquisition of an undertaking or unlisted company or companies and any of the four ratios mentioned above for the purpose of classifying transactions equals or exceeds 100 per cent in respect of it.[10] An acquisition is a reverse takeover if taken together with other acquisitions during the preceding 12 months it will result in a change in the power to control the acquiring company by the introduction of a new majority shareholder or group of shareholders.[10] A very substantial acquisition or a reverse takeover must be approved by the shareholders of the acquiring company by an ordinary resolution passed at a general meeting before it is carried out, and any contract for the acquisition must be made conditional on that approval being given.[11] When the intended transaction is notified to the Stock Exchange, the Quotations Committee will suspend the listing of the acquiring company's securities until approval of the transaction is given by a general meeting, and upon that approval being given the listing will be cancelled, but will normally be restored on the company publishing full listing particulars appropriate for an introduction[12] of all its shares and debt

9 Ibid, Section 6, Chapter 1, para 3.4.
10 Ibid, Section 6, Chapter 1, para 2 (see p 129, above).
11 Ibid, Section 6, Chapter 1, para 7.
12 For the contents of listing particulars on an introduction of securities on the Stock Exchange, see p 90, above.

securities to listing.[11] However, if the transaction is in substance a merger of two companies or undertakings of similar size engaged in the same line of business, and there will be no material change in the directors or management of the companies involved or in voting control, and the merged company or acquiring company is suitable for listing, the Quotations Committee may lift the suspension of listing when full information about the transaction has been published, and it will not then be necessary to apply for a restored listing or to publish listing particulars, although approval of the transaction by a general meeting of the acquiring company will still be required before the transaction is carried out.[11] If in any case of a very substantial acquisition or reverse takeover the general meeting of the acquiring company does not approve the transaction, it cannot proceed, and any contract for the acquisition will be determined for non-fulfilment of the condition it must contain making it dependent on shareholder approval; a suspension of the company's listing will thereupon be lifted as no longer required.

Class 2 and Class 3 transactions

Class 2 and Class 3 transactions are defined by employing the same ratios as are used for Class 1 transactions.[13] If any of the four applicable ratios equals or exceeds 5 per cent but the transaction is not within Class 1, it will fall into Class 2.[14] The only step which the acquiring or disposing company must then take is to deliver six copies of an announcement of the transaction to the Company Annnouncements Office for publication to the market and by the press as soon as possible after the terms of the transaction have been agreed.[15] The contents of the announcement are the same as those in an announcement of a Class 1 transaction.[16] There is no need to send a circular to shareholders of the acquiring or disposing company or to obtain their approval, unless the transaction also falls within Class 4. Class 3 transactions are similarly defined by employing the four ratios which are used for Class 1 and 2 transactions.[13] If all those ratios are less than 5 per cent, no announcement or circular to shareholders and no approval of the transaction by a general meeting is required, unless the transaction also falls within Class 4.[17] However, an announcement must be sent to the Company Announcements Office for publication if the consideration for an acquisition includes shares or debt securities for which a listing will be sought.[18] The announcement need only state the number of securities which will be issued and brief details of the assets which are being acquired, but if it is necessary to avoid shareholders being misled, the announcement must also set out the aggregate value of the consideration for the acquisition and its components (eg issues of shares or debt securities), any arrangement for deferred payment, and the value of the assets being acquired.[18]

---

13 See p 128, above.
14 The Stock Exchange: *Admission of Securities to Listing*, Section 6, Chapter 1, para 4.1.
15 Ibid, Section 6, Chapter 1, paras 2 and 4.2.
16 See p 129, above.
17 The Stock Exchange: *Admission of Securities to Listing*, Section 6, Chapter 1, paras 2 and 5.1 and 2.
18 Ibid, Section 6, Chapter 1, para 5.2.

Class 4 transactions

Class 4 transactions are defined not by their size or proportion to the acquiring or disposing company's assets or profits, but by reference to the interest of one or more directors or substantial shareholders of the company or their associates in the transaction. An associate of a director or substantial shareholder is defined in similar terms to the definition in the Companies Acts of a person who is connected with a director.[19] The following are associates of a director or substantial shareholder, namely (a) his or her spouse or child under the age of 18 years; (b) a trustee of any trust of which the director or substantial shareholder or his spouse or minor child is a beneficiary or would be a beneficiary if discretionary powers were exercised in his favour; (c) a company in which the interests of a director or substantial shareholder together with the interests of his spouse and minor children extend to its issued equity share capital carrying at least 30 per cent of the voting power exercisable at general meetings, or carrying the power to appoint or control the appointment of a majority of its directors.[20] If a substantial shareholder is a company, its associates are (i) its subsidiaries, parent company and subsidiaries of its parent company; and (ii) any other company in which the substantial shareholder and companies in the same group are together interested in issued equity share capital carrying in the aggregate at least 30 per cent of the voting power exercisable at general meetings, or carrying the power to appoint or control the appointment of a majority of the directors.[20]

A transaction is a Class 4 transaction (whether it also falls into Class 1, 2 or 3 or not) if it is: (a) an acquisition or disposal of assets by the listed company or any of its subsidiaries from or to a director or substantial shareholder of the listed company or an associate of such a director or substantial shareholder; or (b) a transaction under which the listed company or any of its subsidiaries is to take an interest in another company any part of whose equity share capital has been or is to be acquired by a director of the listed company or an associate of such a director; or (c) a transaction one of whose principal purposes or consequences is the granting of credit or the making of a loan by the listed company or any of its subsidiaries to a director or substantial shareholder of the listed company or to an associate of such a director or substantial shareholder, but excluding the grant of credit on normal commercial terms in the ordinary and usual course of business; or (d) a takeover by the listed company or any of its subsidiaries the acceptance of which could result in a significant acquisition from a director or substantial shareholder of the listed company or from an associate of such a director or substantial shareholder; there is no quantitative definition of a significant acquisition, but it is interpreted as meaning significant in relation to the total number of shares for which the takeover offer is made, or significant in relation to the resulting shareholding which the director or substantial shareholder and their associates would hold in the acquiring company if the takeover were successful (ie on a takeover by an exchange of shares); or (e) the acceptance by the listed company or any of its subsidiaries of a takeover offer which would result in a significant

19 Companies Act 1980, s 64 (now Companies Act 1985, s 346).
20 The Stock Exchange: *Admission of Securities to Listing*, Section 6, Chapter 1, para 1.2.

disposal to a director or substantial shareholder of the listed company or an associate of such a director or substantial shareholder (eg by the acceptance giving a director or substantial shareholder the power through the offeror company to control the listed company).[1]

The Quotations Committee normally requires a circular to be sent to the shareholders of a listed company if a Class 4 transaction is proposed (whatever the size of the transaction), and also normally requires the approval of the transaction by the shareholders of the listed company passing an ordinary resolution approving it at a general meeting.[1] The Committee may require that the director, substantial shareholder or associate who is interested in the transaction shall not vote at the general meeting called to approve the transaction and that a statement that he may not vote shall be included in the circular sent to shareholders.[1] The circular must give full particulars of the transaction to which it relates, the name of the director or substantial shareholder who, or whose associate, is interested in the transaction and of the associate too if he is interested, and also the extent of the interest of the director, substantial shareholder or associate.[2] Sufficient information about the transaction should be included to show that it is fair and reasonable, and the advantages and disadvantages of it to the company must be pointed out so as to enable shareholders to reach their own conclusion.[2] If the transaction involves the acquisition or disposal of an asset by the listed company, an independent valuation will be required if the worth of the asset lies primarily in its capital value as distinct from its revenue generating capacity, and in all cases the opinion of an independent expert that the transaction is fair and reasonable so far as the shareholders' interests are concerned must be included in the circular.[2] A circular in respect of a Class 4 transaction must contain certain items of information required in listing particulars, but it will not constitute listing particulars since there is no application for the admission or restoration of the listed company's securities to listing, and listing particulars will be required only where a very substantial acquisition is involved. The circular must in addition to information about the transaction, set out the following information required in listing particulars, namely, the name and registered or head office of the company; a statement that experts whose reports or statements are contained in the circular have consented to their inclusion; the names of persons who are directly or indirectly interested in 5 per cent or more of the company's issued capital; a summary of material contracts entered into by the company within the previous two years; an address in the City of London where certain documents relating to the company may be inspected; if the transaction relates to a merger, division or takeover of a company or the acquisition of the whole or part of an undertaking or its assets, a statement of the aggregate consideration for the transaction and its components and any consequential variation in the remuneration of the listing company's directors; a statement of any significant change in the financial or trading position of the listed company or the group of companies to which it belongs since the end of the last financial year for which the company has published audited accounts, or since the publication of its most recent interim report; details of directors'

1 The Stock Exchange: *Admission of Securities to Listing*, Section 6, Chapter 1, para 6.1.
2 Ibid, Section 6, Chapter 1, para 6.2.

actual and proposed service contracts with the listed company and companies in the same group; and particulars of directors' interests in significant or unusual transactions with such companies if they have been entered into or were not wholly fulfilled at any time during or since the company's last complete financial year; and each director's beneficial and other interests in shares and debentures of the listed company and other companies in the same group.[2] Where applicable, the same statements as to the potential income tax and capital transfer tax liability of the company must also be included in the circular as in listing particulars.[2] If the transaction also falls within Class 1, the circular must also contain the additional information required under the rules relating to that Class.[2]

A Class 4 transaction must be reported to and approved by the shareholders of a listed company before a contract is entered into to carry it out, and a copy of the draft contract must be supplied to the Quotations Committee.[1] Nevertheless, a takeover offer may be made by a listed company even though it involves a Class 4 transaction, but the offer must be made conditional on the consent of the listed company's shareholders being given to the transaction.[1] The Quotations Department must be informed of the proposed transaction as soon as its principal terms have been provisionally agreed upon, and the instructions of the Quotations Committee must be sought as to the despatch of circulars to shareholders and the holding of a general meeting to approve the transaction.[1] If the transaction may result in any persons (particularly substantial shareholders) coming under an obligation under the City Code on Takeovers and Mergers to make a general offer to acquire all the outstanding shares carrying voting rights of the listed company or any other company,[3] the Panel on Takeovers and Mergers must also be consulted so that a mandatory offer will be made concurrently with the transaction.[1] This would be the situation if the listed company disposed of voting shares it held in another company to one or more of its directors or substantial shareholders who already held so many voting shares in the other company that the acquisition imposed an obligation on him under the City Code to make an offer for the remaining voting shares of the other company. A mandatory bid would also be called for if the listed company acquired equity shares in another company by arrangement with one or more of its directors or substantial shareholders who already held equity shares in the other company so that the combined holdings of the listed company and the directors or substantial shareholders attained the level for a mandatory bid.

CONTINUING OBLIGATIONS OF LISTED PUBLIC AUTHORITY ISSUERS

The continuing obligations imposed on states, regional and local authorities of states and public international bodies (other than member states of

---

3 City Code on Takeovers and Mergers, Rule 9.1. A mandatory bid is called for if a person and persons acting in concert with him make an acquisition of shares which results in their total holding in the company being one which carries 30 per cent or more of the voting rights exercisable at general meetings, or if having acquired a total holding carrying between 30 and 50 per cent of such voting rights, they or any of them acquire further shares which carry more than 2 per cent of such voting rights.

the European Community and their regional and local authorities) by the Admission Directive in respect of their listed debt securities[4] are repeated in the Stock Exchange rules, and are extended to member states and their regional and local authorites.[5] Additionally, certain of the continuing obligations which are imposed on listed companies by the Stock Exchange rules alone are also imposed on such public authorities in respect of their listed debt securities, namely, the obligation to notify the Company Announcements Office of proposed payments of interest and decisions to pass interest payments, of proposed drawings of securities for redemption or repayment, and of the amount of debt securities outstanding after any purchase or drawing;[6] such public authorities are also subject to the obligation to supply the Company Announcements Office with six copies of all announcements made by the issuer[7] and to the same obligations as are imposed on listed companies to certify instruments of transfer of their debt securities, to issue split letters of allotment and to issue certificates in respect of registered debt securities within 14 days after transfers are lodged.[8]

Although the Admission Directive treats public international bodies (such as the World Bank, the International Development Association and the European Investment Bank) in the same way as sovereign states and their regional and local authorities in imposing continuing obligations in connection with issues of their debt securities, the Stock Exchange rules segregate them and class them together with (i) companies and other corporations established or governed by special legislation of a member state of the European Community to exercise a state monopoly in carrying on their businesses if their borrowings are unconditionally guaranteed by such a member state or one of its federal component units (eg a *Land* of the Federal Republic of West Germany), and (ii) corporations (other than companies) established by special legislation of a member state whose activities are confined by law to raising funds under state control by the issue of debt securities and to financing production by means of the proceeds of such issues and resources provided by the member state, and whose debt securities are treated in law as debt securities issued or guaranteed by the member state.[9] By the Stock Exchange rules all these bodies, whether public international bodies or companies or corporations governed by the law of a member state, must conform to the same obligations in connection with issues of listed debt securities as are imposed on companies which have issued listed debt securities.[10] This, of course, is essential in the case of companies and corporations governed by the law of a member state in order to comply with the Admission Directive, and the only exemption which may be given by national law under the Directive is that companies and other corporations which are nationals of member states may be permitted not to publish details of new loan issues which they make and major new developments in their activities which may signifi-

4 See p 45, above.
5 The Stock Exchange: *Admission of Securities to Listing*, Section 5, Chapter 4, paras 1, 2 and 9.
6 Ibid, Section 5, Chapter 4, paras 3 to 5.
7 Ibid, Section 5, Chapter 4, para 6.
8 Ibid, Section 5, Chapter 4, paras 7 and 8 (see p 126, above).
9 Ibid, Section 2, Chapter 2, para 1(*b*) and (*c*) and Section 5, Chapter 3, Title.
10 Ibid, Section 5, Chapter 3, paras 3, 4, 6, 8 to 12 and 15.

cantly affect their ability to meet their commitments.[11] In fact the Stock Exchange rules do not give even this limited exemption.

In addition to imposing the obligations set out in the Admission Directive, the Stock Exchange rules also oblige issuers in the present category to notify to the Company Announcements Office all information necessary to enable the holders of their debt securities and the public to appraise their financial position and to avoid the establishment of a false market in their securities, in the same way as a listed company must do.[12] An issuer in the present category must also notify the Company Announcements Office immediately of any decision to pass interest payments and of any proposed change in its share or loan capital, including the redemption, repurchase or cancellation of debt securities, and it must supply copies of its annual accounts and reports to the Stock Exchange for use by its statistical services.[13] If debt securities of the issuer are in bearer form, it must publish a notice in at least one leading London newspaper of the availability of its audited annual accounts and reports on publication and, where applicable, the availability of the audited annual accounts and reports of its parent company or corporation, of any other company or corporation which has guaranteed the debt securities and of any company into whose securities the debt securities are convertible, or for whose securities they are exchangeable, or whose securities are the subject of subscription rights attached to the debt securities.[14] Likewise, the issuer must advertise in a leading London newspaper the current availability of any right in connection with an issue of securities to holders of the bearer debt securities (eg subscription or conversion rights) and the procedure for voting on resolutions affecting holders of the securities which are currently being considered.[14]

SANCTIONS FOR CONTINUING OBLIGATIONS

The obligations imposed on companies and other issuers of listed securities by the Admission Directive and the Interim Reports Directive as given effect in United Kingdom law by the Stock Exchange (Listing) Regulations are obligations created by law, and in theory, therefore, are enforceable by any interested party applying to the court for an appropriate injunction if the obligation is to abstain from certain acts, or for a mandatory injunction if the obligation is to do certain acts. A member of a company or corporation or a holder of its listed debt securities would have a sufficient interest for this purpose,[15] and it would appear that the Council of the Stock Exchange would also have a sufficient interest as the competent authority designated to enforce the directives.[16]

In fact the effective sanction to ensure that companies and other issuers do fulfil the obligations imposed on them by the Admission Directive and

11 Admission Directive, art 8; The Stock Exchange (Listing) Regulations 1984, reg 6 and Sch 2, para 2.
12 The Stock Exchange: *Admission of Securities to Listing*, Section 5, Chapter 3, para 1.
13 Ibid, Section 5, Chapter 3, paras 5, 7 and 14.
14 Ibid, Section 5, Chapter 3, para 13.
15 *Jenkin v Pharmaceutical Society of Great Britain* [1921] 1 Ch 392.
16 The Stock Exchange (Listing) Regulations 1984, reg 4(1).

by the Stock Exchange rules is the power of the Quotations Committee to suspend or terminate a listing for the relevant securities. The Admission Directive empowers the Quotations Committee (acting on behalf of the Council of the Stock Exchange) to suspend a listing if the smooth operation of the market is, or may be, temporarily jeopardised (eg by a false market resulting from a listed company failing to make an appropriate announcement about its affairs), or where the protection of investors so requires (eg failure to publish a half-yearly report within the time limit allowed).[17] Furthermore, the Quotations Committee may terminate a listing if it is satisfied that owing to special circumstances normal regular dealings in a listed security are no longer possible.[18] The Admission Directive is not specific as to how serious the circumstances must be to justify a cancellation of a listing, but it would clearly be warranted if a listed issuer failed persistently to fulfil the obligations imposed on it by the Admission Directive or the Stock Exchange rules which supplement the directive, particularly where the issuer's default has resulted in a continuing false market or the risk of detriment to investors.

The Stock Exchange rules provide more generally than the Admission Directive that the Council of the Stock Exchange (acting through the Quotations Committee) may prohibit dealings in any listed security for any reason whatsoever,[19] and the Stock Exchange's manual, *Admission of Securities to Listing*, amplifies this by stating that the Committee may at any time suspend or cancel a listing, whether requested by the issuer or not, and will not hesitate to do so to protect investors and ensure an orderly market.[20] The manual adds that the continuation of a suspension for a prolonged period without the issuer taking adequate action to obtain restoration of the listing is likely to lead the Quotations Committee to cancel the listing.[20] There appears to be no inconsistency between the Admission Directive and the Stock Exchange rules despite the unlimited discretion which the latter appear to confer on the Quotations Committee to suspend or cancel a listing for any reason. It is implied in the Stock Exchange rules that the Committee's powers may be exercised only for proper purposes, namely, the preservation of a properly functioning market and the protection of investors, and these purposes are no wider than those expressed in the Admission Directive.

It would seem that before cancelling a listing the Quotations Committee must give the issuer an opportunity to present arguments and evidence in opposition to the proposed cancellation, and this will be particularly so when the grounds for the cancellation are alleged infringements of the Admission Directive or the related Stock Exchange rules.[1] It is less certain that the Quotations Committee would be bound to do this if it were proposed to suspend a listing. This is because the need for a suspension is often urgent, so that there is no time for the consideration of the issuer's submissions, and because a suspension can speedily be terminated. Nevertheless, it would seem that the Committee would be bound to

17 Admission Directive, art 14(1).
18 Ibid, art 14(2).
19 Rules and Regulations of the Stock Exchange, r 165(1) (now The Stock Exchange Rules (1984 Edition), para 545–2).
20 The Stock Exchange: *Admission of Securities to Listing*, Section 1, Chapter 1, para 15.
 1 *Ridge v Baldwin* [1964] AC 40.

consider an application by the issuer for the termination of a suspension and to consider the arguments and evidence submitted in support of the application.

The Admission Directive requires decisions of the Quotations Committee suspending or terminating a listing of securities to be subject to review by the courts,[2] and an application for review is available in any case under the general principles of English law. The form of the proceedings may depend on whether the challenged decision involves a question of law or fact arising under the Stock Exchange (Listing) Regulations or the three directives or the implementation of the directives by the Quotations Committee, or whether, on the other hand, only the Stock Exchange's own rules are involved. In the former case the application to the court will be one initiated by an ex parte application for leave to apply on motion for judicial review of the Quotations Committee's decision,[3] but in the latter case it would appear that the application must be by way of ordinary civil proceedings for an injunction or a declaratory judgment.[4] On the other hand, it could be argued that because the Quotations Committee's power to suspend or terminate a listing is now dervied from the Stock Exchange (Listing) Regulations 1984, and the Admission Directive, it is acting as a public authority exercising legal powers in ordering a suspension or termination whatever its reasons for doing so may be, and so its decision may in all cases be challenged by an application for judicial review.[4]

2 Admission Directive, art 15(1).
3 Supreme Court Act 1981, s 31(1) (51 Halsbury's Statutes (3rd edn) 625); RSC, Ord 53, r 1.
4 See p 24, above.

APPENDIX

The Stock Exchange (Listing) Regulations 1984 (1984/716)

Citation, commencement and extent
1.—(1) These regulations may be cited as The Stock Exchange (Listing) Regulations 1984.

(2) *(a)* To the extent that these regulations relate to the conditions of admission of securities to official listing they shall come into operation, in relation only to securities offered by or on behalf of a Minister of the Crown or a body corporate controlled by a Minister of the Crown or a subsidiary of such a body corporate within the meaning of section 154 of the Companies Act 1948, on the tenth day after the day on which they are made;

(b) in all other respects they shall come into operation on 1 January 1985.

(3) These regulations extend to Northern Ireland.

(4) For the purpose of paragraph (2) of this regulation, a body is controlled by a Minister of the Crown if a Minister of the Crown is entitled to exercise or control the exercise of more than one half of the voting rights attributable to its ordinary share capital which are exercisable in all circumstances at general meetings.

Interpretation
2.—(1) In these regulations, unless the context otherwise requires, the following expressions have the following meanings—

'the Admission directive' means Council Directive No 79/279/EEC co-ordinating the conditions for the admission of securities to official stock exchange listing(**a**);

'admission to official listing' means admission of securities to the Official List of The Stock Exchange and 'offical listing' shall be construed accordingly;

'the Companies Acts' means the Companies Act 1948 and the Companies Act (Northern Ireland) 1960;

'the Council' means the Council of The Stock Exchange;

'the directives' means the Admission directive, the Interim Reports directive and the Listing Particulars directive;

'the Interim Reports directive' means Council Directive No 82/121/EEC on information to be published on a regular basis by companies the shares of which have been admitted to official stock exchange listing(**b**);

'the Listing Particulars directive' means Council Directive No 80/390/EEC co-ordinating the requirements for the drawing-up, scrutiny and distribution of the listing particulars to be published for the admission of securities to official stock exchange listing(**c**);

(**a**) OJ No L 66, 16. 3. 1979, p 21.
(**b**) OJ No L 48, 20. 2. 1982, p 26.
(**c**) OJ No L 100, 17. 4. 1980, p 1.

and references to an article or other provision of any of the directives shall be taken as a reference to that article or other provision as set out in Schedule 1 to these regulations.

(2) Expressions used in the directives shall, unless the context otherwise requires, have the same meaning in these regulations as in the directives.

Conditions of admission to official listing and obligations of companies and other issuers
3.—(1) Subject to regulation 6 below, the requirements of the directives as regards—
  (*a*) the conditions of admission of securities to official listing;
  (*b*) the obligations of issuers of securities admitted to official listing;
  (*c*) in relation to interim reports, the obligations of companies the shares of which are admitted to official listing,
shall have effect and be applied accordingly.

(2) Companies and other issuers shall accordingly be subject to the obligations referred to in paragraph (1) of this regulation whether admission preceded or follows the date these regulations come into force.

(3) Nothing in these regulations shall affect any power of the Council, whether under the Deed of Settlement of The Stock Exchange or otherwise, whether a power to impose more stringent or additional conditions or obligations or any other power, so long as any such power is not exercised in a manner inconsistent with the directives.

Competent authority
4.—(1) The Council shall be the competent authority for all purposes under the directives and shall have all the powers required to be conferred on or which member states are permitted to confer on such competent authority by the directives.

(2) The Council may arrange for the discharge of its functions as competent authority by any committee, sub-committee, officer or employee of the Council.

(3) The restrictions referred to in Article 19 of the Admission directive and Article 25 of the Listing Particulars directive shall apply to persons employed by or formerly employed by the Council in the exercise of its functions as competent authority.

Listing particulars
5.—(1) The obligation referred to in paragraph 1 of Article 4 of the Listing Particulars directive shall be incumbent upon the persons referred to in paragraph 2 of that Article.

(2) In the event of non-compliance with or contravention of the obligation referred to in paragraph 1 of Article 4 of the Listing Particulars directive a person referred to in paragraph 2 of that Article shall not incur any liability by reason of the non-compliance or contravention if—
  (*a*) as regards any matter not disclosed he proves that he was not cognisant thereof; or
  (*b*) he proves that the non-compliance or contravention arose from an honest mistake of fact on his part; or
  (*c*) the non-compliance or contravention was in respect of matters which in the opinion of the court dealing with the case were immaterial or was otherwise such as ought, in the opinion of that court, having regard to all the circumstances of the case, reasonably to be excused.

(3) Nothing in this regulation shall limit or diminish any liability which any person may incur under the general law apart from these regulations.

Member State options
6. Schedule 2 to these regulations shall have effect for the purpose of determining the extent to which and the manner in which provisions of the directives shall apply for the purposes of these regulations.

Interaction with other law relating to issues and offers
7.—(1) Where application has been made to the Council for admission of any securities to official listing, and the Council has approved the applicable listing particulars, then—

(a) a form of application for any of those securities, if issued with a document which sets out the approved listing particulars or indicates where they can be obtained or inspected, need not have with it the prospectus otherwise required by the Companies Acts;

(b) in relation to an offer of any of those securities for subscription or purchase, made by means of such a document as above-mentioned, provisions of the Companies Acts otherwise applicable with respect to prospectuses and their contents, or with respect to the consequences attending the issue of a prospectus, or the inclusion of any statement in, or the omission of anything from, a prospectus shall not apply;

(c) if the approved listing particulars have been published in accordance with the directives, and an offer of any of the securities for subscription or purchase is made by means of a document which does not set out the published listing particulars but indicates where they can be obtained or inspected, the validity of the offer, or of any transaction entered into by reference to it, shall not be impugned on the grounds of absence of notice, or insufficient notice, of any matter comprised in the particulars;

(d) for the purposes of any provision (other than in the Companies Acts) which depends for its operation on a prospectus complying with any requirement of those Acts, a prospectus setting out the approved listing particulars shall be deemed to comply with that requirement and, if delivered to the registrar of companies in England and Wales for registration, to have been so delivered in pursuance of section 41 of the Companies Act 1948.

(2) Where application has been made to the Council for admission of any securities to official listing, then in relation to any offer of those securities for subscription or sale—

(a) section 423(2) of the Companies Act 1948 (offer of shares or debentures of oversea company deemed not an offer to the public if made to professional investor) shall apply for the purposes of Part II of that Act as well as for those of Part X; and

(b) section 371(2) of the Companies Act (Northern Ireland) 1960 (provision corresponding to section 423(2)) shall apply for the purposes of Part II of that Act as well as for those of Part XI of it.

(3) A document relating to securities which have been admitted to official listing, or in respect of which listing particulars have been approved by the Council, shall not be subject to the restrictions in relation to distribution imposed by section 14(1) of the Prevention of Fraud (Investments) Act 1958 or section 13(1) of the Prevention of Fraud (Investments) Act (Northern Ireland) 1940 (circulars relating to investments), if—

(a) it contains nothing but matter which the directives require (in whatever terms) to be made generally available; or *(b)* it is subject to any requirement of the directives (however expressed) that it be submitted to the Council for clearance and has been so submitted and cleared.

(4) Section 39 of the Companies Act 1948 and section 39 of the Companies Act (Northern Ireland) 1960 (both of which sections provide for a stock exchange certificate relaxing prospectus requirements where application is made for official listing) are hereby repealed, and also—

(a) in the Companies Act 1948—
:   (i) in section 38(1) and (3), the words 'Subject to the next following section' (twice),
    (ii) in section 41(1)*(b)*(i), the words from 'or, if in the case of a prospectus' to 'memorandum of that contract', and
    (iii) in section 50, subsection (7);
(b) in the Prevention of Fraud (Investments) Act 1958—
:   (i) in section 2(2)*(b)*, *(c)* and *(d)*, the words 'or by section thirty-nine of that Act' (three times), and
    (ii) in section 14(2)*(a)* and *(b)*, the same words (twice);
(c) in the Companies Act (Northern Ireland) 1960—
:   (i) in section 38(1), the words 'Subject to section thirty-nine',
    (ii) in section 38(3), 'and section thirty-nine',
    (iii) in section 41(1)*(b)*(i), the words from 'or, if in the case of a prospectus' to 'memorandum of that contract', and
    (iv) in section 50, subsection (7);
(d) in the Prevention of Fraud (Investments) Act (Northern Ireland) 1940—
:   (i) in section 2(2)*(b)*, *(c)* and *(d)*, the words 'or by section thirty-nine of that Act' (three times), and
    (ii) in section 13(2)*(a)* and *(b)*, the same words (twice).

(5) On or before the date of publication of listing particulars in accordance with the directives, a copy of the listing particulars shall be delivered to the registrar of companies in England and Wales or in Scotland, as the case may be, or, in the case of a company incorporated in Northern Ireland, to the registrar of companies in Northern Ireland.

(6) Any document which is published as, or containing, listing particulars shall, on the face of it, state that a copy of those listing particulars have been delivered for registration as required by this regulation.

(7) If any such document is published without a copy of the relevant listing particulars having being delivered under this regulation to the registrar, the issuer and every person who is knowingly a party to the publication of the particulars shall be liable on summary conviction to a fine not exceeding one-fifth of the statutory maximum, or £2000, whichever is the lesser, or on conviction after continued contravention, a default fine not exceeding one-fiftieth of the statutory maximum, or £100, whichever is the lesser.

(8) In this regulation, 'statutory maximum'—
(a) in relation to England and Wales and Scotland has the meaning given by section 74 of the Criminal Justice Act 1982,
(b) in relation to Northern Ireland, has the same meaning as in the Companies (Northern Ireland) Order 1981(**a**), as for the time being in force;
and this regulation shall be an enactment to which section 80(2) of the Companies Act 1980 and Article 81(2) of the Companies (Northern Ireland) Order 1981 (meaning of 'default fine') apply.

(**a**) SI 1981/83 (NI 19).

(9) For the avoidance of doubt, it is hereby declared that, save as provided in this regulation, nothing in these regulations shall affect any obligation on issuers of securities admitted to official listing imposed or to be imposed by or under any other enactment.

Liability

8.—(1) Neither the Council nor any other person shall be liable in damages by reason only of non-compliance with or contravention of any obligation (other than that referred to in paragraph 1 of Article 4 of the Listing Particulars directive) imposed by or by virtue of these regulations, nor shall the Council be so liable in respect of anything done or omitted to be done by it in connection with its functions as competent authority unless the act or omission complained of was done or omitted to be done in bad faith.

(2) No transaction shall be void or voidable by reason only of the fact that it was entered into in contravention of, or not in conformity with, these regulations.

SCHEDULES

SCHEDULE 1—THE DIRECTIVES

Regulation 2

The Admission directive

COUNCIL DIRECTIVE

of 5 March 1979

coordinating the conditions for the admission of securities to official stock exchange listing

(79/279/EEC)

THE COUNCIL OF THE EUROPEAN COMMUNITIES.

Having regard to the Treaty establishing the European Economic Community, and in particular Articles 54 (3) (g) and 100 thereof,

Having regard to the proposal from the Commission ([1]),

Having regard to the opinion of the European Parliament ([2]),

Having regard to the opinion of the Economic and Social Committee ([3]),

Whereas the coordination of the conditions for the admission of securities to official listing on stock exchanges situated or operating in the Member States is likely to provide equivalent protection for investors at Community level, because of the more uniform guarantees offered to investors in the various Member States; whereas it will facilitate both the admission to official stock exchange listing, in each such State, of securities from other Member States and the listing of any given security on a number of stock exchanges in the Community; whereas it will accordingly make for greater interpenetration of national securities markets and therefore contri-

bute to the prospect of establishing a European capital market;

Whereas such coordination must therefore apply to securities, independently of the legal status of their issuers, and must therefore also apply to securities issued by non-member States or their regional or local authorities or international public bodies; whereas this Directive therefore covers entities not covered by the second paragraph of Article 58 of the Treaty and goes beyond the scope of Article 54 (3) (g) while directly affecting the establishment and functioning of the common market within the meaning of Article 100;

Whereas there should be the possibility of a right to apply to the courts against decisions by the competent national authorities in respect of the application of this Directive, although such right to apply must not be allowed to restrict the discretion of these authorities;

Whereas, initially, this coordination should be sufficiently flexible to enable account to be taken of present differences in the structures of securities markets in the Member States and to enable the Member States to take account of any specific situations with which they may be confronted;

([1]) OJ No C 56, 10. 3. 1976, p 3.
([2]) OJ No C 238, 11. 10. 1976, p 38.
([3]) OJ No C 204, 30. 8. 1976, p 5.

Whereas, for this reason, coordination should first be limited to the establishment of minimum conditions for the admission of securities to official listing on stock exchanges situated or operating in the Member States, without however giving issuers any right to listing;

Whereas, this partial coordination of the conditions for admission to official listing constitutes a first step towards subsequent closer alignment of the rules of Member States in this field,

HAS ADOPTED THIS
DIRECTIVE:

SECTION I
General provisions

Article 1

1. This Directive concerns securities which are admitted to official listing or are the subject of an application for admission to official listing on a stock exchange situated or operating within a Member State.

2. Member States may decide not to apply this Directive to:

— units issued by collective investment undertakings other than the closed-end type,
— securities issued by a Member State or its regional or local authorities.

Article 2

For the purposes of applying this Directive:

(a) collective investment undertakings other than the closed-end type shall mean unit trusts and investment companies:

— the object of which is the collective investment of capital provided by the public, and which

operate on the principle of risk spreading, and

— the units of which are, at the request of holders, repurchased or redeemed, directly or indirectly, out of the assets of these undertakings. Action taken by such undertakings to ensure that the stock exchange value of its units does not significantly vary from their net asset value shall be regarded as equivalent to such repurchase or redemption;

(b) units shall mean securities issued by collective investment undertakings as representing the rights of participants in the assets of such undertakings;

(c) European unit of account shall mean the unit of account as defined in Article 10 of the Financial Regulation of 21 December 1977 applicable to the general budget of the European Communities (¹).

Article 3

Member States shall ensure that:

— securities may not be admitted to official listing on any stock exchange situated or operating within their territory unless the conditions laid down by this Directive are satisfied, and that

— issuers of securities admitted to such official listing, whether admission takes place before or after the date on which this Directive is implemented, are subject to the obligations provided for by this Directive.

Article 4

1. The admission of securities to official listing shall be subject to the conditions set out in Schedules A and B to this Directive, relating to shares and debt securities respectively.

(¹) OJ No L 356, 31. 12. 1977, p 1.

2. The issuers of securities admitted to official listing must fulfil the obligations set out in Schedules C and D to this Directive, relating to shares and debt securities respectively.

3. Certificates representing shares may be admitted to official listing only if the issuer of the shares represented fulfils the conditions set out in I (1) to I (3) of Schedule A and the obligations set out in Schedule C and if the certificates fulfil the conditions set out in II (1) to II (6) of Schedule A.

Article 5

1. Subject to the prohibitions provided for in Article 6 and in Schedules A and B, the Member States may make the admission of securities to official listing subject to more stringent conditions than those set out in Schedules A and B or to additional conditions, provided that these more stringent and additional conditions apply generally for all issuers or for individual classes of issuer and that they have been published before application for admission of such securities is made.

2. Member States may make the issuers of securities admitted to official listing subject to more stringent obligations than those set out in Schedules C and D or to additional obligations, provided that these more stringent and additional obligations apply generally for all issuers or for individual classes of issuer.

3. Member States may, under the same conditions as those laid down in Article 7, authorize derogations from the additional or more stringent conditions and obligations referred to in paragraphs 1 and 2 hereof.

4. Member States may, in accordance with the applicable national rules require issuers of securities admitted to official listing to inform the public on a regular basis of their financial position and the general course of their business.

Article 6

Member States may not make the admission to official listing of securities issued by companies or other legal persons which are nationals of another Member State subject to the condition that the securities must already have been admitted to official listing on a stock exchange situated or operating in one of the Member States.

Article 7

Any derogations from the conditions for the admission of securities to official listing which may be authorized in accordance with Schedules A and B must apply generally for all issuers where the circumstances justifying them are similar.

Article 8

Member States may decide not to apply the conditions set out in Schedule B and the obligations set out in A (4) (a) and (c) of Schedule D in respect of applications for admission to official listing of debt securities issued by companies and other legal persons which are nationals of a Member State and which are set up by, governed by or managed pursuant to a special law where repayments and interest payments in respect of those securities are guaranteed by a Member State or one of its federal states.

SECTION II

Authorities competent to admit securities to official listing

Article 9

1. Member States shall designate the national authority or authorities competent to decide on the admission of securities to official listing on a stock exchange situated or operating within their territories and shall ensure that

this Directive is applied. They shall inform the Commission accordingly, indicating, if appropriate, how duties have been allocated.

2. Member States shall ensure that the competent authorities have such powers as may be necessary for the exercise of their duties.

3. Without prejudice to the other powers conferred upon them, the competent authorities may reject an application for the admission of a security to official listing if, in their opinion, the issuer's situation is such that admission would be detrimental to investors' interests.

Article 10

By way of derogation from Article 5, Member States may, solely in the interests of protecting the investors, give the competent authorities power to make the admission of a security to official listing subject to any special condition which the competent authorities consider appropriate and of which they have explicitly informed the applicant.

Article 11

The competent authorities may refuse to admit to official listing a security already officially listed in another Member State where the issuer fails to comply with the obligations resulting from admission in that Member State.

Article 12

Without prejudice to any other action or penalties which they may contemplate in the event of failure on the part of the issuer to comply with the obligations resulting from admission to official listing, the competent authorities may make public the fact that an issuer is failing to comply with those obligations.

Article 13

1. An issuer whose securities are admitted to official listing shall provide the competent authorities with all the information which the latter consider appropriate in order to protect investors or ensure the smooth operation of the market.

2. Where protection of investors or the smooth operation of the market so requires, an issuer may be required by the competent authorities to publish such information in such a form and within such time limits as they consider appropriate. Should the issuer fail to comply with such requirement, the competent authorities may themselves publish such information after having heard the issuer.

Article 14

1. The competent authorities may decide to suspend the listing of a security where the smooth operation of the market is, or may be, temporarily jeopardized or where protection of investors so requires.

2. The competent authorities may decide that the listing of the security be discontinued where they are satisfied that, owing to special circumstances, normal regular dealings in a security are no longer possible.

Article 15

1. Member States shall ensure decisions of the competent authorities refusing the admission of a security to official listing or discontinuing such a listing shall be subject to the right to apply to the courts.

2. An applicant shall be notified of a decision regarding his application for admission to official listing within six months of receipt of the application or, should the competent authority require

any further information within that period, within six months of the applicant's supplying such information.

3. Failure to give a decision within the time limit specified in paragraph 2 shall be deemed a rejection of the application. Such rejection shall give rise to the right to apply to the courts provided for in paragraph 1.

Article 16

Where an application for admission to official listing relates to certificates representing shares, the application shall be considered only if the competent authorities are of the opinion that the issuer of the certificates is offering adequate safeguards for the protection of investors.

SECTION III

Publication of the information to be made available to the public

Article 17

1. The information which issuers of a security admitted to official listing in a Member State are required to make available to the public in accordance with the requirements of Schedules C and D shall be published in one or more newspapers distributed throughout the Member State or distributed widely therein or shall be made available to the public either in writing in places indicated by announcements to be published in one or more newspapers distributed throughout the Member State or widely distributed therein or by other equivalent means approved by the competent authorities. The issuers must simultaneously send such information to the competent authorities.

2. The information referred to in paragraph 1 shall be published in the official language or languages, or in one of the official languages or in another language provided that in the Member State in

question the official language or languages or such other language is or are customary in the sphere of finance and accepted by the competent authorities.

SECTION IV

Cooperation between Member States

Article 18

1. The competent authorities shall cooperate wherever necessary for the purpose of carrying out their duties and shall exchange any information required for that purpose.

2. Where applications are to be made simultaneously or within short intervals of one another for admission of the same securities to official listing on stock exchanges situated or operating in more than one Member State, or where an application for admission is made in respect of a security already listed on a stock exchange in another Member State, the competent authorities shall communicate with each other and make such arrangements as may be necessary to expedite the procedure and simplify as far as possible the formalities and any additional conditions required for admission of the security concerned.

3. In order to facilitate the work of the competent authorities, any application for the admission of a security to official listing on a stock exchange situated or operating in a Member State must state whether a similar application is being or has been made in another Member State, or will be made in the near future.

Article 19

1. Member States shall provide that all persons employed or formerly employed by the competent authorities shall be bound by professional secrecy. This means that any confidential information received in the course of their duties may not be divulged to any per-

son or authority except by virtue of provisions laid down by law.

2. Paragraph 1 shall not, however, preclude the competent authorities of the various Member States from exchanging information as provided for in this Directive. Information thus exchanged shall be covered by the obligation of professional secrecy to which the persons employed or formerly employed by the competent authorities receiving the information are subject.

SECTION V

Contact Committee

Article 20

1. A Contact Committee (hereinafter called 'the Committee') shall be set up alongside the Commission. Its function shall be:

(a) without prejudice to Articles 169 and 170 of the EEC Treaty to facilitate the harmonized implementation of this Directive through regular consultations on any practical problems arising from its application and on which exchanges of view are deemed useful;
(b) to facilitate the establishment of a concerted attitude between the Member States on the more stringent or additional conditions and obligations which, pursuant to Article 5 of this Directive, they may lay down at national level;
(c) to advise the Commission, if necessary, on any supplements or amendments to be made to this Directive or on any adjustments to be made in accordance with Article 21.

2. It shall not be the function of the Committee to appraise the merits of decisions taken by the competent authorities in individual cases.

3. The Committee shall be composed of persons appointed by the Member States and of representatives of the Commission. The chairman shall be a representative of the Commission. Secretarial services shall be provided by the Commission.

4. Meetings of the Committee shall be convened by its chairman, either on his own initiative or at the request of one Member State delegation. The Committee shall draw up its rules of procedure.

Article 21

1. For the purpose of adjusting, in the light of the requirements of the economic situation, the minimum amount of the foreseeable market capitalization laid down in the first paragraph of I (2) of Schedule A, the Commission shall submit to the Committee a draft of the measures to be taken. The Committee shall deliver its opinion within the period laid down by its chairman. Its decisions shall require 41 votes in favour, the votes of the Member States being weighted as provided for in Article 148 (2) of the Treaty.

2. When the Committee has delivered an opinion in favour of the draft of the measures envisaged by the Commission the latter shall adopt them.

Where the opinion of the Committee is not in accordance with the draft of the measures envisaged by the Commission or where the Committee has not delivered an opinion within the required period, the Commission shall without delay lay before the Council, which shall act by qualified majority, a proposal concerning the measures to be taken.

Where the Council fails to act on the proposal within three months of its receipt, the measures proposed shall be adopted by the Commission.

SECTION VI

Final provisions

Article 22

1. [*Date of implementation substituted by directive 82/148/EEC* (**a**)]

2. As from the notification of this Directive, the Member States shall communicate to the Commission the texts of the main laws, regulations and administrative provisions which they adopt in the field covered by this Directive.

Article 23

This Directive is addressed to the Member States.

(**a**) OJ No L 62, 5. 3. 82, p 22.

SCHEDULE A

CONDITIONS FOR THE ADMISSION OF SHARES TO OFFICIAL LISTING ON A STOCK EXCHANGE

I. Conditions relating to companies for the shares of which admission to official listing is sought

1. *Legal position of the company*

The legal position of the company must be in conformity with the laws and regulations to which it is subject, as regards both its formation and its operation under its statutes.

2. *Minimum size of the company*

The foreseeable market capitalization of the shares for which admission to official listing is sought or, if this cannot be assessed, the company's capital and reserves, including profit or loss, from the last financial year, must be at least one million European units of account.

However, Member States may provide for admission to official listing, even when this condition is not fulfilled, provided that the competent authorities are satisfied that there will be an adequate market for the shares concerned.

A higher foreseeable market capitalization or higher capital and reserves may be required by a Member State for admission to official listing only if another regulated, regularly operating, recognized open market exists in that State and the requirements for it are equal to or less than those referred to in the first paragraph.

The condition set out in the first paragraph shall not be applicable for the admission to official listing of a further block of shares of the same class as those already admitted.

The equivalent in national currency of one million European units of account shall initially be that applicable on the date on which the Directive is adopted.

If, as a result of adjustment of the equivalent of the European unit of account in national currency, the market capitalization expressed in national currency remains for a period of one year at least 10% more or less than the value of one million European units of account the Member State must, within the 12 months following the expiry of that period, adjust its laws, regulations or administrative provisions to comply with the first paragraph.

3. *A company's period of existence*

A company must have published or filed its annual accounts in accordance with national law for the three financial years preceding the application for official listing. By way of exception, the competent authorities may derogate from this condition where such derogation is desirable in the interests of the company or of investors and where the competent authorities are satisfied that investors have the necessary information available to be able to arrive at an informed judgment on the company and the shares for which admission to official listing is sought.

II. Conditions relating to the shares for which admission to official listing is sought

1. *Legal position of the shares*

The legal position of the shares must be in conformity with the laws and regulations to which they are subject.

2. *Negotiability of the shares*

The shares must be freely negotiable.

The competent authorities may treat shares which are not fully paid up as freely negotiable, if arrangements have been made to ensure that the negotiability of such shares is not restricted and that dealing is made open and proper by providing the public with all appropriate information.

The competent authorities may, in the case of the admission to official listing of shares which may be acquired only subject to approval, derogate from the first paragraph only if the use of the approval clause does not disturb the market.

3. *Public issue preceding admission to official listing*

Where public issue precedes admission to official listing, the first listing may be made only after the end of the period during which subscription applications may be submitted.

4. *Distribution of shares*

A sufficient number of shares must be distributed to the public in one or more Member States not later than the time of admission.

This condition shall not apply where shares are to be distributed to the public through the stock exchange. In that event, admission to official listing may be granted only if the competent authorities are satisfied that a sufficient number of shares will be distributed through the stock exchange within a short period.

Where admission to official listing is sought for a further block of shares of the same class, the competent authorities may assess whether a sufficient number of shares has been distributed to the public in relation to all the shares issued and not only in relation to this further block.

However, by way of derogation from the first paragraph, if the shares are admitted to official listing in one or more non-Member States, the competent authorities may provide for their admission to official listing if a sufficient number of shares is distributed to the public in the non-Member State or States where they are listed.

A sufficient number of shares shall be deemed to have been distributed either when the shares in respect of which application for admission has been made are in the hands of the public to the extent of at least 25% of the subscribed capital represented by the class of shares concerned or when, in view of the large number of shares of the same class and the extent of their distribution to the public, the market will operate properly with a lower percentage.

5. *Listing of shares of the same class*

The application for admission to official listing must cover all the shares of the same class already issued.

However, Member States may provide that this condition shall not apply to applications for admission not covering all the shares of the same class already issued where the shares of that class for which admission is not sought belong to blocks serving to maintain control of the company or are not negotiable for a certain time under agreements, provided that the public is informed of such situations and that there is no danger of such situations prejudicing the interests of the holders of the shares for which admission to official listing is sought.

6. *Physical form of shares*

For the admission to official listing of shares issued by companies which are nationals of another Member State and which shares have a physical form it is necessary and sufficient that their physical form comply with the standards laid down in that other Member State. Where the physical form does not conform to the standards in force in the Member State in which admission to official listing is applied for, the competent authorities of that State shall make that fact known to the public.

The physical form of shares issued by companies which are nationals of a non-member State must afford sufficient safeguard for the protection of the investors.

7. *Shares issued by companies from a non-member State*

If the shares issued by a company which is a national of a non-member State are not listed in either the country of origin or in the country in which the major proportion of the shares is held, they may not be admitted to official listing unless the competent authorities are satisfied that the absence of a listing in the country of origin or in the country in which the major proportion is held is not due to the need to protect investors.

SCHEDULE B

CONDITIONS FOR THE ADMISSION OF DEBT SECURITIES TO OFFICIAL LISTING ON A STOCK EXCHANGE

A. ADMISSION TO OFFICIAL LISTING OF DEBT SECURITIES ISSUED BY AN UNDERTAKING

I. Conditions relating to undertakings for the debt securities of which admission to official listing is sought

Legal position of the undertaking

The legal position of the undertaking must be in conformity with the laws and regulations to which it is subject, as regards both its formation and its operation under its statutes.

II. Conditions relating to the debt securities for which admission to official listing is sought

1. *Legal position of the debt securities*

The legal position of the debt securities must be in conformity with the laws and regulations to which they are subject.

2. *Negotiability of the debt securities*

The debt securities must be freely negotiable.

The competent authorities may treat debt securities which are not fully paid up as freely negotiable if arrangements have been made to ensure that the negotiability of these debt securities is not restricted and that dealing is made open and proper by providing the public with all appropriate information.

3. *Public issue preceding admission to official listing*

Where public issue precedes admission to official listing, the first listing may be made only after the end of the period during which subscription applications may be submitted. This provision shall not apply in the case of tap issues of debt securities when the closing date for subscription is not fixed.

4. *Listing of debt securities ranking* pari passu

The application for admission to official listing must cover all debt securities ranking *pari passu.*

5. *Physical form of debt securities*

For the admission to official listing of debt securities issued by undertakings which are nationals of another Member State and which debt securities have a physical form, it is necessary and sufficient that their physical form comply with the standards laid down in that other Member State. Where the physical form does not conform to the standards in force in the Member State in which admission to official listing is applied for, the competent authorities of that State shall make that fact known to the public.

However, the physical form of debt securities issued in a single Member State must conform to the standards in force in that State.

The physical form of debt securities issued by undertakings which are nationals of a non-member State must afford sufficient safeguard for the protection of the investors.

III. Other conditions

1. *Minimum amount of the loan*

The amount of the loan may not be less than 200 000 European units of account. This provision shall not be applicable in the case of tap issues where the amount of the loan is not fixed.

Member States may, however, provide for admission to official listing even when this condition is not fulfilled, where the competent authorities are satisfied that there will be a sufficient market for the debt securities concerned.

The equivalent in national currency of 200 000 European units of account shall initially be that applicable on the date on which this Directive is adopted.

If as a result of adjustment of the equivalent of the European unit of account in national currency the minimum amount of the loan expressed in national currency remains, for a period of one year, at least 10% less than the value of 200 000 European units of account the Member State must, within the 12 months following the expiry of that period, amend its laws, regulations and administrative provisions to comply with the first paragraph.

2. *Convertible or exchangeable debentures, and debentures with warrants*

Convertible or exchangeable debentures and debentures with warrants may be admitted to official listing only if the related shares are already listed on the same stock exchange or on another regulated, regularly operating, recognized open market or are so admitted simultaneously.

However, Member States may, by way of derogation from the first paragraph, provide for the admission to official listing of convertible or exchangeable debentures or debentures with warrants, if the competent authorities are satisfied that holders have at their disposal all the information necessary to form an opinion concerning the value of the shares to which these debt securities relate.

B. ADMISSION TO OFFICIAL LISTING OF DEBT SECURITIES ISSUED BY A STATE, ITS REGIONAL OR LOCAL AUTHORITIES OR A PUBLIC INTERNATIONAL BODY

1. *Negotiability of the debt securities*

The debt securities must be freely negotiable.

2. *Public issue preceding admission to official listing*

Where public issue precedes admission to official listing, the first listing may be made only after the end of the period during which subscription applications may be submitted. This provision shall not apply where the closing date for subscription is not fixed.

3. *Listing of debt securities ranking* pari passu

The application for admission to official listing must cover all the securities ranking *pari passu*.

4. *Physical form of debt securities*

For the admission to official listing of debt securities which are issued by a Member State or its regional or local authorities in a physical form, it is necessary and sufficient that such physical form comply with the standards in force in that Member State. Where the physical form does not comply with the standards in force in the Member State where admission to official listing is applied for, the competent authorities of that State shall bring this situation to the attention of the public.

The physical form of debt securities issued by non-member States or their regional or local authorities or by public international bodies must afford sufficient safeguard for the protection of the investors.

SCHEDULE C

OBLIGATIONS OF COMPANIES WHOSE SHARES ARE ADMITTED TO OFFICIAL LISTING ON A STOCK EXCHANGE

1. *Listing of newly issued shares of the same class*

Without prejudice to the second paragraph of II(5) of Schedule A, in the case of a new public issue of shares of the same class as those already officially listed, the company shall be required, where the new shares are not automatically admitted, to apply for their admission to the same listing, either not more than a year after their issue or when they become freely negotiable.

2. *Treatment of shareholders*

(a) The company shall ensure equal treatment for all shareholders who are in the same position.

(b) The company must ensure, at least in each Member State in which its shares are listed, that all the necessary facilities and information are available to enable shareholders to exercise their rights. In particular, it must:

—inform shareholders of the holding of meetings and enable them to exercise their right to vote,

—publish notices or distribute circulars concerning the allocation and payment of dividends, the issue of new shares including allotment, subscription, renunciation and conversion arrangements,

—designate as its agent a financial institution through which shareholders may exercise their financial rights, unless the company itself provides financial services.

3. *Amendment of the instrument of incorporation or the statutes*

(a) A company planning an amendment to its instrument of incorporation or its statutes must communicate a draft thereof to the competent authorities of the Member States in which its shares are listed.

(b) That draft must be communicated to the competent authorities no later than the calling of the general meeting which is to decide on the proposed amendment.

4. *Annual accounts and annual report*

(a) The company must make available to the public, as soon as possible, its most recent annual accounts and its last annual report.

(b) If the company prepares both annual own and annual consolidated accounts, it must make them available to the public. In that event the competent authorities may authorize the company only to make available to the public either the own or the consolidated accounts, provided that the accounts which are not made available to the public do not contain any significant additional information.

(c) If the annual accounts and reports do not comply with the provision of Council Directives concerning companies' accounts and if they do not give a true and fair view of the company's assets and liabilities, financial position and profit or loss, more detailed and/or additional information must be provided.

5. *Additional information*

(a) The company must inform the public as soon as possible of any major new developments in its sphere of activity which are not public knowledge and which may, by virtue of their effect on its assets and liabilities or financial position or on the general course of its business, lead to substantial movements in the prices of its shares.

The competent authorities may, however, exempt the company from this requirement, if the disclosure of particular information is such as to prejudice the legitimate interests of the company.

(b) The company must inform the public without delay of any changes in the rights attaching to the various classes of shares.

(c) The company must inform the public of any changes in the structure (shareholders and breakdown of holdings) of the major holdings in its capital as compared with information previously published on that subject as soon as such changes come to its notice.

6. *Equivalence of information*

(a) A company whose shares are officially listed on stock exchanges situated or operating in different Member States must ensure that equivalent information is made available to the market at each of these exchanges.

(b) A company whose shares are officially listed on stock exchanges situated or operating in one or more Member States and in one or more non-member States must make available to the markets of the Member State or States in which its shares are listed information which is at least equivalent to that which it makes available to the markets of the non-member State or States in question, if such information may be of importance for the evaluation of the shares.

SCHEDULE D

OBLIGATIONS OF ISSUERS WHOSE DEBT SECURITIES ARE ADMITTED TO OFFICIAL LISTING ON A STOCK EXCHANGE

A. DEBT SECURITIES ISSUED BY AN UNDERTAKING

1. *Treatment of holders of debt securities*

(a) The undertaking must ensure that all holders of debt securities ranking *pari passu* are given equal treatment in respect of all the rights attaching to those debt securities.

Provided they are made in accordance with national law, this condition shall not prevent offers of early repayment of certain debt securities being made to holders by an undertaking in derogation from the conditions of issue and in particular in accordance with social priorities.

(b) The undertaking must ensure that at least in each Member State where its debt securities are officially listed all the facilities and information necessary to enable holders to exercise their rights are available. In particular, it must:

—publish notices or distribute circulars concerning the holding of meetings of holders of debt securities, the payment of interest, the exercise of any conversion, exchange, subscription or renunciation rights, and repayment,

—designate as its agent a financial institution through which holders of debt securities may exercise their financial rights, unless the undertaking itself provides financial services.

2. *Amendment of the instrument of incorporation or the statutes*

(a) An undertaking planning an amendment to its instrument of incorporation or its statutes affecting the rights of holders of debt securities must forward a draft thereof to the competent authorities of the Member States in which its debt securities are listed.

(b) That draft must be communicated to the competent authorities no later than the calling of the meeting of the body which is to decide on the proposed amendment.

3. *Annual accounts and annual report*

(a) The undertaking must make available to the public as soon as possible its most recent annual accounts and its last annual report the publication of which is required by national law.

(b) If the undertaking prepares both annual own and annual consolidated accounts, it must make them available to the public. In that event, however, the competent authority may authorize the undertaking only to make available to the public either the own accounts or the consolidated accounts, provided that the accounts which are not made available do not contain any significant additional information.

(c) If the accounts and reports do not comply with the provisions of Council Directives concerning undertakings' accounts and if they do not give a true and fair view of the undertaking's assets and liabilities, financial position and results, more detailed and/or additional information must be provided.

4. *Additional information*

(a) The undertaking must inform the public as soon as possible of any major new developments in its sphere of activity which are not public knowledge and which may significantly affect its ability to meet its commitments.

The competent authorities may, however, exempt the undertaking from this obligation at its request if the disclosure of particular information would be such as to prejudice the legitimate interests of the undertaking.

(b) The undertaking must inform the public without delay of any change in the rights of holders of debt securities resulting in particular from a change in loan terms or in interest rates.

(c) The undertaking must inform the public without delay of new loan issues and in particular of any guarantee or security in respect thereof.

(d) Where the debt securities officially listed are convertible or exchangeable debentures, or debentures with warrants, the undertaking must inform the public without delay of any changes in the rights attaching to the various classes of shares to which they relate.

5. *Equivalence of information*

(a) An undertaking the debt securities of which are officially listed on stock exchanges situated or operating in different Member States must ensure that equivalent information is made available to the market at each of these exchanges.

(b) An undertaking the debt securities of which are officially listed on stock exchanges situated or operating in one or more Member States and in one or more non-member States must make available to the markets of the Member State or Member States in which its debt securities are listed information which is at least equivalent to that which it makes available to the markets of the non-member State or States in question, if such information may be of importance for the evaluation of the debt securities.

B. DEBT SECURITIES ISSUED BY A STATE OR ITS REGIONAL OR LOCAL AUTHORITIES OR BY A PUBLIC INTERNATIONAL BODY

1. *Treatment of holders of debt securities*

(a) States, their regional or local authorities and public international bodies must ensure that all holders of debt securities ranking *pari passu* are given equal treatment in respect of all the rights attaching to those debt securities.

Provided they are made in accordance with national law, this condition shall not prevent offers of early repayment of certain debt securities being made to holders by an issuer in derogation from the conditions of issue and in particular in accordance with social priorities.

(b) States, their regional or local authorities and public international bodies must ensure that at least in each Member State in which their debt securities are officially listed all the facilities and information necessary to enable holders of debt securities to exercise their rights are available. In particular, they must:

—publish notices or distribute circulars concerning the holding of meetings of holders of debt securities, the payment of interest and redemption,

—designate as their agents financial institutions through which holders of debt securities may exercise their financial rights.

2. *Equivalence of information*

a) States, their regional or local authorities and public international bodies the debt securities of which are officially listed on stock exchanges situated or operating in different Member States must ensure that equivalent information is made available to the market at each of these exchanges.

(b) States, their regional or local authorities and public international bodies the debt securities of which are officially listed on stock exchanges situated or operating in one or more Member States and in one or more non-member States must make available to the markets of the Member State or Member States in which their debt securities are listed information which is at least equivalent to that which they make available to the markets of the non-member State or States in question, if such information may be of importance for the evaluation of the debt securities.

COUNCIL DIRECTIVE
of 17 March 1980

coordinating the requirements for the drawing up, scrutiny and distribution of the listing particulars to be published for the admission of securities to official stock exchange listing

(80/390/EEC)

THE COUNCIL OF THE EUROPEAN COMMUNITIES,

Having regard to the Treaty establishing the European Economic Community, and in particular Articles 54(3)(g) and 100 thereof,

Having regard to the proposal from the Commission[1],

Having regard to the opinion of the European Parliament[2],

Having regard to the opinion of the Economic and Social Committee[3],

Whereas the market in which undertakings operate has been enlarged to embrace the whole Community and this enlargement involves a corresponding increase in their financial requirements and extension of the capital markets on which they must call to satisfy them; whereas admission to official listing on stock exchanges of Member States of securities issued by undertakings constitutes an important means of access to these capital markets; whereas furthermore exchange restrictions on the purchase of securities traded on the stock exchanges of another Member State have been eliminated as part of the liberalization of capital movements;

Whereas safeguards for the protection of the interests of actual and potential investors are required in most Member States of undertakings offering their securities to the public, either at the time of their offer or of their admission to official stock exchange listing; whereas such safeguards require the provision of information which is sufficient and as objective as possible concerning the financial circumstances of the issuer and particulars of the securities for which admission to official listing is requested; whereas the form under which this information is required usually consists of the publication of listing particulars;

Whereas the safeguards required differ from Member State to Member State, both as regards the contents and the layout of the listing particulars and the efficacy, methods and timing of the check on the information given therein; whereas the effect of these differences is not only to make it more difficult for undertakings to obtain admission of securities to official listing on stock exchanges of several Member States but also to hinder the acquisition by investors residing in one Member State of securities listed on stock exchanges of other Member States and thus to inhibit the financing of the undertakings and investment throughout the Community;

Whereas these differences should be eliminated by coordinating the rules and regulations without necessarily making them completely uniform, in order to achieve an adequate degree of equivalence in the safeguards required in each Member State to ensure the provision

[1] OJ No C 131, 13. 12. 1972, p 61.
[2] OJ No C 11, 7. 2. 1974, p 24.
[3] OJ No C 125, 16. 10. 1974, p 1.

of information which is sufficient and as objective as possible for actual or potential security holders; whereas at the same time, taking into account the present degree of liberalization of capital movements in the Community and the fact that a mechanism for checking at the time the securities are offered does not yet exist in all Member States, it would appear sufficient at present to limit the coordination to the admission of securities to official stock exchange listing;

Whereas such coordination must apply to securities independently of the legal status of the issuing undertaking, and accordingly, in so far as this Directive applies to entities to which no reference is made in the second paragraph of Article 58 of the Treaty and goes beyond the scope of Article 54 (3) (g), it must be based also on Article 100,

HAS ADOPTED THIS DIRECTIVE:

SECTION I

General provisions

Article 1

1. This Directive shall apply to securities which are the subject of an application for admission to official listing on a stock exchange situated or operating within a Member State.

2. This Directive shall not apply to:

— units issued by collective investment undertakings other than the closed-end type,

— securities issued by a State or by its regional or local authorities.

Article 2

For purposes of applying this Directive:

(a) 'collective investment undertakings other than the closed-end type' shall mean unit trusts and investment companies:

— the object of which is the collective investment of capital provided by the public, and which operate on the principle of risk spreading, and

— the units of which are, at the holders' request, repurchased or redeemed, directly or indirectly, out of the assets of these undertakings. Action taken by such undertakings to ensure that the stock exchange value of its units does not significantly vary from their net asset value shall be regarded as equivalent to such repurchase or redemption;

(b) 'units of a collective investment undertaking' shall mean securities issued by a collective investment undertaking as representing the rights of participants in the assets of such an undertaking;

(c) 'issuers' shall mean companies and other legal persons and any undertaking whose securities are the subject of an application for admission to official listing on a stock exchange;

(d) 'net turnover' shall comprise the amounts derived from the sale of products and the provision of services falling within the undertaking's ordinary activities, after deduction of sales rebates and of value added tax and other taxes directly linked to the turnover;

(e) 'credit institution' shall mean an undertaking whose business is to receive deposits or other repayable funds from the public and to grant credits for its own account;

(f) 'participating interest' shall mean rights in the capital of other undertakings, whether or not represented by certificates, which, by creating a durable link with those undertakings, are intended to contribute to the activities of the undertaking which holds these rights;

(g) 'annual accounts' shall comprise the balance sheet, the profit and loss account and the notes on the accounts. These documents shall constitute a composite whole.

Article 3

Member States shall ensure that the admission of securities to official listing on a stock exchange situated or operating within their territories is conditional upon the publication of an information sheet, hereinafter referred to as listing particulars.

Article 4

1. The listing particulars shall contain the information which, according to the particular nature of the issuer and of the securities for the admission of which application is being made, is necessary to enable investors and their investment advisers to make an informed assessment of the assets and liabilities, financial position, profits and losses, and prospects of the issuer and of the rights attaching to such securities.

2. Member States shall ensure that the obligation referred to in paragraph 1 is incumbent upon the persons responsible for the listing particulars as provided for in heading 1.1 of Schedules A and B annexed hereto.

Article 5

1. Without prejudice to the obligation referred to in Article 4, Member States shall ensure that, subject to the possibilities for exemptions provided for in articles 6 and 7, listing particulars contain, in as easily analysable and comprehensible a form as possible, at least the items of information provided for in Schedules A, B or C, depending on whether shares, debt securities or certificates representing shares are involved.

2. In the specific cases covered by Articles 8 to 17 the listing particulars are to be drawn up in accordance with the specification given in those Articles, subject to the possibilities for exemp-

tions provided for in Articles 6 and 7.

3. Where certain headings in Schedules A, B and C appear inappropriate to the issuer's sphere of activity or legal form, listing particulars giving equivalent information shall be drawn up by adapting these headings.

Article 6

Member States may allow the authorities responsible for checking the listing particulars within the meaning of this Directive (hereinafter referred to as 'the competent authorities') to provide for partial or complete exemption from the obligation to publish listing particulars in the following cases:

1. where the securities for which admission to official listing is applied for are:

(a) securities which have been the subject of a public issue;

(b) securities issued in connection with a takeover offer;

(c) securities issued in connection with a merger involving the acquisition of another company or the formation of a new company, the division of a company, the transfer of all or part of an undertaking's assets and liabilities or as consideration for the transfer of assets other than cash;

and where, not more than 12 months before the admission of the securities to official listing, a document, regarded by the competent authorities as containing information equivalent to that of the listing particulars provided for by this Directive, has been published in the same Member State. Particulars shall also be published of any material changes which have occurred since such document was prepared. The document must be made available to the public at the registered office of the issuer and at the offices of the financial organizations retained to act as the latter's paying agents, and any particulars of material changes shall be published in accordance with Articles 20(1) and 21(1).

2. where the securities for which admission to official listing is applied for are:

  (a) shares allotted free of charge to holders of shares already listed on the same stock exchange; or

  (b) shares resulting from the conversion of convertible debt securities or shares created after an exchange for exchangeable debt securities, if shares of the company whose shares are offered by way of conversion or exchange are already listed on the same stock exchange; or

  (c) shares resulting from the exercise of the rights conferred by warrants, if shares of the company whose shares are offered to holders of the warrants are already listed on the same stock exchange; or

  (d) shares issued in substitution for shares already listed on the same stock exchange if the issuing of such new shares does not involve any increase in the company's issued share capital;

and, where appropriate, the information provided for in Chapter 2 of Schedule A is published in accordance with Articles 20(1) and 21(1).

3. where the securities for which admission to official listing is applied for are:

  (a) shares of which either the number or the estimated market value or the nominal value or, in the absence of a nominal value, the accounting par value, amounts to less than 10% of the number or of the corresponding value of shares of the same class already listed on the same stock exchange; or

  (b) debt securities issued by companies and other legal persons which are nationals of a Member State and which:

    — in carrying on their business, benefit from State monopolies, and

    — are set up or governed by a special law or pursuant to such a law or whose borrowings are unconditionally and irrevocably guaranteed by a Member State or one of a Member State's federated States; or

  (c) debt securities issued by legal persons, other than companies, which are nationals of a Member State, and

    — were set up by special law, and

    — whose activities are governed by that law and consist solely in:

      (i) raising funds under state control through the issue of debt securities, and

      (ii) financing production by means of the resources which they have raised and resources provided by a Member State, and

    — the debt securities of which are, for the purposes of admission to official listing, considered by national law as debt securities issued or guaranteed by the State; or

  (d) shares allotted to employees, if shares of the same class have already been admitted to official listing on the same stock exchange; shares which differ from each other solely as to the date of first entitlement or dividends shall not be considered as being of different classes; or

  (e) securities already admitted to official listing on another stock exchange in the same Member State; or

  (f) shares issued in consideration for the partial or total renunciation by the management of a limited partnership with a share capital of its statutory rights over the profits, if shares of the same class have already been admitted to official listing on the same stock exchange; shares which differ from each other solely as to the date of first entitlement to dividends shall not be considered as being of different classes; or

(g) supplementary certificates representing shares issued in exchange for the original securities, where the issuing of such new certificates has not brought about any increase in the company's issued capital, and provided that certificates representing such shares are already listed on the same stock exchange, and where:

— in the case of (a), the issuer has complied with the stock exchange publicity requirements imposed by the national authorities and has produced annual accounts and annual and interim reports which these authorities have considered adequate,

— in the case of (e), listing particulars complying with this Directive have already been published, and

— in all the cases referred to in points (a) to (g), information concerning the number and type of securities to be admitted to official listing and the circumstances in which such securities have been issued has been published in accordance with Articles 20(1) and 21(1).

Article 7

The competent authorities may authorize omission from the listing particulars of certain information provided for by this Directive if they consider that:

(a) such information is of minor importance only and is not such as will influence assessment of the assets and liabilities, financial position, profits and losses and prospects of the issuer; or

(b) disclosure of such information would be contrary to the public interest or seriously detrimental to the issuer, provided that, in the latter case, such omission would not be likely to mislead the public with regard to facts and circumstances, knowledge of which is essential for the assessment of the securities in question.

SECTION II

Contents of the listing particulars in certain specific cases

Article 8

1. Where the application for admission to official listing relates to shares offered to shareholders of the issuer on a preemptive basis and shares of the latter are already listed on the same stock exchange, the competent authorities may provide that the listing particulars shall contain only the information provided for by Schedule A:

— in chapter 1,

— in chapter 2,

— in chapter 3, headings 3.1.0, 3.1.5, 3.2.0, 3.2.1, 3.2.6, 3.2.7, 3.2.8, and 3.2.9,

— in chapter 4, headings 4.2, 4.4, 4.5, 4.7.1, and 4.7.2,

— in chapter 5, headings 5.1.4, 5.1.5, and 5.5,

— in chapter 6, headings 6.1, 6.2.0, 6.2.1, 6.2.2, 6.2.3, and

— in chapter 7.

Where the shares referred to in the first subparagraph are represented by certificates, the listing particulars shall contain, at least, subject to Article 16 (2) and (3), in addition to the information mentioned in that subparagraph, that provided for in Schedule C:

— in chapter 1, headings 1.1, 1.3, 1.4, 1.6 and 1.8, and

— in chapter 2.

2. Where the application for admission to official listing relates to convertible debt securities, exchangeable debt securities or debt securities with warrants which are offered on a pre-emptive basis to the shareholders of the issuer and where the latter's shares are already listed on the same stock exchange, the competent authorities may provide that the listing particulars shall contain only:

— information concerning the nature of the shares offered by way of conversion, exchange or subscription and the rights attaching thereto,

— the information provided for in Schedule A and mentioned above in the first subparagraph of paragraph 1, except for that provided for in Chapter 2 of that Schedule,

— the information provided for in Chapter 2 of Schedule B, and

— the conditions of and procedures for conversion, exchange and subscription and the situations in which they may be amended.

3. When published in accordance with Article 20, listing particulars as referred to in paragraphs 1 and 2 shall be accompanied by the annual accounts for the latest financial year.

4. Where the issuer prepares both own and consolidated annual accounts, both sets of accounts shall accompany the listing particulars. However, the competent authorities may allow the issuer to attach to the listing particulars either the own or the consolidated accounts alone, provided that the accounts not attached to the listing particulars furnish no material additional information.

Article 9

1. Where the application for admission to official listing relates to debt securities which are neither convertible, exchangeable, nor accompanied by warrants and are issued by an undertaking which has securities already listed on the same stock exchange, the competent

authorities may provide that the listing particulars shall contain only the information provided for by Schedule B:

— in chapter 1,

— in chapter 2,

— in chapter 3, headings 3.1.0, 3.1.5, 3.2.0 and 3.2.2,

— in chapter 4, heading 4.3,

— in chapter 5, headings, 5.1.2, 5.1.3, 5.1.4 and 5.4,

— in chapter 6, and

— in chapter 7.

2. When published in accordance with Article 20, listing particulars as referred to in paragraph 1 shall be accompanied by the annual accounts for the latest financial year.

3. Where the issuer prepares both own and consolidated annual accounts, both sets of accounts must accompany the listing particulars. However, the competent authorities may allow the issuer to attach to the listing particulars either the own or the consolidated accounts alone, provided that the accounts not attached to the listing particulars furnish no material additional information.

Article 10

Where the application for admission to official listing relates to debt securities nearly all of which, because of their nature, are normally bought and traded in by a limited number of investors who are particularly knowledgeable in investment matters, the competent authorities may allow the omission from the listing particulars of certain information provided for by Schedule B or allow its inclusion in summary form, on condition that such information is not material from the point of view of the investors concerned.

Article 11

1. For the admission of securities, issued by financial institutions, to of-

ficial listing, the listing particulars must contain:

— at least the information specified in Chapters 1, 2, 3, 5 and 6 of Schedules A or B, according to whether the issue is of shares or debt securities, and

— information adapted, in accordance with the rules laid down for that purpose by national law or by the competent authorities, to the particular nature of the issuer of the securities in question and at least equivalent to that specified in Chapters 4 and 7 of Schedules A or B.

2. Member States shall determine the financial institutions to be covered by this Article.

3. The arrangements laid down by this Article may be extended to:

— collective investment undertakings whose units are not excluded from the scope of this Directive by the first indent of Article 1(2).

— finance companies engaging in no activity other than raising capital to make it available to their parent company or to undertakings affiliated to that company, and

— companies holding portfolios of securities, licences or patents and engaging in no activity other than the management of such portfolios.

Article 12

Where the application for admission to official listing concerns debt securities issued in a continuous or repeated manner by credit institutions which regularly publish their annual accounts and which, within the Community, are set up or governed by a special law, or pursuant to such a law, or are subject to public supervision designed to protect savings, the Member States may provide that the listing particulars shall contain only:

— the information provided for in heading 1.1 and Chapter 2 of Schedule B, and

— information concerning any events of importance for the assessment of the securities in question which have occurred since the end of the financial year in respect of which the last annual accounts were published. Such accounts must be made available to the public at the issuer's offices or at those of the financial organizations retained to act as the latter's paying agents.

Article 13

1. For the admission to official listing of debt securities guaranteed by a legal person, listing particulars must include:

— with respect to the issuer, the information provided for in Schedule B, and

— with respect to the guarantor, the information provided for in heading 1.3 and Chapters 3 to 7 of that Schedule.

Where the issuer or guarantor is a financial institution, the part of the listing particulars relating to that financial institution shall be drawn up in accordance with Article 11, without prejudice to the first subparagraph of this paragraph.

2. When the issuer of the guaranteed debt securities is a finance company within the meaning of Article 11 (3), the listing particulars must include:

— with respect to the issuer, the information provided for in Chapters 1, 2 and 3 and in headings 5.1.0 and 5.1.5 and 6.1 of Schedule B, and

— with respect to the guarantor, that provided for in heading 1.3 and Chapters 3 to 7 of that Schedule.

3. Where there is more than one guarantor, the information specified shall be required of each one, however; the competent authorities may allow abridgement of this information with a view to achieving greater comprehensibility of the listing particulars.

4. The guarantee contract must, in the cases referred to in paragraphs 1, 2 and 3, be made available for inspection by the public at the offices of the issuer and at those of the financial organizations retained to act as the latter's paying agents. Copies of the contract shall be provided to any person concerned on request.

Article 14

1. Where the application for admission to official listing relates to convertible debt securities, exchangeable debt securities or debt securities with warrants, the listing particulars must include:

— information concerning the nature of the shares offered by way of conversion, exchange or subscription, and the rights attaching thereto,

— the information provided for in heading 1.3 and Chapters 3 to 7 of Schedule A,

— the information provided for in Chapter 2 of Schedule B, and

— the conditions of and procedures for conversion, exchange or subscription and details of the situations in which they may be amended.

2. When the issuer of the convertible debt securities, the exchangeable debt securities or the debt securities with warrants is not the issuer of the shares, listing particulars must include:

— information concerning the nature of the shares offered by way of conversion, exchange or subscription and the rights attaching thereto, and

— in respect of the issuer of the securities, the information provided for in Schedule B,

— in respect of the issuer of the shares, that provided for in heading 1.3 and Chapters 3 to 7 of Schedule A, and

— the conditions of and procedures for conversion, exchange or subscription and details of the situations in which they may be amended.

However, where the issuer of the debt securities is a finance company within the meaning of Article 11 (3), listing particulars need contain, in relation to that company, only the information provided for in Chapters 1, 2 and 3 and headings 5.1.0 to 5.1.5 and 6.1 of Schedule B.

Article 15

1. Where the application for admission to official listing relates to securities issued in connection with a merger involving the acquisition of another company or the formation of a new company, the division of a company, the transfer of all or part of an undertaking's assets and liabilities, a takeover offer or as consideration for the transfer of assets other than cash, the documents describing the terms and conditions of such operations, as well as, where appropriate, any opening balance sheet, whether or not pro forma, if the issuer has not yet prepared its annual accounts, must, without prejudice to the requirement to publish the listing particulars, be made available for inspection by the public at the offices of the issuer of the securities and at those of the financial organizations retained to act as the latter's paying agents.

2. Where the transaction referred to in paragraph 1 took place more than two years previously, the competent authorities may dispense with the requirement imposed in that paragraph.

Article 16

1. When the application for admission to official listing relates to certificates representing shares, the listing particulars must contain the information, as regards certificates, provided for in Schedule C and the information, as regards the shares represented, provided for in Schedule A.

2. However, the competent authorities may relieve the issuer of the certificates of the requirement to publish details of

its own financial position, when the issuer is:

— a credit institution which is a national of a Member State and is set up or governed by a special law or pursuant to such law or is subject to public supervision designed to protect savings, or

— a subsidiary 95% or more of which is owned by a credit institution within the meaning of the preceding indent, the commitments of which towards the holders of certificates are unconditionally guaranteed by that credit institution and which is subject, *de jure* or *de facto*, to the same supervision, or

— an 'Administratiekantoor' in the Netherlands governed, for the safe custody of the original securities, by special regulations laid down by the competent authorities.

3. In the case of certificates issued by a securities transfer organization or by an auxiliary institution set up by such organization, the competent authorities may dispense with the publication of the information provided for in Chapter 1 of Schedule C.

Article 17

1. Where debt securities for which admission to official listing is applied for benefit, as regards both repayment of the loan and the payment of interest, from the unconditional and irrevocable guarantee of a State or of one of a State's federated States, national legislation or the competent authorities may authorize the abridgement of the information provided for in Chapters 3 and 5 of Schedule B.

2. The possibility of abridgement provided for in paragraph 1 may also be applied to companies set up or governed by a special law or pursuant to such law which have the power to levy charges on their consumers.

SECTION III

Arrangements for the scrutiny and publication of listing particulars

Article 18

1. Member States shall appoint one or more competent authorities and shall notify the Commission of the appointments of such authorities, giving details of any division of powers among them. Member States shall also ensure that this Directive is applied.

2. No listing particulars may be published until they have been approved by the competent authorities.

3. The competent authorities shall approve the publication of listing particulars only if they are of the opinion that they satisfy all the requirements set out in this Directive.

Member States shall ensure that the competent authorities have the powers necessary for them to carry out their task.

4. This Directive shall not affect the competent authorities' liability, which shall continue to be governed solely by the national law.

Article 19

The competent authorities shall decide whether to accept the audit report of the official auditor provided for in heading 1.3 of Schedules A and B or, if necessary, to require an additional report.

The requirement for the additional report must be the outcome of an examination of each case on its merits. At the request of the official auditor and/or of the issuer, the competent authorities must disclose to them the reasons justifying this requirement.

Article 20

1. Listing particulars must be published either:

— by insertion in one or more newspapers circulated throughout the Member State in which the admission to official listing of securities is sought, or widely circulated therein, or

— in the form of a brochure to be made available, free of charge, to the public at the offices of the stock exchange or stock exchanges on which the securities are being admitted to official listing, at the registered office of the issuer and at the offices of the financial organizations retained to act as the latter's paying agents in the Member State in which the admission of securities to official listing is sought.

2. In addition, either the complete listing particulars or a notice stating where the listing particulars have been published and where they may be obtained by the public must be inserted in a publication designated by the Member State in which the admission of securities to official listing is sought.

Article 21

1. Listing particulars must be published within a reasonable period, to be laid down in national legislation or by the competent authorities before the date on which official listing becomes effective.

Moreover, where the admission of securities to official listing is preceded by trading of the pre-emptive subscription rights giving rise to dealings recorded in the official list, the listing particulars must be published within a reasonable period, to be laid down by the competent authorities before such trading starts.

2. In exceptional, properly justified cases, the competent authorities may allow the postponement of the publication of the listing particulars until after:

— the date on which official listing becomes effective, in the case of securities of a class already listed on the same stock exchange issued in consideration of transfers of assets other than cash,

— the date of the opening of trading in pre-emptive subscription rights.

3. If the admission of debt securities to official listing coincides with their public issue and if some of the terms of the issue are not finalized until the last moment, the competent authorities may merely require the publication, within a reasonable period, of listing particulars omitting information as to these terms but indicating how it will be given. Such information must be published before the date on which official listing starts, except where debt securities are issued on a continuous basis at varying prices.

Article 22

Where listing particulars are, or will be, published in accordance with Articles 1 and 3 for the admission of securities to official listing, the notices, bills, posters and documents announcing this operation and indicating the essential characteristics of these securities, and all other documents relating to their admission and intended for publication by the issuer or on his behalf, must first be communicated to the competent authorities. The latter shall decide whether they should be submitted to scrutiny before publication.

The abovementioned documents must state that listing particulars exist and indicate where they are being, or will be, published in accordance with Article 20.

Article 23

Every significant new factor capable of affecting assessment of the securities which arises between the time when the listing particulars are adopted and the time when stock exchange dealings begin shall be covered by a supplement to the listing particulars, scrutinized in the same way as the latter and published in accordance with procedures to be laid down by the competent authorities.

SECTION IV

Cooperation between the Member States

Article 24

1. Where applications for admission of the same securities to official listing on stock exchanges situated or operating within several Member States are made simultaneously, or within short intervals of one another, the competent authorities shall exchange information and use their best endeavours to achieve maximum coordination of their requirements concerning listing particulars, to avoid a multiplicity of formalities and to agree to a single text requiring at the most translation, where appropriate, and the issue of supplements as necessary to meet the individual requirements of each Member State concerned.

2. Where an application for admission to official listing is made for securities which have been listed in another Member State less than six months previously, the competent authorities to whom application is made shall contact the competent authorities which have already admitted the securities to official listing and shall, as far as possible, exempt the issuer of those securities from the preparation of new listing particulars, subject to any need for updating, translation or the issue of supplements in accordance with the individual requirements of the Member State concerned.

Article 25

1. Member States shall provide that all persons employed or formerly employed by the competent authorities shall be bound by professional secrecy.

(¹) OJ No L 66, 16. 3. 1979, p 21.

This means that any confidential information received in the course of their duties may not be divulged to any person or authority except by virtue of provisions laid down by law.

2. Paragraph 1 shall not, however, preclude the competent authorities of the various Member States from exchanging information as provided for in this Directive. Information thus exchanged shall be covered by the obligation of professional secrecy to which the persons employed or formerly employed by the competent authorities receiving the information are subject.

SECTION V

Contact Committee

Article 26

1. The Contact Committee set up by Article 20 of Council Directive 79/279/EEC of 5 March 1979 coordinating the conditions for the admission of securities to official stock exchange listing(¹) shall also have as its function:

(a) without prejudice to Articles 169 and 170 of the EEC Treaty to facilitate the harmonized implementation of this Directive through regular consultations on any practical problems arising from its application on which exchanges of views are deemed useful;

(b) to facilitate consultation between the Member States on the supplements and improvements to the listing particulars which the competent authorities are entitled to require or recommend at national level;

(c) to advise the Commission, if necessary, on any additions or amendments to be made to this Directive.

2. It shall not be the function of the Contact Committee to appraise the merits of decisions taken by the competent authorities in individual cases.

SECTION VI

Final provisions

Article 27

1. [*Date of implementation substituted by directive 82/148/EEC* ª]

2. As from the notification of this Directive, the Member States shall communicate to the Commission the texts of the main laws, regulations and administrative provisions which they adopt in the field covered by this Directive.

Article 28

This Directive is addressed to the Member States.

(ª) OJ No L 62, 5. 3. 82, p 22.

SCHEDULE A

LAYOUT FOR LISTING PARTICULARS FOR THE ADMISSION OF SHARES TO OFFICIAL STOCK EXCHANGE LISTING

CHAPTER 1

Information concerning those responsible for listing particulars and the auditing of accounts

1.1. Name and function of natural persons and name and registered office of legal persons responsible for the listing particulars or, as the case may be, for certain parts of them, with, in the latter case, an indication of those parts.

1.2. Declaration by those responsible referred to in heading 1.1 that, to the best of their knowledge, the information given in that part of the listing particulars for which they are responsible is in accordance with the facts and contains no omissions likely to affect the import of the listing particulars.

1.3. Names, addresses and qualifications of the official auditors who have audited the company's annual accounts for the preceding three financial years in accordance with national law.

Statement that the annual accounts have been audited. If audit reports to the annual accounts have been refused by the official auditors or if they contain qualifications, such refusal or such qualifications shall be reproduced in full and the reasons given.

Indication of other information in the listing particulars which has been audited by the auditors.

CHAPTER 2

Information concerning admission to official listing and the shares for the admission of which application is being made

2.1. Indication that the admission applied for is admission to official listing of shares already marketed or admission to listing with a view to stock exchange marketing.

2.2. Information concerning the shares in respect of which application for official listing is being made:

2.2.0. Indication of the resolutions, authorizations and approvals by virtue of which the shares have been or will be created and/or issued.

Nature of the issue and amount thereof.

Number of shares which have been or will be created and/or issued, if predetermined.

2.2.1. In the case of shares issued in connection with a merger, the division of a company, the transfer of all or part of an undertaking's assets and liabilities, a takeover offer, or as consideration for the transfer of assets other than cash, indication of where the documents describing the terms and conditions of such operations are available for inspection by the public.

2.2.2. A concise description of the rights attaching to the shares, and in particular the extent of the voting rights, entitlement to share in the profits and to share in any surplus in the event of liquidation and any privileges.

Time limit after which dividend entitlement lapses and indication of the party in whose favour this entitlement operates.

2.2.3. Tax on the income from the shares withheld at source in the country of origin and/or the country of listing.

Indication as to whether the issuer assumes responsibility for the withholding of tax at source.

2.2.4. Arrangements for transfer of the shares and any restrictions on their free negotiability (eg clause establishing approval requirement).

2.2.5. Date on which entitlement to dividends arises.

2.2.6. The stock exchanges where admission to official listing is or will be sought.

2.2.7. The financial organizations which, at the time of admission of shares to official listing, are the paying agents of the issuer in the Member States where admission has taken place.

2.3. In so far as it is relevant, information concerning issue and placing, public or private, of the shares in respect of which the application for admission to official listing is made where such issue or placing has been effected within the 12 months preceding admission:

2.3.0. Indication of the exercise of the right of pre-emption of shareholders or of the restriction or withdrawal of such right.

Indication, where applicable, of the reasons for restriction or withdrawal of such right; in such cases, justification of the issue price, where an issue is for cash; indication of the beneficiaries if the restriction or withdrawal of the right of pre-emption is intended to benefit specific persons.

2.3.1. The total amount of the public or private issue or placing and the number of shares offered, where applicable by category.

2.3.2 If the public or private issue or placing were or are being made simultaneously on the markets of two or more States and if a tranche has been or is being reserved for certain of these, indication of any such tranche.

2.3.3. The issue price or the offer or placing price, stating the nominal value or, in its absence, the accounting par value or the amount to be capitalized; the issue premium and the amount of any expenses specifically charged to the subscriber or purchaser.

The methods of payment of the price, particularly as regards the paying-up of shares which are not fully paid.

2.3.4. The procedure for the exercise of any right of pre-emption; the negotiability of subscription rights; the treatment of subscription rights not exercised.

2.3.5. Period of the opening of the issue or offer of shares, and names of the financial organizations responsible for receiving the public's subscriptions.

2.3.6. Methods of and time limits for delivery of the shares, possible creation or provisional certificates.

2.3.7. Names, addresses and descriptions of the natural or legal persons underwriting or guaranteeing the issue for the issuer. Where not all of the issue is underwritten or guaranteed, a statement of the portion not covered.

2.3.8. Indication or estimate of the overall amount and/or of the amount per share of the charges relating to the issue operation, stating the total remuneration of the financial intermediaries, including the underwriting commission or margin, guarantee commission, placing commission or selling agent's commission.

2.3.9. Net proceeds accruing to the issuer from the issue and intended application of such proceeds, eg, to finance the investment programme or to strengthen the issuer's financial position.

2.4. Information concerning admission of shares to official listing:

2.4.0. Description of the shares for which admission to official listing is applied, and in particular the number of shares and nominal value per share, or, in the absence of nominal value, the accounting par value or the total nominal value, the exact designation or class, and coupons attached.

2.4.1. If the shares are to be marketed on the stock exchange and no such shares have previously been sold to the public, a statement of the number of shares made available to the market and of their nominal value, or, in the absence of nominal value, of their accounting par value, or a statement of the total nominal value and, where applicable, a statement of the minimum offer price.

2.4.2. If known, the dates on which the new shares will be listed and dealt in.

2.4.3. If shares of the same class are already listed on one or more stock exchanges, indication of these stock exchanges.

2.4.4. If shares of the same class have not yet been admitted to official listing but are dealt in on one or more other markets which are subject to regulation, are in regular operation and are recognized and open, indication of such markets.

2.4.5. Indication of any of the following which have occurred during the last financial year and the current financial year:

—public takeover offers by third parties in respect of the issuer's shares,

—public takeover offers by the issuer in respect of other companies' shares.

The price or exchange terms attaching to such offers and the outcome thereof are to be stated.

2.5. If, simultaneously or almost simultaneously with the creation of shares for which admission to official listing is being sought, shares of the same class are subscribed for or placed privately or if shares of other classes are created for public or private placing, details are to be given of the nature of such operations and of the number and characteristics of the shares to which they relate.

CHAPTER 3

General information about the issuer and its capital

3.1. General information about the issuer:

3.1.0. Name, registered office and principal administrative establishment if different from the registered office.

3.1.1. Date of incorporation and the length of life of the issuer, except where indefinite.

3.1.2. Legislation under which the issuer operates and legal form which it has adopted under that legislation.

3.1.3. Indication of the issuer's objects and reference to the clause of the memorandum of association in which they are described.

3.1.4. Indication of the register and of the entry number therein.

3.1.5. Indication of where the documents concerning the issuer which are referred to in the listing particulars may be inspected.

3.2. General information about the capital:

3.2.0. The amount of the issued capital, the number and classes of the shares of which it is composed with details of their principal characteristics; the part of the issued capital still to be paid up, and an indication of the number, or total nominal value, and the type of the shares not yet fully paid up, broken down where applicable according to the extent to which they have been paid up.

3.2.1. Where there is authorized but unissued capital or an undertaking to increase the capital, *inter alia* in connection with convertible loans issued or subscription options granted, indication of:

—the amount of such authorized capital or capital increase and, where appropriate, the duration of the authorization,

—the categories of persons having preferential subscription rights for such additional portions of capital,

—the terms and arrangements for the share issue corresponding to such portions.

3.2.2. If there are shares not representing capital, the number and main characteristics of such shares are to be stated.

3.2.3. The amount of any convertible debt securities, exchangeable debt securities or debt securities with warrants, with an indication of the conditions governing and the procedures for conversion, exchange or subscription.

3.2.4. Conditions imposed by the memorandum and articles of association governing changes in the capital and in the respective rights of the various classes of shares, where such conditions are more stringent than is required by law.

3.2.5. Summary description of the operations during the three preceding years which have changed the amount of the issued capital and/or the number and classes of shares of which it is composed.

3.2.6. As far as they are known to the issuer, indication of the natural or legal persons who, directly or indirectly, severally or jointly, exercise or could exercise control over the issuer, and particulars of the proportion of the capital held giving a right to vote.

Joint control shall mean control exercised by more than one company or by more than one person having concluded an agreement which may lead to their adopting a common policy in respect of the issuer.

3.2.7. In so far as they are known to the issuer, indication of the shareholders who, directly or indirectly, hold a proportion of the issuer's capital which the Member States may not fix at more than 20%.

3.2.8. If the issuer belongs to a group of undertakings, a brief description of the group and of the issuer's position within it.

3.2.9. Number, book value and nominal value or, in the absence of a nominal value, the accounting par value of any of its own shares which the issuer or another company in which it has a direct or indirect holding of more than 50% has acquired and is holding, if such securities do not appear as a separate item on the balance sheet.

CHAPTER 4

Information concerning the issuer's activities

4.1.   The issuer's principal activities:

4.1.0. Description of the issuer's principal activities, stating the main categories of products sold and/or services performed.

Indication of any significant new products and/or activities.

4.1.1. Breakdown of net turnover during the past three financial years by categories of activity and into geographical markets in so far as, taking account of the manner in which the sale of products and the provision of services falling within the issuer's ordinary activities are organized, these categories and markets differ substantially from one another.

4.1.2. Location and size of the issuer's principal establishments and summary information about real estate owned. Any establishment which accounts for more than 10% of turnover or production shall be considered a principal establishment.

4.1.3. For mining, extraction of hydrocarbons, quarrying and similar activities in so far as significant, description of deposits, estimate of economically exploitable reserves and expected period of working.

Indication of the periods and main terms of concessions and the economic conditions for working them.

Indication of the progress of actual working.

4.1.4. Where the information given pursuant to headings 4.1.0 to 4.1.3 has been influenced by exceptional factors, that fact should be mentioned.

4.2. Summary information regarding the extent to which the issuer is dependent, if at all, on patents or licences, industrial, commercial or financial contracts or new manufacturing processes, where such factors are of fundamental importance to the issuer's business or profitability.

4.3. Information concerning policy on the research and development of new products and processes over the past three financial years, where significant.

4.4. Information on any legal or arbitration proceedings which may have or have had a significant effect on the issuer's financial position in the recent past.

4.5 Information on any interruptions in the issuer's business which may have or have had a significant effect on the issuer's financial position in the recent past.

4.6. Average numbers employed and changes therein over the past three financial years, if such changes are material, with, if possible, a breakdown of persons employed by main categories of activity.

4.7. Investment policy:

4.7.0. Description, with figures, of the main investments made, including interests such as shares, debt securities, etc, in other undertakings over the past three financial years and the months already elapsed of the current financial year.

4.7.1. Information concerning the principal investments being made with the exception of interests being acquired in other undertakings.

Distribution of these investments geographically (home and abroad).

Method of financing (internal or external).

4.7.2. Information concerning the issuer's principal future investments, with the exception of interests to be acquired in other undertakings on which its management bodies have already made firm commitments.

CHAPTER 5

Information concerning the issuer's assets and liabilities, financial position and profits and losses

5.1. Accounts of the issuer:

5.1.0. The last three balance sheets and profit and loss accounts drawn up by the company set out as a comparative table. The notes on the annual accounts for the last financial year.

The draft listing particulars must be filed with the competent authorities not more than 18 months after the end of the financial year to which the last annual accounts published relate. The competent authorities may extend that period in exceptional cases.

5.1.1. If the issuer prepares consolidated annual accounts only, it shall include those accounts in the listing particulars in accordance with heading 5.1.0.

If the issuer prepares both own and consolidated annual accounts, it shall include both sets of accounts in the listing particulars in accordance with heading 5.1.0. However, the competent authorities may allow the issuer to include either the own or the consolidated annual accounts, on condition that the accounts which are not included do not provide any significant additional information.

5.1.2. The profit or loss per share of the issuing company, for the financial year, arising out of the company's ordinary activities, after tax, for the last three financial years, where the company includes its own annual accounts in the listing particulars.

Where the issuer includes only consolidated annual accounts in the listing particulars, it shall indicate the consolidated profit or loss per share, for the financial year, for the last three financial years. This information shall appear in addition to that provided in accordance with the preceding subparagraph where the issuer also includes its own annual accounts in the listing particulars.

If in the course of the abovementioned period of three financial years the number of shares in the issuing company has changed as a result, for example, of an increase or decrease in capital or the rearrangement or splitting of shares, the profit or loss per share referred to in the first and second paragraph above shall be adjusted to make them comparable; in that event the adjustment formulae used shall be disclosed.

5.1.3. The amount of the dividend per share for the last three financial years, adjusted, if necessary, to make it comparable in accordance with the third subparagraph of heading 5.1.2.

5.1.4. Where more than nine months have elapsed since the end of the financial year to which the last published own annual and/or consolidated annual accounts relate, an interim financial statement covering at least the first six months shall be included in the listing particulars or appended to them. If such an interim financial statement is unaudited, that fact must be stated.

Where the issuer prepares consolidated annual accounts, the competent authorities shall decide whether the interim financial statement to be submitted must be consolidated or not.

Any significant change which has occurred since the end of the last financial year or the preparation of the interim financial statement must be described in a note inserted in the listing particulars or appended thereto.

5.1.5. If the own or consolidated annual accounts do not comply with the Council Directives on undertakings' annual accounts and do not give a true and fair view of the issuer's assets and liabilities, financial position and profits and losses, more detailed and/or additional information must be given.

5.1.6. A table showing the sources and application of funds over the past three financial years.

5.2. Individual details listed below relating to the undertakings in which the issuer holds a proportion of the capital likely to have a significant effect on the assessment of its own assets and liabilities, financial position or profits and losses.

The items of information listed below must be given in any event for every undertaking in which the issuer has a direct or indirect participating interest, if the book value of that participating interest represents at least 10% of the capital and reserves or accounts for at least 10% of the net profit or loss of the issuer or, in the case of a group, if the book value of that participating interest represents at least 10% of the consolidated net assets or accounts for at least 10% of the consolidated net profit or loss of the group.

The items of information listed below need not be given provided that the issuer proves that its holding is of a purely provisional nature.

Similarly, the information required under points (e) and (f) may be omitted where the undertaking in which a participating interest is held does not publish its annual accounts.

Pending subsequent coordination of provisions relating to consolidated annual accounts, the Member States may authorize the competent authorities to permit the omission of the information prescribed in points (d) to (j) if the annual accounts of the undertakings in which the participating interests are held are consolidated into the group annual accounts or if the value attributable to the interest under the equity method is disclosed in the annual accounts, provided that, in the opinion of the competent authorities, the omission of that information is not likely to mislead the public with regard to the facts and circumstances, knowledge of which is essential for the assessment of the security in question.

The information provided for under points (g) and (j) may be omitted if, in the opinion of the competent authorities, such omission does not mislead investors.

(a) Name and registered office of the undertaking.

(b) Field of activity.

(c) Proportion of capital held.

(d) Issued capital.

(e) Reserves.

(f) Profit or loss arising out of ordinary activities, after tax, for the last financial year.

(g) Value at which the issuer obliged to publish listing particulars shows shares held in its accounts.

(h) Amount still to be paid up on shares held.

(i) Amount of dividends received in the course of the last financial year in respect of shares held.

(j) Amount of the debts owed to and by the issuer with regard to the undertaking.

5.3.   Individual details relating to the undertakings not referred to in heading 5.2 in which the issuer holds at least 10% of the capital. These details may be omitted when they are of negligible importance for the purpose of the objective set in Article 4 of this Directive:

(a) name and registered office of the undertaking;

(b) proportion of capital held.

5.4.   When the listing particulars comprise consolidated annual accounts, disclosure:

(a) of the consolidation principles applied. These shall be described explicitly where the Member State has no laws governing the consolidation of annual accounts or where such principles are not in conformity with such laws or with a generally accepted method in use in the Member State in which the stock exchange on which admission to official listing is requested is situated or operates;

(b) of the names and registered offices of the undertakings included in the consolidation, where that information is important for the purpose of assessing the assets and liabilities, the financial position and the profits and losses of the issuer. It is sufficient to distinguish them by a sign in the list of undertakings of which details are required in heading 5.2;

(c) for each of the undertakings referred to in (b):

—the total proportion of third-party interests, if annual accounts are consolidated globally;

—the proportion of the consolidation calculated on the basis of interests, if consolidation has been effected on a *pro rata* basis.

5.5.   Where the issuer is a dominant undertaking forming a group with one or more dependent undertakings, the details provided for in Chapters 4 and 7 shall be given for that issuer and group,

The competent authorities may permit the provision of that information for the issuer alone or for the group alone, provided that the details which are not provided are not material.

5.6.   If certain information provided for under Schedule A is given in the annual accounts provided in accordance with this Chapter, it need not be repeated.

CHAPTER 6

Information concerning administration, management and supervision

6.1.   Names, addresses and functions in the issuing company of the following persons and an indication of the principal activities performed by them outside that company where these are significant with respect to that company:

(a) members of the administrative, management or supervisory bodies;

(b) partners with unlimited liability, in the case of a limited partnership with a share capital;

(c) founders, if the company has been established for fewer than five years.

6.2. Interests of the members of the administrative, management and supervisory bodies in the issuing company:

6.2.0. Remuneration paid and benefits in kind granted, during the last completed financial year under any heading whatsoever, and charged to overheads or the profit appropriation account, to members of the administrative, management and supervisory bodies, these being total amounts for each category of body.

The total remuneration paid and benefits in kind granted to all members of the administrative, management and supervisory bodies of the issuer by all the dependent undertakings with which it forms a group must be indicated.

6.2.1. Total number of shares in the issuing company held by the members of its administrative, management and supervisory bodies and options granted to them on the company's shares.

6.2.2. Information about the nature and extent of the interests of members of the administrative, management and supervisory bodies in transactions effected by the issuer which are unusual in their nature or conditions (such as purchases outside normal activity, acquisition or disposal of fixed asset items) during the preceding financial year and the current financial year. Where such unusual transactions were concluded in the course of previous financial years and have not been definitively concluded, information on those transactions must also be given.

6.2.3. Total of all the outstanding loans granted by the issuer to the persons referred to in heading 6.1(a) and also of any guarantees provided by the issuer for their benefit.

6.3. Schemes for involving the staff in the capital of the issuer.

CHAPTER 7

Information concerning the recent development and prospects of the issuer

7.1. Except in the event of a derogation granted by the competent authorities, general information on the trend of the issuer's business since the end of the financial year to which the last published annual accounts relate, in particular:

—the most significant recent trends in production, sales and stocks and the state of the order book, and

—recent trends in costs and selling prices.

7.2. Except in the event of a derogation granted by the competent authorities, information on the issuer's prospects for at least the current financial year.

SCHEDULE B

LAYOUT FOR LISTING PARTICULARS FOR THE ADMISSION OF DEBT SECURITIES TO OFFICIAL STOCK EXCHANGE LISTING

CHAPTER 1

Information concerning those responsible for listing particulars and the auditing of accounts

1.1.   Names and addresses of the natural or legal persons responsible for the listing particulars or, as the case may be, for certain parts of them with, in the latter case, an indication of those parts.

1.2.   Declaration by those responsible, as referred to in heading 1.1, that, to the best of their knowledge, the information given in that part of the listing particulars for which they are responsible is in accordance with the facts and contains no omissions likely to affect the import of the listing particulars.

1.3.   Names, addresses and qualifications of the official auditors who have audited the annual accounts for the preceding three financial years in accordance with national law.

Statement that the annual accounts have been audited. If audit reports on the annual accounts have been refused by the official auditors or if they contain qualifications, such refusal or such qualifications must be reproduced in full and the reasons given.

Indication of other information in the listing particulars which has been audited by the auditors.

CHAPTER 2

Information concerning loans and the admission of debt securities to official listing

2.1.   Conditions of the loan:

2.1.0.   The nominal amount of the loan; if this amount is not fixed, a statement to this effect be made.

The nature, number and numbering of the debt securities and the denominations.

2.1.1.   Except in the case of continuous issues, the issue and redemption prices and the nominal interest rate; if several interest rates are provided for, an indication of the conditions for changes in the rate.

2.1.2.   Procedures for the allocation of any other advantages; the method of calculating such advantages.

2.1.3.   Tax on the income from the debt securities withheld at source in the country of origin and/or the country of listing.

Indication as to whether the issuer assumes responsibility for the withholding of tax at source.

2.1.4. Arrangements for the amortization of the loan, including the repayment procedures.

2.1.5. The financial organizations which, at the time of admission to official listing are the paying agents of the issuer in the Member State of admission.

2.1.6. Currency of the loan; if the loan is denominated in units of account, the contractual status of these; currency option.

2.1.7. Time limits:

(a) period of the loan and any interim due dates;

(b) the date from which interest becomes payable and the due dates for interest;

(c) the time limit on the validity of claims to interest and repayment of principal;

(d) procedures and time limits for delivery of the debt securities, possible creation of provisional certificates.

2.1.8. Except in the case of continuous issues, an indication of yield. The method whereby that yield is calculated shall be described in summary form.

2.2.   Legal information:

2.2.0. Indication of the resolutions, authorizations and approvals by virtue of which the debt securities have been or will be created and/or issued.

Type of operation and amount thereof.

Number of debt securities which have been or will be created and/or issued, if predetermined.

2.2.1. Nature and scope of the guarantees, sureties and commitments intended to ensure that the loan will be duly serviced as regards both the repayment of the debt securities and the payment of interest.

Indication of the places where the public may have access to the texts of the contracts relating to these guarantees, sureties and commitments.

2.2.2. Organization of trustees or of any other representation for the body of debt security holders.

Name and function and description and head office of the representative of the debt security holders, the main conditions of such representation and in particular the conditions under which the representative may be replaced.

Indication of where the public may have access to the contracts relating to these forms of representation.

2.2.3. Mention of clauses subordinating the loan to other debts of the issuer already contracted or to be contracted.

2.2.4. Indication of the legislation under which the debt securities have been created and of the courts competent in the event of litigation.

2.2.5. Indication as to whether the debt securities are registered or bearer.

2.2.6. Any restrictions on the free transferability of the debt securities.

2.3. Information concerning the admission of the debt securities to official listing.

2.3.0. The stock exchanges where admission to official listing is, or will be, sought.

2.3.1. Names, addresses and description of the natural or legal persons underwriting or guaranteeing the issue for the issuer. Where not all of the issue is underwritten or guaranteed, a statement of the portion not covered.

2.3.2. If the public or private issue or placing were or are being made simultaneously on the markets of two or more States and if a tranche has been or is being reserved for certain of these, indication of any such tranche.

2.3.3. If debt securities of the same class are already listed on one or more stock exchanges, indication of these stock exchanges.

2.3.4. If debt securities of the same class have not yet been admitted to official listing but are dealt in one or more other markets which are subject to regulation, are in regular operation and are recognized and open, indication of such markets.

2.4. Information concerning the issue if it is concomitant with official admission or if it took place within the three months preceding such admission.

2.4.0. The procedure for the exercise of any right of pre-emption; the negotiability of subscription rights; the treatment of subscription rights not exercised.

2.4.1. Method of payment of the issue or offer price.

2.4.2. Except in the case of continuous debt security issues, period of the opening of the issue or offer and any possibilities of early closure.

2.4.3. Indication of the financial organizations responsible for receiving the public's subscriptions.

2.4.4. Reference, where necessary, to the fact that the subscriptions may be reduced.

2.4.5. Except in the case of continuous debt security issues, indication of the net proceeds of the loan.

2.4.6. Purpose of the issue and intended application of its proceeds.

CHAPTER 3

General information about the issuer and its capital

3.1. General information about the issuer.

3.1.0. Name, registered office and principal administrative establishment if different from the registered office.

3.1.1. Date of incorporation and the length of life of the issuer, except where indefinite.

3.1.2. Legislation under which the issuer operates and legal form which it has adopted under that legislation.

3.1.3. Indication of the issuer's objects and reference to the clause in the memorandum of association in which they are described.

3.1.4. Indication of the register and of the entry number therein.

3.1.5. Indication of where the documents concerning the issuer which are referred to in the listing particulars may be inspected.

3.2.   General information about capital:

3.2.0. The amount of the issued capital and the number and classes of the securities of which it is composed with details of their principal characteristics.

The part of the issued capital still to be paid up, with an indication of the number, or total nominal value, and the type of securities not yet fully paid up, broken down where applicable according to the extent to which they have been paid up.

3.2.1. The amount of any convertible debt securities, exchangeable debt securities or debt securities with warrants, with an indication of the conditions governing and the procedures for conversion, exchange or subscription.

3.2.2. If the issuer belongs to a group of undertakings, a brief description of the group and of the issuer's position within it.

3.2.3. Number, book value and nominal value or, in the absence of a nominal value, the accounting par value of any of its own shares which the issuer or another company in which the issuer has a direct or indirect holding of more than 50% has acquired and is holding, if such securities do not appear as a separate item on the balance sheet, in so far as they represent a significant part of the issued capital.

CHAPTER 4

Information concerning the issuer's activities

4.1.   The issuer's principal activities.

4.1.0. Description of the issuer's principal activities, stating the main categories of products sold and/or services performed.

Indication of any significant new products and/or activities.

4.1.1. Net turnover during the past two financial years.

4.1.2. Location and size of the issuer's principal establishments and summary information about real estate owned. Any establishment which accounts for more than 10% of turnover or production shall be considered a principal establishment.

4.1.3. For mining, extraction of hydrocarbons, quarrying and similar activities in so far as significant, description of deposits, estimate of economically exploitable reserves and expected period of working.

Indication of the periods and main terms of concessions and the economic conditions for working them.

Indication of the progress of actual working.

4.1.4. Where the information given pursuant to headings 4.1.0 to 4.1.3 has been influenced by exceptional factors, that fact should be mentioned.

4.2. Summary information regarding the extent to which the issuer is dependent, if at all, on patents or licences, industrial, commercial or financial contracts or new manufacturing processes, where such factors are of fundamental importance to the issuer's business or profitability.

4.3. Information on any legal or arbitration proceedings which may have or have had a significant effect on the issuer's financial position in the recent past.

4.4. Investment policy:

4.4.0. Description, with figures, of the main investments made, including interests such as shares, debt securities, etc, in other undertakings, over the past three financial years and the months already elapsed of the current financial year.

4.4.1. Information concerning the principal investments being made with the exception of interests being acquired in other undertakings.

Distribution of these investments geographically (home and abroad).

Method of financing (internal or external).

4.4.2. Information concerning the issuer's principal future investments, with the exception of interests to be acquired in other undertakings, on which its management bodies have already made firm commitments.

CHAPTER 5

Information concerning the issuer's assets and liabilities, financial position and profits and losses

5.1. Accounts of the issuer:

5.1.0. The last two balance sheets and profit and loss accounts drawn up by the issuer set out as a comparative table. The notes on the annual accounts for the last financial year.

The draft listing particulars must be filed with the competent authorities not more than 18 months after the end of the financial year to which the last annual accounts published relate. The competent authorities may extend that period in exceptional cases.

5.1.1. If the issuer prepares consolidated annual accounts only, it shall include those accounts in the listing particulars in accordance with heading 5.1.0.

If the issuer prepares both own and consolidated annual accounts, it shall include both sets of accounts in the listing particulars in accordance with heading 5.1.0. However, the competent authorities may allow the issuer to include either the own or the consolidated annual accounts, on condition that the accounts which are not included do not provide any significant additional information.

5.1.2. Where more than nine months have elapsed since the end of the financial year to which the last published own annual and/or consolidated annual accounts relate, an interim financial statement covering at least the first six months shall be included in the listing particulars or appended to them. If the interim financial statement is unaudited, that fact must be stated.

Where the issuer prepares consolidated annual accounts, the competent authorities shall decide whether the interim financial statement to be submitted must be consolidated or not.

Any significant change which has occurred since the end of the last financial year or the preparation of the aforementioned interim financial statement must be described in a note inserted in or appended to the listing particulars.

5.1.3. If the own annual or consolidated annual accounts do not comply with the Council Directives on undertakings' annual accounts and do not give a true and fair view of the issuer's assets and liabilities, financial position and profits and losses, more detailed and/or additional information must be given.

5.1.4. Indication as at the most recent date possible (which must be stated) of the following, if material:

—the total amount of any loan capital outstanding, distinguishing between loans guaranteed (by the provision of security or otherwise, by the issuer or by third parties) and loans not guaranteed,

—the total amount of all other borrowings and indebtedness in the nature of borrowing, distinguishing between guaranteed and unguaranteed borrowings and debts,

—the total amount of any contingent liabilities.

An appropriate negative statement shall be given, where relevant, in the absence of any such loan capital, borrowings and indebtedness and contingent liabilities.

If the issuer prepares consolidated annual accounts, the principles laid down in heading 5.1.1. shall apply.

As a general rule, no account should be taken of liabilities between undertakings within the same group, a statement to that effect being made if necessary.

5.1.5. A table showing the sources and application of funds over the past three financial years.

5.2.　Individual details listed below relating to the undertakings in which the issuer holds a proportion of the capital likely to have a significant effect on the assessment of its own assets and liabilities, financial position or profits and losses.

The items of information listed below must be given in any event for every undertaking in which the issuer has a direct or indirect participating interest, if the book value of that participating interest represents at least 10% of the capital and reserves or accounts for at least 10% of the net profit or loss of the issuer, or in the case of a group, if the book value of that participating interest represents at least 10% of the consolidated net assets or accounts for at least 10% of the consolidated net profit or loss of the group.

The items of information listed below need not be given provided that the issuer proves that its holding is of a purely provisional nature.

Similarly, the information required under points (e) and (f) may be omitted where the undertaking in which a participating interest is held does not publish its annual accounts.

Pending coordination of provisions relating to consolidated annual accounts, the Member States may authorize the competent authorities to permit the omission of the information prescribed in points (d) to (h) if the annual accounts of the undertakings in which the participating interests are held are consolidated into the group annual accounts or if the value attributable to the interest under the equity method is disclosed in the annual accounts, provided that in the opinion of the competent authorities, the omission of that information is not likely to mislead the public with regard to the facts and circumstances knowledge of which is essential for the assessment of the security in question.

(a) Name and registered office of the undertaking.

(b) Field of activity.

(c) Proportion of capital held.

(d) Issued capital.

(e) Reserves.

(f) Profit or loss arising out of ordinary activities, after tax, for the last financial year.

(g) Amount still to be paid up on shares held.

(h) Amount of dividends received in the course of the last financial year in respect of shares held.

5.3.　When the listing particulars comprise consolidated annual accounts, disclosure:

(a) of the consolidation principles applied. These shall be described explicitly where the Member State has no laws governing the consolidation of annual accounts or where such principles are not in conformity with such laws or with a generally accepted method in use in the Member State in which the stock exchange on which admission to official listing is requested is situated or operates;

(b) of the names and registered offices of the undertakings included in the consolidation, where that information is important for the purpose of assessing the assets and liabilities, the financial position and the profits and losses of the issuer. It is sufficient to distinguish them by a sign in the list of companies for which details are required in heading 5.2;

(c) for each of the undertakings referred to in (b):

—the total proportion of third-party interests, if annual accounts are consolidated globally,

—the proportion of the consolidation calculated on the basis of interests, if consolidation has been effected on a *pro rata* basis.

5.4. Where the issuer is a dominant undertaking forming a group with one or more dependent undertakings, the details provided for in Chapters 4 and 7 shall be given for that issuer and group.

The competent authorities may permit the provision of that information for the issuer alone or for the group alone, provided that the details which are not provided are not material.

5.5. If certain information provided for under Schedule B is given in the annual accounts provided in accordance with this Chapter, it need not be repeated.

CHAPTER 6

Information concerning administration, management and supervision

6.1. Names, addresses and functions in the issuing undertaking of the following persons, and an indication of the principal activities performed by them outside that undertaking where these are significant with respect to that undertaking:

(a) members of the administrative management or supervisory bodies;

(b) partners with unlimited liability, in the case of a limited partnership with a share capital.

CHAPTER 7

Information concerning the recent development and prospects of the issuer

7.1. Except in the event of a derogation granted by the competent authorities, general information on the trend of the issuer's business since the end of the financial year to which the last published annual accounts relate, in particular:

—the most significant recent trends in production, sales and stocks and the state of the order book, and

—recent trends in costs and selling prices.

7.2. Except in the event of a derogation granted by the competent authorities, information on the issuer's propsects for at least the current financial year.

SCHEDULE C

LAYOUT FOR LISTING PARTICULARS FOR THE ADMISSION OF
CERTIFICATES REPRESENTING SHARES TO OFFICIAL STOCK
EXCHANGE LISTING

CHAPTER 1

General information about the issuer

1.1.   Name, registered office and principal administrative establishment if different from the registered office.

1.2.   Date of incorporation and length of life of the issuer, except where indefinite.

1.3.   Legislation under which the issuer operates and legal form which it has adopted under that legislation.

1.4.   The amount of the issued capital and the number and classes of the securities of which it is composed with details of their principal characteristics.

The part of the issued capital still to be paid up, with an indication of the number, or total nominal value, and the type of the securities not yet fully paid up, broken down where applicable according to the extent to which they have been paid up.

1.5.   Indication of the principal holders of the capital.

1.6.   Names, addresses and functions in the issuing body of the following persons, and an indication of the principal activities performed by them outside that body where these are significant with respect to that body, and also the functions held:

(a) members of the administrative, management or supervisory bodies;

(b) partners with unlimited liability, in the case of a limited partnership with a share capital.

1.7.   The company's objects. If the issue of certificates representing shares is not the sole object of the company, the nature of its other activities must be described, those of a purely trustee nature being dealt with separately.

1.8.   A summary of the annual accounts relating to the last completed financial year.

Where more than nine months have elapsed since the end of the last financial year to which the last published own annual and/or consolidated annual accounts relate, an interim financial statement covering at least the first six months shall be included in the listing particulars or appended to them. If the interim financial statement is unaudited, that fact must be stated.

Where the issuer prepares consolidated annual accounts, the competent authorities shall decide whether the interim financial statement to be submitted must be consolidated or not.

Any significant change which has occurred since the end of the last financial year or the preparation of the interim financial statement must be described in a note inserted in the listing particulars or appended thereto.

CHAPTER 2

Information on the certificates themselves

2.1.   Legal status:

Indication of the rules governing the issue of the certificates and mention of the date and place of their publication.

2.1.0.   Exercise of and benefit from the rights attaching to the original securities, in particular voting rights—conditions on which the issuer of the certificates may exercise such rights, and measures envisaged to obtain the instructions of the certificate holders—and the right to share in profits and any liquidation surplus.

2.1.1.   Bank or other guarantees attached to the certificates and intended to underwrite the issuer's obligations.

2.1.2.   Possibility of obtaining the conversion of the certificates into original securities and procedure for such conversion.

2.2.   The amount of the commissions and costs to be borne by the holder in connection with:

—the issue of the certificate,

—the payment of the coupons,

—the creation of additional certificates,

—the exchange of the certificates for original securities.

2.3.   Transferability of the certificates:

(a) The stock exchanges where admission to official listing is, or will be, sought;

(b) Any restrictions on the free transferability of the certificates.

2.4.   Supplementary information for admission to official listing:

(a) If the certificates are to be placed on a stock exchange the number of certificates made available to the market and/or the total nominal value; the minimum sale price, if such a price is fixed;

(b) Date on which the new certificates will be listed, if known.

2.5.   Indication of the tax arrangements with regard to any taxes and charges to be borne by the holders and levied in the countries where the certificates are issued.

2.6.   Indication of the legislation under which the certificates have been created and of the courts competent in the event of litigation.

COUNCIL DIRECTIVE

of 15 February 1982

on information to be published on a regular basis by companies the shares of which have been admitted to official stock exchange listing

(82/121/EEC)

THE COUNCIL OF THE EUROPEAN COMMUNITIES

Having regard to the Treaty establishing the European Economic Community, and in particular Articles 54 (3) (g) and 100 thereof,

Having regard to the proposal from the Commission ([1]),

Having regard to the opinion of the European Parliament ([2]),

Having regard to the opinion of the Economic and Social Committee ([3]),

Whereas Council Directive 80/390/EEC of 17 March 1980 coordinating the requirements for the drawing up, scrutiny and distribution of the listing particulars to be published for the admission of securities to official stock exchange listing ([4]) seeks to ensure improved protection of investors and a greater degree of equivalence in the protection provided, by coordinating requirements as to the information to be published at the time of admission;

Whereas, in the case of securities admitted to official stock exchange listing, the protection of investors requires that the latter be supplied with appropriate regular information throughout the entire period during which the securities are listed; whereas coordination of requirements for this regular information has similar objectives to those envisaged for the listing particulars, namely to improve such protection and to make it more equivalent, to facilitate the listing of these securities on more than one stock exchange in the Community, and in so doing to contribute towards the establishment of a genuine Community capital market by permitting a fuller interpenetration of securities markets;

Whereas, under Council Directive 79/279/EEC of 5 March 1979 coordinating the conditions for the admission of securities to official stock exchange listing ([5]), listed companies must as soon as possible make available to investors their annual accounts and report giving information on the company for the whole of the financial year; whereas the fourth Directive 78/660/EEC ([6]) has coordinated the laws, regulations and administrative provisions of the Member States concerning the annual accounts of certain types of companies;

Whereas companies should also, at least once during each financial year, make available to investors reports on their activities; whereas this Directive can, consequently, be confined to coordinating the content and distribution of a single report covering the first six months of the financial year;

([1]) OJ No C 29, 1. 2. 1979, p 5 and OJ No C 210, 16. 8. 1980, p 5.
([2]) OJ No C 85, 8. 4. 1980, p 69.
([3]) OJ No C 53, 3. 3. 1980, p 54.
([4]) OJ No L 100, 17. 4. 1980, p 1.
([5]) OJ No L 66, 16. 3. 1979, p 21
([6]) OJ No L 222, 14. 8. 1978, p 11.

194

Whereas, however, in the case of ordinary debentures, because of the rights they confer on their holders, the protection of investors by means of the publication of a half-yearly report is not essential; whereas, by virtue of Directive 79/279/EEC, convertible or exchangeable debentures and debentures with warrants may be admitted to official listing only if the related shares are already listed on the same stock exchange or on another regulated, regularly operating, recognized open market or are so admitted simultaneously; whereas the Member States may derogate from this principle only if their competent authorities are satisfied that holders have at their disposal all the information necessary to form an opinion concerning the value of the shares to which these debentures relate; whereas, consequently, regular information needs to be coordinated only for companies whose shares are admitted to official stock exchange listing;

Whereas the half-yearly report must enable investors to make an informed appraisal of the general development of the company's activities during the period covered by the report; whereas, however, this report need contain only the essential details on the financial position and general progress of the business of the company in question;

Whereas, in order to take account of difficulties resulting from the current state of laws in certain Member States, companies may be allowed a longer period to implement the provisions of this Directive than that laid down for the adaptation of national laws;

Whereas, so as to ensure the effective protection of investors and the proper operation of stock exchanges, the rules relating to regular information to be published by companies, the shares of which are admitted to official stock exchange listing within the Community, should apply not only to companies from Member States, but also to companies from non-member countries.

HAS ADOPTED THIS DIRECTIVE:

SECTION I

General provisions and scope

Article 1

1. This Directive shall apply to companies the shares of which are admitted to official listing on a stock exchange situated or operating in a Member State, whether the admission is of the shares themselves or of certificates representing them and whether such admission precedes or follows the date on which this Directive enters into force.

2. This Directive shall not, however, apply to investment companies other than those of the closed-end type.

For the purposes of this Directive 'investment companies other than those of the closed-end type' shall mean investment companies:

— the object of which is the collective investment of capital provided by the public, and which operate on the principle of risk spreading, and

— the shares of which are, at the holders' request, repurchased or redeemed, directly or indirectly, out of those companies' assets. Action taken by such companies to ensure that the stock exchange value of their shares does not significantly vary from their net asset value shall be regarded as equivalent to such repurchase or redemption.

3. The Member States may exclude central banks from the scope of this Directive.

Article 2

The Member States shall ensure that the companies publish half-yearly reports on their activities and profits and losses during the first six months of each financial year.

Article 3

The Member States may subject companies to obligations more stringent than those provided for by this Directive or to additional obligations, provided that they apply generally to all companies or to all companies of a given class.

SECTION II

Publication and contents of the half-yearly report

Article 4

1. The half-yearly report shall be published within four months of the end of the relevant six-month period.

2. In exceptional, duly substantiated cases, the competent authorities shall be permitted to extend the time limit for publication.

Article 5

1. The half-yearly report shall consist of figures and an explanatory statement relating to the company's activities and profits and losses during the relevant six-month period.

2. The figures, presented in table form, shall indicate at least:

— the net turnover, and

— the profit or loss before or after deduction of tax.

These terms shall have the same meanings as in the Council Directives on company accounts.

3. The Member States may allow the competent authorities to authorize companies, exceptionally and on a case-by-case basis, to supply estimated figures for profits and losses, provided that the shares of each such company are listed officially in only one Member State. The use of this procedure must be indicated by the company in its report and must not mislead investors.

4. Where the company has paid or proposes to pay an interim dividend, the figures must indicate the profit or loss after tax for the six-month period and the interim dividend paid or proposed.

5. Against each figure there must be shown the figure for the corresponding period in the preceding financial year.

6. The explanatory statement must include any significant information enabling investors to make an informed assessment of the trend of the company's activities and profits or losses together with an indication of any special factor which has influenced those activities and those profits or losses during the period in question, and enable a comparison to be made with the corresponding period of the preceding financial year.

It must also, as far as possible, refer to the company's likely future development in the current financial year.

7. Where the figures provided for in paragraph 2 are unsuited to the company's activities, the competent authorities shall ensure that appropriate adjustments are made.

Article 6

Where a company publishes consolidated accounts it may publish its half-yearly report in either consolidated or unconsolidated form. However, the Member States may allow the competent authorities, where the latter consider that the form not adopted would have contained additional material information, to require the company to publish such information.

Article 7

1. The half-yearly report must be published in the Member State or Member States where the shares are admitted to official listing by insertion in one or more newspapers distributed throughout the State or widely distributed

therein or in the national gazette, or shall be made available to the public either in writing in places indicated by announcement to be published in one or more newspapers distributed throughout the State or widely distributed therein, or by other equivalent means approved by the competent authorities.

2. A half-yearly report must be drawn up in the official language or languages or in one of the official languages or in another language, provided that, in the Member State concerned, such official language or languages or such other language are customary in the sphere of finance and are accepted by the competent authorities.

3. The company shall send a copy of its half-yearly report simultaneously to the competent authorities of each Member State in which its shares are admitted to official listing. It shall do so not later than the time when the half-yearly report is published for the first time in a Member State.

Article 8

Where the accounting information has been audited by the official auditor of the company's accounts, that auditor's report and any qualifications he may have shall be reproduced in full.

SECTION III

Powers of the competent authorities

Article 9

1. Member States shall appoint one or more competent authorities and shall notify the Commission of the appointment of such authorities, giving details of any division of powers among them. Member States shall also ensure that this Directive is applied.

2. The Member States shall ensure that the competent authorities have the necessary powers to carry out their task.

3. Where particular requirements of this Directive are unsuited to a company's activities or circumstances, the competent authorities shall ensure that suitable adaptations are made to such requirements.

4. The competent authorities may authorize the omission from the half-yearly report of certain information provided for in this Directive if they consider that disclosure of such information would be contrary to the public interest or seriously detrimental to the company, provided that, in the latter case, such omission would not be likely to mislead the public with regard to facts and circumstances knowledge of which is essential for the assessment of the shares in question.

The company or its representatives shall be responsible for the correctness and relevance of the facts on which any application for such exemption is based.

5. Paragraphs 3 and 4 shall also apply to the more stringent or additional obligations imposed pursuant to Article 3.

6. If a company governed by the law of a non-member country publishes a half-yearly report in a non-member country, the competent authorities may authorize it to publish that report instead of the half-yearly report provided for in this Directive, provided that the information given is equivalent to that which would result from the application of this Directive.

7. This Directive shall not affect the competent authorities' liability, which shall continue to be governed solely by national law.

SECTION IV

Cooperation between Member States

Article 10

1. The competent authorities shall cooperate whenever necessary for the purpose of carrying out their duties and shall exchange any information required for that purpose.

2. Where a half-yearly report has to be published in more than one Member State, the competent authorities of these Member States shall, by way of derogation from Article 3, use their best endeavours to accept as a single text the text which meets the requirements of the Member State in which the company's shares were admitted to official listing for the first time or the text which most closely approximates to that text. In cases of simultaneous admission to official listing on two or more stock exchanges situated or operating in different Member States, the competent authorities of the Member States concerned shall use their best endeavours to accept as a single text the text of the report which meets the requirements of the Member State in which the company's head office is situated; if the company's head office is situated in a non-member country, the competent authorities of the Member States concerned shall use their best endeavours to accept a single version of the report.

SECTION V

Contact Committee

Article 11

1. The Contact Committee set up by Article 20 of Directive 79/279/EEC shall also have as its function:

(a) without prejudice to Articles 169 and 170 of the Treaty to facilitate the harmonized implementation of this Directive through regular consultations on any practical problems arising from its application on which exchanges of views are deemed useful;

(b) to facilitate consultation between the Member States on the more stringent or additional obligations which they may impose pursuant to Article 3 with a view to the ultimate convergence of obligations imposed in all Member States, in accordance with Article 54 (3) (g) of the Treaty;

(c) to advise the Commission, if necessary, on any additions or amendments to be made to this Directive; in particular, the Committee shall consider the possible modification of Articles 3 and 5 in the light of progress towards the convergence of obligations referred to in (b) above.

2. Within five years of notification of this Directive, the Commission shall, after consulting the Contact Committee, submit to the Council a report on the application of Articles 3 and 5 and on such modifications as it would be possible to make thereto.

SECTION VI

Final provisions

Article 12

1. Member States shall bring into force the measures necessary to comply with this Directive not later than 30 June 1983. They shall forthwith inform the Commission thereof.

2. Member States may postpone application of the measures referred to in paragraph 1 until 36 months from the date on which they bring such measures into force.

3. As from the notification of this Directive, Member States shall communicate to the Commission the main provi-

sions of the laws, regulations and administrative provisions which they adopt in the field governed by this Directive.

Article 13

This Directive is addressed to the Member States.

SCHEDULE 2—MEMBER STATE OPTIONS
Regulation 6

1. The Admission directive shall not apply to units issued by collective investment undertakings other than of the closed-end type or securities issued by a member state or by its regional or local authorities.

2. The conditions and obligations referred to in Article 8 of the Admission directive shall not apply to the securities issued by persons referred to in that Article.

3. Shares may be admitted to official listing where the condition referred to in the second indent of paragraph 2 in Part I of Schedule A to the Admission directive is not fulfilled provided that the requirements of that paragraph are met.

4. Debt securities may be admitted to official listing where the condition referred to in the second indent of paragraph 1 of Part III of Section A of Schedule B to the Admission directive is not fulfilled, provided that the requirements of that paragraph are met.

5. Convertible or exchangeable debentures and debentures with warrants may be admitted to official listing if the requirement in the second indent of paragraph 2 in Part III of Section A of Schedule B to the Admission directive is satisfied.

6. It is hereby determined that no financial institutions are to be covered by Article 11 of the Listing Particulars directive.

7. It shall not be necessary for listing particulars relating to the securities referred to in Article 12 of the Listing Particulars directive to contain any information other than the information referred to in that Article.

8. The publication referred to in paragraph 2 of Article 20 of the Listing Particulars directive shall be The Stock Exchange Weekly Official Intelligence.

9. For the purposes of paragraph 3.2.7. of Schedule A to the Listing Particulars directive the proportion of the issuer's capital shall be 5%.

10. Nothing in these regulations shall apply to a central bank so far as they implement the Interim Reports directive.